WE-NARRATIVES

THEORY AND INTERPRETATION OF NARRATIVE
James Phelan and Katra Byram, Series Editors

WE-NARRATIVES

COLLECTIVE STORYTELLING
IN CONTEMPORARY FICTION

Natalya Bekhta

THE OHIO STATE UNIVERSITY PRESS

COLUMBUS

Library of Congress Cataloging-in-Publication Data

Names: Bekhta, Natalya, author.

Title: We-narratives : collective storytelling in contemporary fiction / Natalya Bekhta.

Other titles: Theory and interpretation of narrative series.

Description: Columbus : The Ohio State University Press, [2020] | Series: Theory and interpretation of narrative | Includes bibliographical references and index. | Summary: "By reading a range of contemporary novels and short stories by Jeffrey Eugenides, Joshua Ferris, Toby Litt, Zakes Mda, Joyce Carol Oates, and Julie Otsuka, and focusing on narrative innovation and experimentation by Margaret Atwood, William Faulkner, and Susan Sontag, this book tackles questions of the formal and performative significance of the first-person plural voice in contemporary fiction"—Provided by publisher.

Identifiers: LCCN 2020000038 | ISBN 9780814214411 (cloth) | ISBN 081421441X (cloth) | ISBN 9780814278055 (ebook) | ISBN 0814278051 (ebook)

Subjects: LCSH: Fiction—20th century—History and criticism. | Grammar, Comparative and general—Pronoun. | Storytelling in literature. | Narration (Rhetoric)

Classification: LCC PN3503 .B426 2020 | DDC 809.3/923—dc23

LC record available at https://lccn.loc.gov/2020000038

Cover design by Andrew Brozyna
Text design by Juliet Williams
Type set in Adobe Minion Pro

Моїм батькам,
Тамарі й Івану Бехтам

CONTENTS

Acknowledgments   ix

INTRODUCTION   Telling a Story in the Plural   1

CHAPTER 1   We-Narrative: The First-Person Plural Narrative Situation   21

CHAPTER 2   We-Discourses: The We-Pronoun and Its Indicative and
             Performative Uses in Fiction   47

CHAPTER 3   Plural Narrators: Collective Voices, Lyric Progression,
             and Direct Speech by Groups   67

CHAPTER 4   Plural Perspective: Group Ethos, Narrators-Voyeurs,
             and Diegetic Levels   103

CHAPTER 5   Collective Knowledge: Epistemological Possibilities of
             We-Narrators, Gossip, and Unreliability   133

CHAPTER 6   Us versus Them: Community Dynamics in We-Narratives   165

Conclusion   177

Works Cited   185

Index   197

ACKNOWLEDGMENTS

DURING MY WORK on this book, I have accumulated a large debt of gratitude to my colleagues, friends, and family across Ukraine, Germany, Finland, the UK, and the US. Without their continuous support, both material and immaterial, my research would not have been possible. I also wish to acknowledge my institutional homes: Justus Liebig University Giessen in Germany, where the bulk of this book was written, as well as the University of Helsinki, in Finland, where I was able to finalize the manuscript. It all started, really, many years ago at the National Ivan Frankó University in Lviv, Ukraine.

I wish to wholeheartedly thank Ansgar Nünning, who played a crucial intellectual role at the stage when this project was finding focus; Greta Olson, who was this book's dedicated and generous commentator; and Heta Pyrhönen, whose support advanced the last versions of it. James Phelan and Peter Rabinowitz at The Ohio State University Press provided invaluable editorial and theoretical insight that shaped the book into what it is now. Ana Jimenez-Moreno offered reassuring guidance through the publication process. Marco Caracciolo's thoughtful comments made me see many of my arguments anew. Madeleine LaRue's meticulous copyediting added clarity to my prose and thoughts. My gratitude goes to René Dietrich, whose reading group changed my approach to theory; Christine Schwanecke; and everyone in the IPP IX. I am grateful to Maria Sruk, and Ivan Žgela, for welcoming me so warmly when I first came to Giessen. Rose Lawson and Ann van de

Veire, thank you for all the help, *Kuchen,* and tea. The many members of the KW club made me willing to brave Giessen for the sake of their company, intellectual generosity, and that weekly Wednesday evening: Thank you, Farzad Boobani, Tobias Gabel and Stephanie Brückel, Mirjam Horn-Schott and Matthias Schott, Francis Ipgrave, Tim Kurtzweil, Ana Fabíola Maurício and Henrique Frederico Rocha, Reinhard Möller, Alexander Scherr, Jutta Weingarten and Andreas Klöber. Theresa Beilschmidt, Christin Grunert, Katharina Kreuder-Sonnen, Christina Norwig, thank you for keeping our community alive long after Giessen. Gero Guttzeit and Daniel Hartley, two people whose ideas influenced this book the most, thank you for the thrill of theory debate, rhetoric, politics, and your friendship.

To my family, the most immediate and selfless community of support, I am forever grateful: my parents, Tamara and Ivan Bekhta, who taught me how to read, English, *and* how to read narratologically—this book is dedicated to them. Markó. Vira and Oleksandr Krynytski. Sofia and Anton Bekhta. Larysa Dovbenko. Aulikki, Esko, Leena, Tatu. Matti Kangaskoski, thank you for being my most honest critic and an infinitely patient listener during the years in which this book was written.

Theirs and many other voices are recorded, in one way or another, in the book that follows.

Work on this book has been partly funded by the Kone Foundation (Finland).

Parts of the introduction, chapter 1, and chapter 2 draw on material previously published in "We-Narratives: The Distinctiveness of Collective Narration" (*Narrative* 25, no. 2 [2017]: 164–81) and in "Emerging Narrative Situations: A Definition of We-Narratives Proper" (in *Emerging Vectors of Narratology,* ed. Per Krogh Hansen et al., 101–26 [Berlin: de Gruyter, 2017]).

Telling a Story in the Plural

STORIES ARE a social phenomenon and thus collective; they are composed and shared as part of a communal practice. Yet, the literal act of story*telling* is an individual performance, if we think of it as an instance of oral narration. It is, of course, possible to speak in turns or for a cacophony of voices to speak simultaneously, but one can only chant, recite, or sing in unison; it is not possible to tell a story in such a way. Even in the literary field, when an authors' collective writes a novel, that novel's fictional voices habitually emanate from individual characters. Nevertheless, there are exceptions to this literary convention: narratives that create genuinely plural voices that have no individual speaker behind them and that emanate from groups, communities, collectives, or nations. Such narratives can be constructed using one technique in particular, that of narration by the first-person *plural,* which creates a storytelling voice that is neither an implicit singular speaker nor an aggregation of many individual voices. Instead, this form expresses multiple subjectivities in their unity. This technique is the focus of this book. Plural narration, performed by a group itself, gives rise to a new narrative situation: we-narrative. By tracing we-narrative's distinctive elements and effects, I propose to make available a mode of narratological analysis that illuminates the existence in narrative fiction of this *structurally* and *compositionally* plural, collective way of telling.

A voice that is collective not just in an abstract sense, but in the literal situation of speech production, is a remarkable (fictional) possibility. China

Miéville literalizes this possibility in his novel *Embassytown* (2011) by imagining a new theory of language and beings who speak from two mouths simultaneously, conveying one mind and one meaning. Genuine we-narratives, I argue, approach a similar idea of a shared voice—although from a less fantastical angle—by constructing group narrators out of various types of everyday communities. This is especially true for the novels and short stories examined here: contemporary we-narratives in English.[1] Such narratives often choose communities as their protagonists and narrators, be it a group of friends, a small suburban neighborhood, a settlement, or a town. Consequently, many of the themes and plot structures in these texts revolve around conflicts of a communal nature, such as the confrontation between a community and an outsider or misfit. A suburban neighborhood scrutinizes a family who has just moved to their town in Joyce Carol Oates's novel *Broke Heart Blues* (1999). In Jeffrey Eugenides's *The Virgin Suicides* (1993), a reclusive family with four mysterious daughters fascinates and disturbs a group of boys—and through them, the rest of the neighborhood. This motif reappears in Hanna Pittard's *The Fates Will Find Their Way* (2011). Precarity, a defining condition of many contemporary communities, becomes the topic of Joshua Ferris's novel *Then We Came to the End* (2007), collectively told by a group of office workers. A lyrical chorus of Japanese immigrant women in the US testify to the hardships of immigration in Julie Otsuka's *The Buddha in the Attic* (2011). TaraShea Nesbit similarly describes a closed community through the plural female voice of *The Wives of Los Alamos* (2014), which can be compared to Kate Walbert's *Our Kind* (2005). Chang-rae Lee's *On Such a Full Sea* (2014), where a post-apocalyptic colony narrates "our" life through the life of "our" rebel, resonates with Zakes Mda's *Ways of Dying* (1995), which allegorically voices a nation's pursuit of a better future through its protagonist couple. The most often cited early example of a we-narrative, however, is William Faulkner's 1930 Gothic tale "A Rose for Emily," which, in one sense, is a story of complex social dynamics between insiders and outsiders within a small-

---

1. Whereas the history of we-narration in Anglophone fiction can be traced back to the late nineteenth century, over the past two decades there seems to have been a considerable increase in novels that use this storytelling voice, making it a contemporary phenomenon. Susan Lanser (1992) traces the early beginnings of the communal voice in fiction in Elizabeth Gaskell's *Cranford* (1853), Sarah Orne Jewett's *The Country of the Pointed Firs* (1896), and Marguerite Audoux's *L'Atelier de Marie-Claire* (1920), with the first full-blown we-voice appearing in Monique Wittig's *Les Guérillères* (1969). Brian Richardson, in *Unnatural Voices* (2006), finds an early example of we-narration in Joseph Conrad's *The Nigger of the 'Narcissus': A Tale of the Sea* (1897). It is important to note, however, that there is no statistical data to make definitive claims about the current rise of we-narratives—neither in Anglophone fiction nor elsewhere.

town community. The tropes of communal expression used in "A Rose for Emily" can be found in many of the above-mentioned works, which, in turn, serve as direct inspiration for their successors and slowly but surely develop the repertoire of narrative techniques that give voice to collectives.

Despite the regular appearance of we-narratives and a number of critical discussions of this phenomenon in narratology,[2] narrative theory has yet to do justice to the plural voice in fiction. The starting point of this book is the observation that the we-voice has generally been treated with suspicion: as an unreliable I-narrator, hiding behind a mask of collectivity, or as an "unnatural," impossible construction in contradistinction to the "natural" I-voice. I argue instead that we-narrators, in the full sense of the term as specified below, present an independent type of character narrators—*group* characters with *collective* voices—that differ in crucial ways from first-person narrators. Such character narrators are groups, not individuals. Consequently, the techniques for narrating and expressing their actions, mental states, and relations with other characters are different from those of singular characters. The effects they produce and the types of readerly engagement they require are likewise distinct. Narrative fiction, I argue, constitutes one of the sites of expression of human collectives and a place where collective subjectivities can be imagined, constructed, and given voice. This book offers a definition and discussion of a prominent technique of collective storytelling—we-narration—and of the narrative situation this technique creates—we-narrative.

To justify these opening claims and to give an initial sense of what I propose to define as a we-narrative, I shall begin with Faulkner's "A Rose for Emily" and its critical reception. As mentioned above, Faulkner's we-narrator relies on a set of characteristics and techniques that become paradigmatic to we-narratives and that are ubiquitous in recent texts. At the same time, however, this story's most striking formal feature, its plural narrator, has gone uncommented by many literary scholars and critics. This oversight lies partly in the peculiar nature of the first-person plural reference (of which more in chapter 2) and partly in the lack of a theoretical model that would consider plural narrators a possibility. Recognizing community as the narrator in "A Rose for Emily," however, opens up an array of thematic implications.

---

2. I am referring to the groundbreaking work by Lanser and Uri Margolin, as well as an extensive overview of experimental voices in fiction by Richardson in *Unnatural Voices*. More recent contributions to discussion include articles by Amit Marcus (2008a, 2008b, 2008c), Monika Fludernik (2011, 2017), Ruth Maxey (2015), and Jan Alber (2015).

A Paradigmatic Example of We-Narrative: Faulkner's "A Rose for Emily"

"A Rose for Emily" is one in a series of stories Faulkner wrote about his "townspeople" or, more generally, the antebellum South (see Skei 1999, 152). Set in the fictional village of Jefferson, Mississippi, the story opens with the death of Miss Emily Grierson. The village community, having gathered for her funeral, begins to reminisce about Emily's life in Jefferson, and the story's form, true to the gossipy nature of its content, adopts an ethical structure of "us" versus Emily. In other words, the focus of "our" telling about her comes to be on how she fit into "our" village. All the narratorial references are consistently made in the first-person plural, *we*, while all the references to Emily are in the distancing third person and combined with an external perspective. This referential setup, which includes no mention of an "I" in the course of the story, is the first mark of a we-narrative. This setup also invites the reader to adopt the villagers' opinions on the narrated events, as well as their shock upon discovering, after finally entering Emily's secluded house, that she had murdered her lover, Homer Barron, the man she was expected to marry, and kept his corpse in her house for decades, sleeping with it in her bed. The most readily available explanation to this crime is spelled out by the collective narrator: Homer had wanted to leave her, and the murder was a crime of passion, triggered, perhaps, by Emily's mental disorder. But apart from being a Southern Gothic tale, a horror story about necrophilia and madness, "A Rose for Emily" also yields itself to a multitude of other thematic and ethical interpretations.[3]

The variety of thematic readings of the short story, informed by various interpretive approaches, is striking: "A Rose for Emily" has been read as a "pure event without implication" (Lionel Trilling qtd. in Towner and Carothers 2006, 64), "an implied criticism of the South" and "a protest against the North" (Skinner 1985, 43), and a dismantling of "the male revisionist myth of Southern womanhood" (Robertson 2006, 161). Emily's act has been interpreted as misandrist or xenophobic, as directed against her community, against Homer as a man of lower social class (see Towner and Carothers 2006, 63), even as a hate crime, since Homer may have been gay and refused to marry her for

---

3. "Ethics" here refers to the rhetorical effects of a narrative and the reader's emotional and moral responses to and engagement with the narrated. Rhetorical ethics, according to James Phelan, regards literature primarily as a communicative event, "one in which tellers seek to engage and influence their audiences' cognition, emotions, and values" (2007, 203).

this reason (Blythe qtd. in Towner and Carothers, 63).[4] While some of these explanations seem more convincing than others, Faulkner's story insists on ambiguity, as Towner and Carothers (63) observe, and thus can sustain open speculations or detective-like solutions. However, it is curious that most of these interpretations ignore a centrally important factor, a crucial clue: They scarcely, if at all, consider the formal subtlety of "A Rose for Emily," namely its plural narration. The plural nature of the story's narrator is what allows competing interpretations to be sustained: A small, intimate community like Jefferson's would be able to convincingly house competing opinions, as some of them become incorporated into circles of gossip and others are elevated to the status of common knowledge. In her village, Emily's image devolves from a desired bride to orphan to "fallen" woman to mad spinster; since the narrator is virtually everybody else in town, there is no voice to challenge this image. The reader's emotional and ethical involvement in Emily's position are consequences of the reader's ethical engagement with the narrating community's fluctuating position and judgments.

It is therefore striking that the plurality of Faulkner's narrator has often been treated as an extension of a first-person singular narrator who speaks on behalf of the group: an anonymous narrator-neighbor (Kempton 1947, 104); a male "spokesman for the community" (Brooks 1983, 8); "the elderly narrator, possibly contemporary with Miss Emily" (Skinner 1985, 43); "an unidentified citizen of Jefferson" (Towner and Carothers 2006, 64). Even in Brian Richardson's investigation, which is dedicated specifically to we-narratives, this narrator is described as a clearly gendered "rural voice that speaks for the higher class of white males" (2006, 47).[5] One reason for this singularization and gendering of the we-narrator is, arguably, analytical: A he-reference to the we-narrator betrays the influence of the classical conception of the narrator-figure as always exclusively singular and, following that, of the same gender as the author unless otherwise explicitly stated. Second, being the story's protagonist, Emily overshadows the community who narrates, since "we" occupy the position of the observers. With narrator-observers, as James Phelan notes, "our interest ultimately is in the characters other than the character narrator—it's Ahab, Gatsby, and charming Billy rather than Ishmael, Nick, or McDermott's narrator that are at the center of their respective narratives" (2005, 199). How-

---

4. I am indebted to Theresa M. Towner and James B. Carothers's (2006) meticulous work on Faulkner's stories for many of the references in my overview of the critical response to "A Rose for Emily."

5. Even when the peculiar plural composition of the narratorial voice is recognized, the narrator is still described by the singular *he*-pronoun for convenience's sake, as in Sullivan's essay (1971, 175).

ever, as a synthetic element of this narrative,[6] the plural we-narrator is crucial for the understanding of the precise ways in which "A Rose for Emily" manages to affect its readers. Understood in collective terms, such a narrator also obviates the need for certain interpretively unproductive questions regarding the "real" identity of the speaker, the vagueness of "his" exact physical placement in the village, "his" seemingly inconsistent emotional involvement in the events narrated, or the implausible sources of "his" knowledge.[7]

When the text offers no clues for resolving these issues in singular terms, what is to be gained from approaching them as elements of a communal narrative voice? Let us first look at the construction of the communal narrator. Like most we-narratives, Faulkner's short story makes it impossible to identify a singular narrator,[8] let alone his or her gender. In a rare exception to the critical consensus, Alice Robertson similarly concludes that, despite numerous theories about the identity of the unnamed narrator of Jefferson, "in reality, the narrator's identity remains nebulous because there is simply not enough evidence within the text to prove either case" (2006, 164). Indeed, sometimes women are explicitly excluded from the we-group, but so are men, the younger generation, older people, tax officials, the druggist, and Emily's neighbor—that is, any number of members of the Jefferson community. This is, after all, the peculiarity of we-reference: "We" stands in for a community, but, such a community being diverse, made up of different ages, genders, opinions, and judgments, it is necessary to occasionally single out some members of the collectivity to describe their particular stance on the event in question. The referent of the "we" is thus inherently ambiguous and unstable. In any given passage in the story, "we" can be "all" or just "some of us." But

6. To refer to the effects and functions of different narrative elements here and in what follows, I rely on Phelan's classification of narrative components into mimetic, thematic, and synthetic. The mimetic component invokes "an audience's interest in the characters as possible people and in the narrative world as like our own" (2005, 20). "Responses to the thematic component involve an interest in the ideational function of the characters and in the cultural, ideological, philosophical, or ethical issues" (20), and responses to the synthetic component are those to the formal construction of the characters and the narrative. Usually, "when both the mimetic and the synthetic components of the protagonist are emphasized, the thematic component of both character and narrative gets foregrounded" (15). We-narrators who are protagonists, for example, often offer meta-comments on (i.e., foreground the synthetic aspect of) their plural nature, thus making their thematic significance as communal or collective voices even more prominent (see Mda's novel *Ways of Dying*, discussed in chapter 5).

7. See Skei (1999, 155) for an example of a summary based on the assumption that its narrator is singular and male.

8. But, as the example of *deadkidsongs* (Litt 2001) will demonstrate, this is not always the case: Litt's multiperson novel combines various narrative situations and, in the chapters written in the we-narrative mode, its effect relies heavily on the possibility of a singular speaker behind the "we" (a group of four boys) and the denial of his identification.

on the whole, this we-narrator strongly implies a community, the entire town. Notice, for example, how the communal frame of reference "our whole town" in the following examples becomes differentiated into the men and women of the community:

> (1) **Our whole town** went to her funeral: **the men** through a sort of respectful affection for a fallen monument, **the women** mostly out of curiosity to see the inside of her house. (Faulkner 1995a, 119)[9]

> (1') So the next day **we all said**, "She will kill herself"; and we said it would be the best thing. . . . Then **some of the ladies** began to say that it was a disgrace to the town and a bad example to the young people. **The men** did not want to interfere. (126)

"We," the town, describe "our" communal actions, which are then followed by the necessary qualifications as to what various subgroups did or said. Similarly, whenever one part of the Jefferson community is singled out with the help of the third-person reference, it is subsequently referred to as "we" and thus reincorporated into the collective, as in the following examples (2) through (4). This practice diversifies the communal voice, but also points to its complex construction and the different social strands of which "we" consists and the various subgroups from which "we" draw "our" knowledge.

> (2) But there were still **others, older people,** who said that even grief could not cause a real lady to forget *noblesse oblige*—without calling it *noblesse oblige*. **They** just **said**, "Poor Emily." (124–25)

> (2') When she had first begun to be seen with Homer Barron, **we had said**, "She will marry him. . . . Later **we said**, "Poor Emily." (126)

In example (2), the pronoun "they" refers to the older people of the town gossiping about Emily's affair with Homer in section 3 of the story. Later, in section 4, "we" continue to gossip about Emily and Homer (2') using the same words as the "older people," thus uniting the narrative voice throughout the story. First, the gossiping is described impersonally, in the third person, but later "we" do not hide the fact that "we" are the ones gossiping.

---

9. Here and in following examples from "A Rose for Emily," the bold emphasis is mine. Similarly, all emphasis in bold throughout the book is mine, with italics reserved for original emphasis.

(3) On the first of the year **they mailed her** a tax notice. (120)

(3') Each December **we sent her** a tax notice. (128)

"They" (3) refers in section 1 to a "deputation" from the newer generation on the Board of Aldermen of the town. But when this episode is mentioned again in example (3'), which comes from section 4, "we" are engaging in the same action, making it apparent that "they" in (3) are part of "us." The same change of reference happens in (4):

(4) And, as we had expected all along, within three days Homer Barron was back in town. **A neighbor saw** the Negro man admit him at the kitchen door at dusk one evening.
    And that was the last **we saw** of Homer Barron. (127)

As can be seen from examples (1) through (4), whenever certain members of the community are singled out, they are either embedded into the we-narrator's frame of reference (women and men of "our town" in example (1)) or merge back into the we-community at a later point in the narration ((2') through (4)). As soon as one of "us" witnesses or hears something, it becomes part of the communal pool of knowledge.

Generally, fluctuation between collective and individual characters (both group members and outsiders) is a nearly indispensable feature of narrative progression in the "we" mode. As Margolin observes: "No literary 'we' narrative moves entirely on the global institutional level of, for example, 'our party' or 'our university,' with its nondistributive properties and actions" (2001, 251). Dramatization of the we-narrator as a character usually involves some particularizations, such as singling out certain subgroups or individuals that might be viewed as exemplary of some aspect of "our" collectivity. In "A Rose for Emily," these are groups within the village—women, men, older people, officials, and so on. Despite its occasional singling out of separate members of the community, the communal narrator nonetheless clearly distinguishes itself from outsiders: Emily and her family, Homer Barron, the Northerners, the contractors. They, the outsiders, are always referred to in the third person, even though the degree to which they are removed from "us" may differ. Emily, for example, used to be part of Jefferson's community, and so "our" concern for "poor Emily" may at times be interpreted as a wish for her to regain her social status, whereas "we" are outwardly hostile to Homer, an alien in Jefferson. Of course, belonging can be a fluctuating condition, one perceived differently even by members of the same group. While the "we" of Jefferson never includes Emily, third-person references to out-of-town outsiders are emphasized by other linguistic markers, such as the derogative terms "nigger" and "Yankee": "The construction company came with niggers and mules and machinery, and a foreman named Homer Barron, a Yankee" (Faulkner 1995a, 124). Elsewhere in the story, the narrator is careful to use the then-polite term "Negro"; the cruder word's appearance here is, possibly, to further stress the outsider status of the workers, to make "a class distinction between town-dwelling blacks, including house servants [all members of the community, NB], and the gang of black laborers" (Towner and Carothers 2006, 70). Such references are not incorporated into the "we" later on, unlike the references to the members of "our" community. Outsiders and boundaries, it has been noted, are defining markers of a community (A. Cohen 1985, 12): Community is a group of people who identify themselves as part of one group on the basis of a common feature (or features) *and* through a significant distinction to members of other groups. In other words, the act of symbolically constructing a community as a separate entity involves recognizing who belongs and who does not.

Besides the exclusionary they-references, the we-narrator's position as a *communal* character is consolidated with the help of descriptions of collective action. For example, in the final section 5 of the story—which Skei (1999, 155) interprets as the only passage in which the anonymous single narrator is present—all of "us" seem to be physically present at the scene (the whole village has gathered at Emily's house for her funeral). This scene also resumes the chronological narration of the story, after a string of associative digressions that started after they came to her funeral in the first paragraph in section 1:

> For a long while we just stood there, looking down at the profound and fleshless grin. . . . Then we noticed that in the second pillow was the indentation of a head. One of us lifted something from it, and leaning forward, that faint and invisible dust dry and acrid in the nostrils, we saw a long strand of iron-gray hair.[10] (Faulkner 1995a, 130)

The last section of the story contributes significantly to the creation of the *character* we-narrator: Not only does the narrator function as an exclusive focalizer in this passage, but it also engages in a truly collective action (e.g.,

---

10. The communal narrator repeats the exact wording of earlier descriptions of Emily's hair: "Up to the day of her death at seventy-four it [her hair, NB] was still that vigorous iron-gray, like the hair of an active man" (Faulkner 1995a, 127–28). But "we" do not spell out the inference (i.e., it was Emily who slept next to the corpse).

a physical action performed simultaneously by all members). It "becomes an actor, physically present in the story" (Richardson 2006, 47): "We" stood there, "we" all leaned forward to see what one of "us" had in their hand. This physical embodiment of the we-narrator relies here on collective terms and thus ensures that the narrator is not reduced to a singularity, either in this passage or in the rest of the narrative.

In short, then, recognizing the theoretical possibility of plural narrators, corroborated by textual evidence, makes possible an analysis of "A Rose for Emily" that takes into consideration the communal origins of the narrating voice, and with it, the politics of inclusion and exclusion, normative beliefs and practices, and so on. It allows us to omit theoretical speculations about which member of the community might be the narrator and facilitates the recognition of the small-town ideology that permeates the telling of Emily's story. The community claims to know everything—it is, after all, the source of common knowledge—and tells a detailed (omniscient) story in which it is also personally (homodiegetically) invested, creating an irreducible tension between fact and assumption. For the reader, the complex ethical consequences of this short story thus arise from an interplay between two groups of relations: (1) the community's ethical relation to Emily and to the telling and (2) the reader's relation to the narrating community, their judgments, and their telling, as well as to Emily herself.

Since Emily is presented exclusively through the we-narrator's external perspective—necessary to achieve the surprising ending—"our" account of the state of things is the only information the reader has, and so the reader is invited to become a detective alongside the narrator, investigating Emily's life. More generally, an external perspective on the main character, as Franz Karl Stanzel observes, complicates any potential sympathy the reader might feel toward her, because the less we know about this character's motives for her actions and behaviors, the less we are inclined "to feel understanding, forbearance, tolerance, and so on, in respect to the conduct of this character" (1984, 128). But in the case of "A Rose for Emily," because the external perspective is that of a conservative, small-town community, a sympathetic response to Emily's character, at least in a contemporary reader, may become possible *despite* the we-narrator's increasingly harsh judgments of her—especially if the reader recognizes the largely unfavorable social conditions in which Emily lived. Such a reader may dissociate herself from the we-narrator's communal values, which, as Robertson observes (2006, 159), include patronizing control, a constrictive class structure ("a lady would never marry a 'day laborer'"), and rigid gender prescriptions. These may be, at least partly, the reasons for Emily's social decline and her murder of Homer: A respectable Southern lady cannot work—so what to do when she is orphaned? She cannot be single; how would she sustain herself? She cannot have lovers—but what if she does, and a Northerner at that? At the same time, the Jefferson community often seems to genuinely care about Emily, complicating any such straightforward interpretation and suggesting that both Emily and her town are caught up in the shift between the old and new values of the post–Civil War South (see Robertson 2006, 159). On the one hand, then, the communal narrator's conservative values may create a progressive image of Emily *ex negativo*. On the other hand, this plural narrating voice often can successfully pass as authoritative, because its statements come across as common knowledge and universally accepted judgments. This makes it difficult for the reader to pinpoint the reasons for the narrator's changing attitudes toward Emily, nor can the reader adopt an unambiguous ethical stance toward the story's conclusion. The story thus structurally registers the complex dynamics between individuals and communities in general.

"A Rose for Emily" can be considered a paradigmatic we-narrative, with its communal narrator, small-town setting, and outsider protagonist, as well as its structure of associative chronology and the manner in which the narrator constructs communal knowledge and ethical evaluations. Moreover, the reversal of the central/peripheral relation between the individual agent (Emily) and the collective (Jefferson community) is a crucial characteristic of this story and another key feature of we-narratives (Margolin 2000, 594–95). Such features, shared by other works discussed in this book, are defining of the narrative situation dominated by a plural narrating voice—of we-narrative.

Definition of We-Narrative

The analysis above has made prominent a number of characteristics that can now be summarized into an extended definition of we-narrative:

> We-narrative is defined by the narrator speaking, acting, and thinking as a collective narrative agent and possessing a collective subjectivity, which the narrative performatively creates and maintains throughout its course. In other words, the we-narrator is a collective character narrator whose voice does not imply an "I"; in we-narrative a group, not an individual, is telling the story. The first-person plural pronoun is therefore used in what I term the "performative mode": The narrator's consistent self-reference as "we" produces a sense of the group as a separate unit, reinforces its solidarity, and removes any possible implications of an "I" speaker behind the "we." To put

this in formal terms, we-narrative is a narrative situation[11] where the defining element is "person, *plural.*" For *most* intents and purposes, such a narrator can be described as identical with the characters in terms of the realms of existence, or homodiegetic, although this distinction does not hold for plural narrators to the extent that it usually does for singular ones. In linguistic terms, the morphological peculiarity of the pronoun "we" offers a very flexible designation for the narrator, which can at any point in the narrative expand or contract, including or excluding various referents from its scope.

I shall now unpack the elements of this definition. First of all, I claim that we-narrative is defined by its group narrator because I rely on the rhetorical conception of narrative as a communicative act: as "somebody telling somebody else on some occasion and for some purpose(s) that something happened" (Phelan 2017, 5). Thus, the figure of the teller becomes distinctive if "somebody" turns into "somebod*ies.*" This rhetorical definition applies to narrative both generally in its function as a symbolically significant social practice—in this case, as a rhetorical act—*and* specifically to the form of narrative as a represented situation of telling, which is characteristic of many fictional texts. Still, literary narrative is perceivably more complex than the structure of represented telling and requires further description. To this end, I combine the rhetorical approach with the category of narrative situation as conceptualized by Franz Karl Stanzel. Within Stanzel's theory, literary narrative can be defined as a mediated artistic presentation of experience ("what happened," in Phelan's definition).[12] Stanzel sees "mediacy" (*Mittelbarkeit*, where *mittelbar* also translates as "indirect") as the generic characteristic of any narrative—a characteristic that derives from a more fundamental epistemological quality,

---

11. Technically, of course, "narrative" cannot be equated with "narrative situation." I am using the phrase "we-narrative" as a shorthand designation for the first-person plural narrative situation. Stanzel himself, emphasizing constant modifications of narrative situations in a novel, "from chapter to chapter or from paragraph to paragraph" (1984, 47), grants that if it is possible to determine a predominant narrative situation in a novel, the novel can be described in terms of this situation—for example, "the authorial novel" (46).

12. I should note that all symbolic forms are shaped by and shaping of human experience, understood here broadly as any phenomenon in the perceived reality. The distinctiveness of the narrative mediation lies in its temporal structure. A convincing case for temporality has been made by Richard Walsh, who offers a minimal definition of narrative as "the semiotic articulation of linear temporal sequence" (2017, 473). Effects of causality, experientiality, progress, and so on are therefore viewed as products of the sense-making moves made possible by such structure. Without going into the specifics of three interrelated distinctions of narrative as a product, process, and mode of comprehension or cognition, suffice it to say that in this combination of definitions, narrative can be viewed as an articulation of temporally structured experience. See also chapter 3.

the Kantian view that "we do not apprehend the world in itself, but rather as it passes through the medium of an observing mind" (1984, 4). In these terms, story-as-experience is conceived and formally expressed, or *mediated,* via one of the available modes of literary representation: "*Narration* in the true sense of mediacy, that is, the reader has the impression that he is confronted by a personalized narrator" (i.e., somebody telling somebody else) or "direct or immediate *presentation,* that is, the reflection of the fictional reality in the consciousness of a character" (Stanzel 1984, 48).[13] One of these two modes (teller or reflector) in a dialectic combination with the categories of person (homo- or heterodiegetic, to use Genette's shorthand terms) and perspective (internal or external) produce certain recognizable forms of narratives, or narrative situations.[14] On the basis of this theoretical background, we-narrative may thus be defined concisely as a first-person (re)presentation (*Darstellung*) of some collective or shared experience (in a philosophical sense) as if it were told, enacted, and thought by a group acting as a character.

Stanzel's model is particularly valuable in that it provides a means to describe a narrative form in its totality and resolves a terminological confusion between "narrative" and "narration" in the existing work on we-narratives. In the following chapters, I discuss in more detail how viewing we-narrative as a narrative situation helps to establish its structurally significant features—that is, the defining ones—thereby delimiting a we-narrative from other uses of we-discourses in fiction and making explicit its *own* conventions of narration and rhetorical effects.[15] Anticipating that discussion, I want to note here that

---

13. This distinction, as Paul Hernadi observes in his introduction to Stanzel's *Theory of Narrative,* reflects the one originating in Plato's diegesis and mimesis (see Stanzel 1984, 65) and known under various names: subjective versus objective narration (Spielhagen), telling versus showing (Friedman), and texts with speakers versus texts without speakers (Doležel), to name the most common ones.

14. A classification within these distinctions, however, calls for some qualifications: In terms of person, I consider the grammatical category of number in addition to the narrator's relation to the narrated; in terms of perspective, a combination of internal and external ones within the same narrative level *and* the same narrative instance is possible, changing mode from teller to reflector and vice versa.

15. To be clear, I rely on the notion of narrative situation in order to delimit we-narrative as a separate narrative form, but it is not my aim to revise the Typological Circle of narrative situations itself—its revision has been attempted by others and has proved a daunting and unsuccessful task. Besides an attempt to update the Circle via inclusion of second-person narrative undertaken by Fludernik (e.g., 1994b; see Reitan 2011 for a summary and a well-thought-out critique), I have in mind Richardson's (1994, 324) attempt to place we-narrative on it. Richardson's proposal, while schematizing the relationship between "we" and other narrative modes metaphorically, does not comply with the classificatory principles of the Circle and thus cannot be regarded as a modification.

the narrative situation of the first-person *plural* is defined by the category of person, similarly to Stanzel's first-person narrative. This category refers to an initial distinction between (a) narrators involved in the storyworld (homodiegesis) and (b) narrators who are not involved (heterodiegesis), which further defines these narrators as either (a) physically embodied and present in the storyworld, possessing an autonomous system of deictic reference, and motivated to tell their story for existential reasons, or (b) only minimally physically present outside the narrated storyworld (or not at all), in which case the deictic planes of their narrations and of the storyworld are separate, and their telling is motivated by impersonal, aesthetic reasons. We-narrators can indeed be readily described as involved in the storyworld, or homodiegetic, with all the subsequent implications. However, as will become clear later on, the distinction of person (homo-/heterodiegesis) does not apply to plural narrators to the same extent that it does to I-narrators. While "we" are, on the one hand, physically involved in the narrated action as a group, on the other hand, "we" also possess a more abstract, disembodied level of existence as a supra-individual entity. The "we" of Jefferson in "A Rose for Emily" is described as physically present in Emily's house in the last section of the story, but for the most part, "we" are the abstract community, approaching embodiment only in "our" individual members. Because of the personal involvement, "we" can be existentially invested in the telling, but at the same time "we" can also adopt a position of the voice of common sense and transpersonal authority. This is why I suggest modifying the category of person to "person, *plural*." In most cases, it is possible to describe a we-narrator within this category as a homodiegetic narrator, and occasional exceptions to that role can be explained, for example, as paralepses. Nevertheless, in chapters 3 and 4, I test the usefulness of a more radical approach to classifying narrators, suggested by Richard Walsh (2007), in an attempt to move beyond the division of homo-/heterodiegesis. Both Stanzel's and Genette's categories of narrative were influenced by Saussurean linguistics, which established the meaning of sign through oppositional pairs. For Stanzel, the category of person was one such opposition aimed at establishing the difference between so-called first- and third-person narratives. But if we-narrators are a distinct, third type of fictional tellers and there exists an *another*-person narrative, then the logic of the oppositional *pair* is disrupted, and we-narratives may be classified in modified or even new terms.

I have now briefly discussed the elements of narrative, narrative situation, and person from the definition above. This leaves the issues of the pronoun and the meaning of collective. As the performativity of the "we" in we-narrative should be minimally clear already from the definition (and will be discussed at length in chapter 2), I shall focus here on the we-narrator as a collective subject. In my claim that a certain, performative use of the we-reference in fiction constructs a collective character, I rely on a sociological meaning of collectivity. In his book *The Philosophy of Sociality* (2007), Raimo Tuomela shows the irreducible difference between three modes of human social interaction: individuals acting as "private" persons in the "I-mode" (3), individuals acting in a progroup fashion but still pursuing their own goals ("the progroup I-mode," 3), and individuals acting in the we-mode (or "the group mode," 3). The we-mode differs from the I-mode in patterns of thinking, feeling, and acting:

> Central parts of the social world—including social groups, social practices, and social institutions—conceptually (and, typically, functionally) require we-mode thinking and acting and, more broadly, the full we-perspective. In turn, we-mode thinking and acting require and are (conceptually and factually) based on thinking and acting as a group member and therefore thinking and acting for a group reason (in a full-blown sense requiring the satisfaction of the Collectivity Condition). (13)

The Collectivity Condition refers here to the supraindividual sense of the group, "the idea of the group members necessarily 'standing or falling together'" (16) when it comes to, for example, actions, opinions, and beliefs that concern the group. There is a difference between two or more individuals acting for one and the same reason (acting in the I-mode, as an aggregated private construction) and these individual acting as a group (in the we-mode, as a collective). Tuomela gives a simple example of two individuals going to have lunch at Alfonzo's (46–47): A statement that "We intend to go to Alfonzo's for lunch" can be interpreted as (a) two people having separate intentions to have lunch at Alfonzo's and who might know about each other's intentions. Regardless of whether one of them makes it, the intention of the other one to have lunch is satisfied. Or it can be interpreted as (b) a "proper we-intention," where "your personal lunch-going intention is to participate in our going to Alfonzo's for lunch" (47). If you do not come, this intention cannot be satisfied by my actions alone. On a bigger scale, the Collectivity Condition

> makes the individual members' collective attitudes and actions in a sense interchangeable and depersonalized, at least in an egalitarian group: It is necessarily the case that if one group member has a (distributive and distributed) collective group attribute, then all the others who occupy a similar

position will have it. Strict individuality is thus blocked and this shows that the Collectivity Condition represents the group level on the level of group members. (48)

Translated into narratological terminology, Tuomela's we-mode theory of social interaction supports my argument for treating the we-narrator under a similar collectivity condition, as a narratorial agent in its own right, capable of acting as a supraindividual unit—an independent character—and exhibiting its own beliefs and other mental states. And, since we-narrator characters are groups whose members are almost never completely disclosed (let alone reduced to a single voice), such characters can be seen as dramatizations of the collective mode of experience in fiction. In other words, we-narrative's rhetorical aim is often to present the sense of groupness from an abstract vantage point, rather than through the eyes of individuals, even if those individuals are acting in the we-mode.

Thus, we-narratives create a narrator whose identity is collective, and this status is structurally significant: It changes the construction of the narrator's knowledge, speech representation, action, and interaction with other characters. The reader has the impression that she is confronted, for example, by a collective statement, a summary of experience and not by one recognizable speaker. That is why instances of we-narration often found in multiperson narratives will not be classified here as we-narratives—they do not induce the representational changes mentioned above. Similarly, the use of "we" on the narratorial level alone is not enough to create a we-narrative (as this is merely an instance of *pluralis auctoris* or a feature of an authorial narrative situation), nor are we-references by an I-narrator limited to the story level (as they will not change the first-person *singular* form of such narratives). We-groups are usually firmly established as characters (main or marginal) by their physical and emotional involvement in the narrated events, which cancels some of the amorphousness of the we-reference: "We" constantly speak about "our" identity, activities, plans, emotions, worries, and more. Its consistent voice, together with its occasional comments to the narratee, strengthen the narrator's role as a group character. An important feature of we-narrators is a group self-image, that is, the awareness of itself as a group (see Margolin 2001, 247).[16]

16. While I largely agree with Margolin's conclusions about formal features of we-narratives, I do, however, disagree with his description of the narrative "we"—as opposed to the lyrical "we"—as always belonging to a single sayer on the highest level of narrative embedding, even if the narrative itself does not suggest there is such an individual sayer (Margolin 1996, 119–20). In his 1996 article, Margolin adheres to the classical view of the narrator and stresses that the narrative "we" speaks only about the group, not for it, which means that the "literary narrative 'we' speech act is hence not a group speech act" (120). I maintain the opposite view.

At the same time, being a plurality (often, a community), "we" is rarely a monolithic character, as it stands in for diverse subgroups. This is where the linguistic peculiarity of the first-person plural pronoun plays a significant role. As Richardson observes: "'We' may represent an intimate or a vast group, and its composition may—and usually does—change during the course of the fiction" (2006, 38). Since we-members may be of different ages and genders and possess varying attitudes and opinions, the we-narrator often singles out these subgroups by references to "some of us," "others of us," or "the rest of us," as well as to individual we-group members. These particularizations shape the narrative fabric of we-narratives as the narration progresses by shifting between the collective and the individual, while nevertheless maintaining the structural dominance of the plural person of the narrator. The we-narrator comes across as a consolidated figure, not least because its self-reference ("we") remains morphologically unchanged, despite the changes in its scope. Furthermore, what distinguishes a full-blown we-narrator from I-narrators and intermediary cases of thematically significant uses of we-reference is the holistic, supraindividual level that this narrator creates. In this sense, as Margolin also observes, "we" is different from "I + you + him/her": "There can obviously be no groups without individuals who embody them, but groups can and do have attributes that belong to the holistic level only" (2000, 598). The we-narrator refers to a collection of individuals who, as a group, necessarily lose their individual properties—the group being "independent of and more important than any of the individuals who compose it" (Hicks 1974, 27). This observation stems from sociological research into everyday, nonfictional groups, but easily extends to their fictional representations.

To sum up, this difference between functioning as individuals and as part of a group underlies my discussion of properties of we-narrators in fiction. I suggest that the representation of groups in we-narratives literalizes the central implication of the group mode by representing groupness not only through individual characters acting in the we-mode, but through groups themselves, which thus function as characters and as narrators. Such character narrators are distinguished by their idiom, are physically embodied in their members, and gain agency through joint actions, joint mental activity, and a shared group ethos. Their group knowledge, beliefs, or attitudes are more than mere aggregates of individual components thereof and thus are not reducible to any individual member of the we-group (e.g., Mathiesen 2007; Hakli, Miller, and Tuomela 2010). It is therefore possible to talk of we-narrators who "think," "feel," and "see" without deeming such collective characters transgressive, impossible, or otherwise "unnatural." This is not to claim that there is a direct correspondence between collective characters and real-world groups, or that groups—and fictional communities, such as the we-narrator of Jefferson—think and feel in any literal sense of individual mind. They are *viewed* as having these capabilities, for example, in sociology (Tuomela 2013, 16)—a view that can be similarly useful for current narratological ventures into the poetics of collective narration. We-narrative offers the possibility of a new type of narrative voice: the voice of a group, community, society, or other collectivity. Importantly, for a narrative to create such a full-blown we-narrator, rather than a progroup I-narrator, it has to create the conditions for its own coming into being, both in structural and in thematic terms. I examine these in detail throughout the book.

Before fully delving into the discussion of we-narratives, I would like to acknowledge my theoretical debts. The definition of we-narrative, which I suggested above and which is the foundation of this book, intervenes into the existing research on narration in the plural with an aim to establish "we-narrative" as a term, elevating it from its role as a loose reference to the various uses of the we-pronoun in fiction. I offer it as a designation of a particular narrative situation, one where the narrator is a we-group, not an "I." (In what follows, this opposition between "we" and "I" also often transforms into the one between "community" and "individual," but, of course, the reverse does not apply: Neither communal nor individual forms of narrative expression have to necessarily take on these pronouns.) In this sense, my treatment of we-narration directly builds on the idea of a communal narrative voice (in the simultaneous form) as conceived by Susan Lanser in her *Fictions of Authority: Women Writers and Narrative Voice* (1992). My approach is also informed by Uri Margolin's extensive work on we- and collective narratives and, in particular, his articles "Telling Our Story: On 'We' Literary Narratives" (1996) and "Telling in the Plural: From Grammar to Ideology" (2000). I must note, however, that Margolin explains we-narration in terms of speech act theory as always rooted in a singular speaker; I adopt a different approach, since many of the narratives work against such a conclusion.

More recently, narration in the plural has been considered from contextualist angles by Brian Richardson and Amit Marcus, who both rely on an ostensive definition of we-narrative. In my work, I extend Richardson's crucial observation that "it is most useful to see the 'we'-narrator as a different kind of figure from the realistic type of first person narrator" (2009, 152); *pace* Richardson, however, I do not consider the we-narrator as "a postmodern first person narrator who refuses to be bound by the epistemological rules of realism" (152), but rather as a distinct first-person *plural* narrator, whose nature it is to possess collective epistemological and other qualities. Marcus uses the term "we-narrative" to refer to various instances of we-reference in fiction (2008c, 2) and avoids a more rigorous definition because of "the scarcity of such narratives" (2008b, 135) and because "some of the most noteworthy ways of employing the first-person plural are best illustrated in texts that alternate between 'we' and other forms of narration" (2008c, 2). But does *any* mention of "we" by the narrator justify calling the form we-narrative, instead of the usual first-person narrative or some other designation? In light of the terminological confusion around different types of plural reference, I have proposed precisely the kind of more rigorous definition that Marcus strives to avoid. The advantages of such a definition, as I argue in chapter 1, include the possibility to recognize the rhetorical effects specific to we-narratives and to distinguish them from those of we-discourses used in other narrative situations; the possibility to identify various ideological implications of narration in the plural that hinge on the opposition between individual and collective; and added clarity in the understanding of how representations of fictional collectives work, without the burden of false interpretive questions of who is *really* speaking when "we" are speaking. To address the complex composition of the we-narrator, I draw on Monika Fludernik's (2011) detailed discussion of referential indeterminacy in you- and we-narratives. Fludernik's definition of we-narratives is also an ostensive one, implying a singular speaker behind the "we" in inclusive ("I + you") or exclusive ("I + she/he/they") variants of we-narratives.[17] It is, however, Fludernik's earlier work on second-person narratives that informs my discussion further: My distinction between two fundamentally different functions of the "we" in literature—namely, indicative and performative—takes its cue from Fludernik's definition of second-person narrative whose aim is "to distinguish it from other uses of the second person in narrative fiction and non-literary texts" (2011, 106; see also Fludernik 1994a). Generally, the following discussion of we-narratives should offer possibilities for a further reconceptualization of current narratological problems and add to the critical vocabulary of forms of contemporary fiction.

This book continues with a development and contextualization of the definition of we-narrative in chapters 1 and 2, while also focusing on the

---

17. In Fludernik's 2018 publication on the "we" in fiction—her most recent one at the time when this book goes into print—she suggests a more explicit formulation: "*We*-narratives are properly texts in which *we* is used consistently to refer to the plural protagonists (and, possibly, speakers or writers)" (172). This still leaves open the question of the status of I-narrators' we-references and whether they qualify as the change in the narrative situation from the regular first person to first-person plural.

differences between a properly narrative form structured around "we" and other discourses that use the first-person plural reference. I then rely on the logic of description of narrative situations and its three elements in order to address the effects of the plural narrating voice on various aspects of narrative. Chapter 3 takes up the element of person (the plural narrator and its consequences), and chapter 4 moves on to perspective (collective focalization). Since in Stanzel's classification the element of mode is the initial distinction on which person and perspective are based, I shall not dedicate a full chapter to the mode of we-narratives. By definition it is the teller mode, as the plural narrator dominates the "we" narrative situation. Therefore, chapter 5, which addresses knowledge construction by we-narrators, only implicitly draws on the distinction of mode in the section on unreliability,[18] without granting it equal footing with person and perspective. Finally, chapter 6 brings all these theoretical strands together in an analysis of Alice Elliott Dark's short story "Watch the Animals" (1999), which is thematically and formally similar to Faulkner's "A Rose for Emily," discussed in the introduction. It thus offers a good test case for the model of analysis of we-narratives developed in the book—and an example of the development of the technique of we-narration since the 1930s.

---

18. The mode distinction between teller and reflector has general repercussions for an understanding of the effects and functions of unreliability (see Stanzel 1984, 147).

CHAPTER 1

We-Narrative

The First-Person Plural Narrative Situation

I APPROACH fictional we-narratives on the basis of three premises: (1) there exists, in fiction, a plural narrating voice that gives expression to collective subjectivity; (2) this voice, manifest in the first-person plural pronoun "we," cannot be reduced to an implicit "I" speaking on behalf of the group behind the "we"; and (3) this voice, dramatized in the "person" of narrator, is at the heart of an independent narrative situation, a we-narrative, that establishes and operates according to its own conventions of narration. Fictional narratives that use the we-reference in this way are relatively rare, but they nevertheless provide enough grounds to claim that there is a distinctive narrative situation, the first-person *plural*. As I mentioned in the opening remarks, narrative theory has yet to do justice to this narrative form, although there is an increased interest in all things collective at the moment. While my discussion occasionally steers to diverse related issues, such as the creation in fiction of group subjectivity or collective consciousness, the guiding interest of this chapter is in the *form of the first-person plural*.

Despite Lanser's groundbreaking work on communal voice in *Fictions of Authority* (1992) and Margolin's theory of collective narrative agents, narration in the plural has been continuously measured by the I-narrator's yardstick. This has led to a confusion, endemic to recent theoretical texts and bibliographies devoted to we-narratives,[1] as to what exactly the term "we-narrative" encompasses. Furthermore, the collective composition of many narrators, as well as the attempts of narrative fiction to create a specific form of expression for collective social experiences, are largely overlooked by narratology. We-narration has been often treated as a "natural" storytelling mode, an extension of everyday we-discourses, or, at another extreme, as an experimental, "unnatural" impossibility. This state of things is, arguably, due to the influence that classical theories of the narrator continue to exert and because of the ubiquity of we-discourses in factual storytelling, which somewhat masks its semantic and artistic potential in fiction. This chapter aims to iron out such issues and position we-narratives, as I propose to define them, in relation to the terms and definitions of collective (and communal), multiperson, and "unnatural" texts.

A Brief Taxonomy of We-Uses: Examples of We-Narratives, First-Person Narratives, and Significant Shifts

An extensive bibliography of literary we-narratives, compiled by Fludernik (2011) of texts analyzed by Marcus, Margolin, Richardson, and Fludernik herself, is a telling example of the confusion over what counts as a we-narrative. The bibliography includes Faulkner's short story "A Rose for Emily" (1930), a paradigmatic example of a we-narrative (see the introduction), together with his "That Will Be Fine" (1935), a first-person narrative (*sensu* Stanzel) in which an I-narrator uses we-references to talk about various joint activities. At the same time, out of the two short stories by "Fernandes" and Joyce Carol Oates (1975), "The Brain of Dr. Vicente" and "Parricide" (a we-narrative and a first-person narrative with extensive passages of we-narration, respectively), only the first is included in the bibliography. Similarly, the bibliography includes Jeffrey Eugenides's novel *The Virgin Suicides* (1993) and Michael Dorris's *A Yellow Raft in Blue Water* (1987). The former is a we-narrative with a communal we-narrator, whereas the latter is a multiperson narrative composed of three sequential first-person narrators whose accounts contribute to a creation of a communal story but formally do not constitute a we-narrative.

Fludernik's bibliography thus uses the term "we-narrative" in at least three senses. These senses may be traced back to Lanser's notion of "communal

---

1. For the bibliographies see Richardson (2006, 141–42), a chronological list in Richardson (2009, 158–59), and Fludernik (2011, 136–41).

voice," introduced in *Fictions of Authority* to complement the categories of authorial and personal voices of narrators in two major narrative situations—authorial and first-person, respectively. Lanser's investigation focuses on the relationship between narrative form and the form-dependent construction of the authority of a narrative voice.[2] Communal narrative voice, for Lanser, is "either a collective voice or a collective of voices that share narrative authority" and can be produced in "a *singular* form in which one narrator speaks for a collective, a *simultaneous* form in which a plural 'we' narrates, and a *sequential* form in which individual members of a group narrate in turn" (1992, 21).[3] The term "we-narrative," it seems, has come to be used in all of these senses—at least as publications by Fludernik, Marcus, and Richardson would suggest. Unlike we-narrative, however, communal narrative comes in a variety of forms and covers a much broader scope. Even though both can have similar effects and implications, they do not necessarily refer to the same narrative technique.

My own definition consciously limits we-narrative to Lanser's simultaneous communal form only, that is, a form of collective or communal narrative in which a "we" narrates.[4] Why this limitation? The purpose of the narratological taxonomy of narrative situations is to give an ideal description of a particular narrative form, its prototype. A single narrator speaking on behalf of communities, multiple narrators who narrate in alternation, or I-narrators who indicatively use the pronoun "we" to refer to themselves together with other characters—these are part of well-theorized narrative situations. The term "we-narrative" (the first-person *plural* narrative situation) implies a structurally distinct narrative form, where the narrator is a plurality, and thus should be used for a designation of this particular form alone.

---

2. Consider, for example, a scale of such authority between (a) personal voice ("I, personally, believe that . . ."), (b) communal ("We believe that . . ."), and (c) authorial ("It is believed that . . ."). Intermediate cases between (a) and (b) are also possible, as when there is singular speaker for the collective, "I think it is safe to say that we all believe that . . . ," or a collection of voices: "I believe that . . ." "I believe this too." "And I think so too."

3. Lanser's (1992) examples are a singular form of communal voice in Elizabeth Gaskell's *Cranford* (1853), sequential narration with communal authority in Louise Erdrich's *Love Medicine* (1984), and Joan Chase's *During the Reign of the Queen of Persia* (1983) as a simultaneous form, which coincides with what I term here "we-voice" and "we-narration."

4. In what follows I shall refer to the we-narrator using plural and singular forms: A "we" that "narrates" or "we" that "narrate." "We" is followed by the predicate in the singular form when, with the help of this pronoun, I refer to the we-narrator as a category or to a group or community. It is followed by the predicate in the plural when the first-person plural pronoun stands in for "us" as characters in their multiplicity. A we-narrative, after all, is precisely a type of narrative that confounds the difference between "is" and "are."

In a nutshell, we-references by the narrator can be found in three contexts:[5] (1) In first-person narratives where "we" is used fairly straightforwardly to refer to the I-narrator plus somebody else. The narrator in this situation is usually (1.1) a single member of a group who speaks about and, if empowered to do so, for the group she represents, or (1.2) several group members who speak individually in turn, but who use "we" to refer to the group and themselves as its members. Narratives of this type are sometimes mistaken for we-narratives, if they use we-references extensively or if they defer disclosing the I-narrator for a long time. (2) In multiperson narratives where no dominant narrative situation can be established and the narration fluctuates between individual and plural references in thematically significant ways. And (3) in narratives in which collective subjectivity dominates and defines the mode of narration. Here, a group is speaking as a whole. This book considers only this last case to be we-narratives.

Three examples may clarify the distinction between we-narrative and other uses of we-discourses in fiction. (The first story by Oates and Faulkner's text are taken from Fludernik's 2011 bibliography.) First, "The Brain of Dr. Vicente" by Joyce Carol Oates (Fernandes and Oates 1975a) is a structurally simple example of what I call a we-narrative. This story describes the death of Dr. Vicente and how his followers (the we-narrator) try to bring him back to life at all costs: They are looking for a "cadaver-donor" for Dr. Vicente's brain. Their efforts, however, remain unsuccessful: Dr. Vicente—or, rather, his brain—is never satisfied with the choices he is offered and rejects every body with the word "Impossible." To give a sense of narration by a we-narrator, I quote the opening three paragraphs in full:

> The brain of Dr. Vicente has been in its air-cooled compartment now for eighteen months. We communicate with the brain by a chemical and electrical process too complex to explain; one of Dr. Vicente's own inventions, made shortly before his death.
>
> We, the half-dozen associates and ex-students of Dr. Vicente's whom he trusted most dearly, think of nothing else but the problem of returning Dr. Vicente to the world. We beg and argue and make threats in order to acquire

---

5. See Margolin (1996, 117–19) for a detailed overview of these situations. Crucially, cases where a singular narrator uses a we-reference depend, in terms of the "informational and epistemic status of what is being said, as well as the illocutionary force of the message" (119), on the narrator's empowerment, that is, whether or not they are speaking for themselves and *about* a group or *for* the group, even if they do not entirely accept the group position. This resonates with Tuomela's (2007) I-mode and we-mode.

cadavers—and you can imagine the competition at our Institute—but when we describe the cadaver-donor to the brain of Dr. Vicente, the brain rejects it.

Of course, the brain cannot see the proposed body and cannot make any judgements based upon the crude sense of sight. Nor can the brain hear, smell, touch, or taste. It communicates to us certain ciphers that are then translated by a computer into our language. For instance, we talked a grieving mother into donating the body of her handsome twenty-year-old son (who was dying from a gunshot wound in the brain—what good fortune!), but when we described this body to the brain of Dr. Vicente it replied in its cipher-language: *Impossible!* (26–27)

The story is told by Dr. Vicente's followers as a collective narrative agent, a well-defined group (the half-dozen associates and ex-students), and the plural voice is never reduced to a single "I" that speaks on behalf of the group. The communal sense of the we-voice is created in several ways: The we-reference is consistent and acquires a performative quality (of which more later); "we," as a character, perform collective actions and share thoughts and feelings; and "we" are firmly established as a narrator, not least because of how "we" explicitly address the narratee. "Our" activities as a collective character are limited to observing the brain, receiving communications from it, and describing the body donors to it—these constitute fairly usual (for a group of researchers) collective actions. The representation of collective speech and thought is also formally straightforward, usually presented in the form of a summary.[6] An interesting passage at the end of the story reveals a possible reason for why this collectivity has been formed: "Even when we are separated from one another and from the Institute, we think constantly about the brain of Dr. Vicente: It weighs upon us in its silence, its sleeplessness, its three pounds of flesh, its bulges and tubes and delicate silky vessels" (28). The short story's we-voice thus creates an image of a communal obsession with the perished genius compared to whom none of "us" ever mattered: "Our" lives and thoughts are consumed with the mystery of the knowledge his brain might contain. Trusting the doctor's plan unconditionally, "we" are collectively blind to the possibility of malfunction or misinterpretation in the communication process, as well as to the reasons for the brain's rejections.

Contrary to the unified we-voice of "The Brain of Dr. Vicente," which draws less attention to itself than to the subject of its narration, Oates's other story from the same collection, "Parricide" (Fernandes and Oates 1975b),

---

6. See also Margolin's (1996, 2000) overview of the techniques of representation of collective actions, speech, and thought.

brings out a tension, inherent in the we-voice, between its collective and individual aspects. The story depends for its meaning chiefly on the juxtaposition of the collective and individual narrating voices and on an elaborate web of innuendos and implications that this interplay produces. Technically, "Parricide" is a first-person narrative with extensive passages of narration in the plural. The plot revolves around an interrogation conducted by Dr. Gouveia of a fourteen-year-old boy called Mário, who is charged with the murder of his father. The short story opens with three of Dr. Gouveia's students entering his office. The opening is narrated in the first-person plural in present tense with an external collective perspective and thus creates a feeling of simultaneity, inviting the reader to participate in the scene on equal terms with the group of students: The reader discovers the room and the boy through "our" eyes as "we" discover and narrate it. "We" establish the setting, describe the boy's appearance, and how the boy and Dr. Gouveia conduct themselves when the latter initiates the conversation. Suddenly, this more or less uninvolved and collective gaze turns into a very personal and individual one: An emotionally charged description of the table at which "we" are sitting serves as a transition into a description of the boy's gaze and the effect it produces on the I-character whose voice suddenly appears:

> The three of us, three young men, sit at the table self-consciously, and are displeased at its ugly, nicked surface and the fact that one of its legs is obviously shorter than the others. The table will wobble slightly if we lean on it. The boy glances at us shyly, his lips twitching as if he wanted to smile.
>
> We do not smile at him. **My heart begins to pound laboriously,** as if I desired something I could not name. (40)

In contrast to the initial generalizing we-voice, the first line of this passage sounds much less general: It seems implausible that the three of "us" are self-conscious, displeased at the table and the boy all at the same time. The I-speaker's sudden comment about his pounding heart suggests that he is the narrator whose feelings were described above (*he* is self-conscious, displeased, and trying to avoid smiling) and who has been masking himself, until now, behind the communal voice. The appearance of a singular voice, however, is immediately contained by the narrative, which regains collective focalization and voice (but without losing the emotional color):

> Thin, with that dark, darkly illuminated skin that stretched across the bones of stark beauty, accenting the bones, drawing attention to the lighter features—the eyes, the eyeballs that seem so white, and the teeth. . . . His

hair is thick and dark, closely curled like tiny curls of wire; it would be fine, frizzy, greasy to the touch. . . . But the rest of his skin is of a dark, even ruddy, olive hue, as if the blood just beneath it were coloring it, warming it **as we stared.** (40–41)

This description serves as a transition from the deeply troubling impact of the boy on the narrator to an attempt to re-establish the anonymous communal perspective. As the passage progresses, its external focalization seems to be no one else's but that one student's. Nevertheless, the passage surprisingly ends with a collective "we stared." Consider a passage two paragraphs below the above quote that solidifies the collective stance:

The boy is listening closely. His breath is not rhythmic, but self-conscious, as if he had to remember to breathe. Perhaps it is because of **our presence, we three students** who cannot help staring. **We are** neatly dressed, in dark suits and ties. **Our hair** is neatly combed, unlike the boy's. **We are not** so dark as he. **We do not** smile and blink so childishly as he, but **our heartbeats quicken along with his.** (41)

Here the we-group, "we three students," is stressed over and over again, and "our" presence permeates the scene. But the mention of "our hair" brings to mind the earlier, intimate description of how the boy's hair would feel to the touch. The smile and the heartbeats, too, harken back to earlier, more personal reflections. Because of the sudden appearance of the "I" in the earlier description of the boy, this passage also has a strong individual note: Even though the narration is in the plural, there is a pronounced "I" behind it. Because of the perspective that orients the passage, this we-voice cannot be plausibly imagined as a truly communal subjectivity.

"Parricide" thus creates an interesting dynamic between its collective and singular passages. One of its techniques is a cataphoric we-reference. The story opens with we-narration, but its singular utterer eventually becomes known, although only after some time, that is, cataphorically, which allows Oates to establish an initial atmosphere of trust and security within the we-group. The narrator, one of the students, seems to hide behind the "we" every time he becomes uncomfortable in his observations of the boy. As the story advances, suspicion that something is amiss with this narrator—going as far as suggestions of pedophilic inclinations and the possibility of his being implicated in the parricide—increasingly arises in the individual outbursts of emotion that the we-narration tries to suppress. When the boy starts talking about a stranger, whose voice and face he cannot remember, who came up to him in the field and gave him an axe, the "I" appears more and more often, with disturbing comments: "My heart is pounding hard; I am tempted to say 'Mário' out loud" (46); "How I would like to caress him, that dark kinky hair, that dark smooth face! I would caress him into silence" (47). Even when the narrator cannot control himself, the we-reference anchors him time and again in the security of the narrated present (he is part of a group of observers of an interrogation, not the one being interrogated), marks him as part of a community, and thus provides access to safe anonymity. But even though its I-narrator is revealed, the we-voice in "Parricide" cannot be reduced to him and the indicative function alone: "We" here does something more than indicating that "I" belongs to the group of students. Although technically, this "we" is uttered by the I-narrator, its (unsuccessful) rhetorical function is to try to erase him. It tries to make his opinions and feelings "objective" where they are intimate and subjective. In this way, the voice performs the narrator's struggle to stay in his safe role as an interrogator/observer, despite his inexplicable urges to shout and get involved.

In contrast to Oates's two short stories, Faulkner's "That Will Be Fine" (1995b) is a first-person narrative that uses we-discourses in a more or less purely indicative manner—that is, in a manner that, according to my definition, does *not* create a plural narrating subject. It opens as follows:

> We could hear the water running into the tub. We looked at the presents scattered over the bed where mamma had wrapped them in the colored paper, with our names on them so Grandpa could tell who they belonged to easy when he would take them off the tree. (265)

The direct speech that comes immediately after this paragraph identifies the I-speaker as a child and introduces his nanny Rosie, making it clear that the "we" in the opening paragraph is an indicative situational reference "'This one is yours,' I said. 'Sho now,' Rosie said. 'You come and get in that tub like your mamma tell you'" (265). The story develops as a typical first-person narrative: A boy tells a story that revolves around his family and thus, unavoidably, includes numerous references to shared activities and situations. Here is another example: "So **I went and bathed** and came back, with the presents all scattered out across mamma's and papa's bed . . . . It would be just tonight and then tomorrow **we would get** on the train . . . and go to Grandpa's, and then tomorrow night and then it would be Christmas and Grandpa would take the presents off the tree and **call out our names**" (266). Even though the narrator's "I" may be absent for extended stretches of the narrative, this fact alone does not make the narrative a we-narrative: I-narrators cannot but use we-references when their belonging to any group needs to be addressed. There is a crucial structural difference, and hence a difference in potential meanings, between a we-narrative, like "The Brain of Dr. Vicente," a first-person narrative with we-references, such as "That Will Be Fine," and intermediate cases, like "Parricide," where the interplay between these two distinct narrative situations produces striking effects.

Collectives, Communities, and We-Narratives

It is thus analytically and interpretively useful to distinguish between we-narrative as a *form* and the rhetorical *effect* of communal or collective voice, character, and subjectivity that this and other forms can create. To put it differently, other types of narrators and narrative forms may also be used to the rhetorical ends of expressing collectivities, as Lanser has persuasively demonstrated. In her research on construction of collectives in factual and fictional narratives, Fludernik (2017, 141–42), for instance, relies on examples from first-person narratives with we-references, from full-blown we-narratives, and from third-person narratives with extensive they-references and plural subjects. This is in line with Margolin's (2000, 593) definition of collective narrative agents, which, as he demonstrates, can be expressed as a variety of pluralities, from plural nouns ("the boys," "a hundred men") and collective terms ("the gang") to plural personal pronouns—"we," but also "they." A "collective narrative" can be created by any of these forms, whereas "we-narrative" is one such form, defined by its plural narrator, as I have suggested above, that embodies the collective voice, often understood more metaphorically, by associating it with a concrete and coherent we-group.

This section focuses on the added meaning that the qualifiers "collective" and "communal" bring to the classification of narrative forms. Whenever a we-narrative constructs a certain effect of groupness, it can be additionally described as a collective or communal we-narrative in an interpretive move that is not without ideological implications. According to Raymond Williams (1985), "communal," derived from "community," has largely positive connotations, being a less general term than "society," less politically charged than "collective," and associated with immediacy.[7] Immediacy, or intimacy, because a community's members live in close proximity, often know each other personally, and/or, at least theoretically, are able meet everyone in the commu-

---

7. See, relatedly, Bonnie Costello's (2012) analysis of how James Merrill's poem "Self-Portrait in a Tyvek™ Windbreaker" ends up cherishing the one-to-one community over larger-scale forms of sociality.

nity. The town of Jefferson in "A Rose for Emily" is a good example here. As a form of social organization, community usually refers to "the more direct, more total and therefore more significant relationships," as opposed to "the more formal, more abstract and more instrumental relationships of *state*, or of *society*" (Williams 1985, 76). Anthony Cohen, in *The Symbolic Construction of Community* (1985), defines community via two opposing features: similarity and difference. It is a group of people whose members "(a) have something in common with each other, which (b) distinguishes them in a significant way from the members of other putative groups" (12). Communities thus realize themselves in opposition to others, via (symbolically constructed) boundaries. No wonder that conflict with outsiders is such a frequent topic in we-narratives with a community as their narrator, even if the distinction between outsiders and insiders is not always straightforward and often very flexible. Since, in small communities, individuals acquire a public image—they "are constituted socially by the stock of public knowledge" (113)—their image fluctuates according to communal judgment.[8] This judgment is adjustable to the point that, if a community member suddenly falls into disgrace, like Faulkner's Emily, personal biographies can be manipulated in the public consciousness to suggest that she was never really "one of us."

But many differences within the community are successfully and routinely contained—this is, in fact, a prerequisite for its existence. Some of the mechanisms of such containment, according to A. Cohen (1985, 20–21), are symbolic forms (placeholders, patterns, ways of behaving) that are shared and that can be imputed with divergent meanings (content) by its members. For example, if Jefferson's community in "A Rose for Emily" is held together by the value it places on honor, what exactly constitutes honorable behavior for each of its members can vary considerably. Community, to quote Cohen once again, "continuously transforms the reality of difference into the appearance of similarity" (21). It is in this nuanced sense that communal—as well as collective—uniformity exists: as a symbolic construction within which individual differences continue to thrive, as long as the shared ethos is strong enough for the members to see past them. Paying attention to the nature of

---

8. Another example may be pertinent here. It comes from a Danish novel, *We, the Drowned* by Carsten Jensen: "We're always coming up with new names for one another. A nickname's a way of stating that no one belongs to himself. You're ours now, it says: We've rechristened you. We know more about you than you know about yourself. We've looked at you and seen more of you than you'll catch in the mirror. Rasmus Arsewhipper, Cat Tormentor, Violin Butcher, Count of the Dunghill, Klaus Bedchamber, Pissy Hans, Kamma Booze, how can any of you imagine we don't know your secrets? . . . Everyone in our town has a story—but it's not the one he tells himself. Its author has a thousand eyes, a thousand ears and five hundred pens that never stop scribbling" (2011, 211).

groups that compose voices in we-narratives, be they communities, collectives, or something else, helps illuminate the ways in which these narratives deal with the complex dynamics of people's joint existence: the constant tension between longing for individuality and togetherness, neutralization of differences in the name of tolerance, and a simultaneous upkeep of borders and divisions into "us" versus "them."

Whereas "community" describes a relatively small social group with, usually, positive connotations, "collective" seems to be a more ambivalent designation that implies acting together for the sake of explicit political agendas. Williams traces the changing meanings of "collective" from a mere description of a gathering, of people acting together, to the "social and political sense of a specific unit" in the early nineteenth century (1985, 69). An interesting example of what exactly is at stake with fictional representations of collectives—rather than communities—is offered by Joel Woller (1999) in his investigation of we-narration in the US documentaries of the Great Depression. Woller compares the negative critical responses to Richard Wright's 1941 photobook *12 Million Black Voices: A Folk History of the Negro in the United States,* which features a classed and racialized we-voice of the oppressed masses, to the overwhelmingly positive reception and canonization of Pare Lorentz's 1930s documentary films about governmental efforts to combat poverty, which are also narrated in the "we." Woller comments that the vast gap between the reception and cultural status of Wright's and Lorentz's work "reflects a bias against attributing agency to oppressed races and exploited classes rather than to paternalistic government and a heroic nation: A bias against dialectical, utopian, and identity-transforming ways of representing community [or, more precisely, collectivity, NB] and agency, and for fixed, mythic, and identity-confirming ways of seeing the same" (341). Using a we-voice, *12 Million Black Voices* drew severe criticism for presuming to speak for others, whereas the ideological implications of Lorentz's first-person plural were all but ignored. The reason for this, as Woller claims, is "a critical double-standard, according to which narrating the collective experience of the mass of the nation in a choral voice is valid and potentially praiseworthy, whereas speaking in the first-person plural for the collective experience of working-class and black masses is, in and of itself, an affront" (360–61). Unless the collective "we" refers to a mythical and valorized "nation," it cannot be treated without suspicion.

Woller's case studies illuminate a more general problem with writing and reading in the "we": an almost automatic distrust for plural voices in current political discourses. "We" is assumed to come from an individual, and the individual cannot speak for the many. Those who can be heard are, consequently, privileged and cannot voice the oppressed. Differences of class, race, and gender are viewed as insurmountable: No one from one camp can speak on behalf of anyone from the other. Interestingly, in the case of political groups, unlike communities, there seems to be a heightened perception of differences rather than their containment. Such a denial of the validity of collective voice is further amplified by the fact that authenticity and truthfulness are generally ascribed only to individual experiences,[9] whereas any collectivity of a meaningful scale seems to provoke fears of authoritarianism and effacing uniformity (Hollywood's dystopias are a telling example). The Hegelian possibility of "unity-in-difference" cannot be imagined; instead, "we" is measured against the ideal of "the more static and less dialectical doctrines . . . of liberal tolerance (or strength-in-diversity)" (Woller 1999, 351). Similarly, writing on the history of collective forms of expression in fiction, Laura Miller observes:

> Modern readers find collective first-person narrators unsettling; the contemporary mind keeps searching for the familiarity of an individual point of view, since it seems impossible that a group could think and feel, let alone act, as one. . . . You could say that the history of Western literature so far has been a journey from the first-person plural to the first-person singular, the signature voice of our time. The solitary first-person narrator—confessional, idiosyncratic, often unreliable—is the choice of novelists . . . . Authenticity can be found only in individual experience. Broader claims to authority are suspect. To presume to speak, as novelists once blithely did, for a nation, a city or, especially, a generation is to invite protest and ridicule. (2004, n.pag.)

This type of suspicion can be also found in narratological analyses of we-narration that reflect the general status of collectives as a controversial mode of social organization. In the time when exploration of collectiveness in fiction becomes an increasingly exciting issue, I believe narratology may benefit from a reflection on the ideology of its analytical categories, which sometimes project a cultural bias onto a narrative text. While a collective of any kind does render individual properties of its members irrelevant, at the same time it does not necessarily create totalitarian uniformity—and the ambiguities of we-narration testify to that.

---

9. An extreme example would be Ayn Rand's work and the continued influence of her individualist and objectivist ideas on modern-day politics (especially in the US; see Gray 2010; Oliver 2014). In her novella *Anthem* (1938), for example, Rand removes the first-person plural pronoun from the new language her characters begin to speak in a liberated world. See also Costello's piece "The Plural of Us: Uses and Abuses of an Ambiguous Pronoun" (2012), which discusses the issue of individuality versus collectivity in detail, while analyzing uses of "we" in poetry in the context of the tenth anniversary of 9/11.

With the above considerations in mind, it is curious to observe that most of the contemporary Anglophone we-narratives analyzed in this book are concerned with communities and small-scale groups. Texts such as Otsuka's *The Buddha in the Attic* or Mda's *Ways of Dying* can be described as narratives that, via small-scale individual and group perspectives, give voice to oppressed masses and nations, oscillating between communal concerns and collective political struggles. Novels such as Eugenides's *The Virgin Suicides* or Oates's *Broke Heart Blues* are more straightforwardly communal, dealing with the drama of memory and longing in suburban neighborhoods. Finally, on an even smaller scale, institutional communities are represented in the form of employees at an advertising agency (Ferris's *Then We Came to the End*), students of a university faculty (Adams's *Many Pretty Toys*), a military-like group of four boys (Litt's *deadkidsongs*), and so on. Communities seem to be readily transformable into novelistic characters. This is perhaps because community, as A. Cohen observes, is "an entity, a reality, invested with all the sentiment attached to kinship, friendship, neighbouring, rivalry, familiarity, jealousy" (1985, 13). As they inform the social processes and relationships of everyday life, these sentiments also inform novelistic conflicts. A good case in point here is the we-narrator in *The Wives of Los Alamos* by Nesbit, who talks about "ourselves" as follows: "We were a group of people connecting both honestly and dishonestly, appearing composed at dusk and bedraggled at daybreak, committed, whether we wanted it or not, to shared conditions of need, agitation, and sometimes joy, which is to say: We were a community" (2014, 77). Describing a we-narrative as communal or as collective is thus an interpretation that captures its chief concerns and narrative conflicts.

Examples of collective we-narratives may be more readily found in proletarian fiction and works of socialist realism. But, as Barbara Foley writes in *Radical Representations: Politics and Form in US Proletarian Fiction, 1929–1941*, however popular the collective narrative form was in Depression-era critical discourses, "critics proved better at heralding the collective novel . . . than at defining it" (1993, 399). One such critic, Granville Hicks, gives his vision of a collective novel:

> The collective novel not only has no individual hero; some group of persons occupies in it a position analogous to that of the hero in conventional fiction. Without lapsing into the mysticism of those pseudo-psychologists who talk about the group-mind, we can see that, under certain circumstances, a group may come into existence that is independent of and more important than any of the individuals who compose it. Such a group could be portrayed through the eyes of a single individual—in other words, in terms of the tra-

ditional novel. But it might be more effective to portray the group as a group, to show forth objectively and unmistakably its independent reality. To do this requires a new technique, the technique of the collective novel. (1974, 27)

Writing in 1934, Hicks effectively produced a version of the definition of collective narrative that Margolin (2000, 591) would suggest in narratological terms sixty years later: To count as a collective narrative agent, a group has to function as a group in a variety of narrative roles (agent, patient, experiencer); it has to have an agency of its own and, in the case of we-narrative, its own voice. Arguably, Hicks was calling for the first-person plural voice to become a new technique of the collective novel.

However, to return to the point with which I opened this section, whether or not we-narration succeeds in creating and expressing a certain group is a different question. "What distinguishes the collective novel," Hicks stresses, is "the sense of the group as a group" (1974, 28). A full-blown, strongly dramatized we-narrator of a supraindividual level would be such an example. But, for instance, the community in Litt's novel *deadkidsongs* (2001) is one in a state of disintegration; not even the narration's persistent recourse to a "we" in the last chapters can save it. *deadkidsongs* is a story about a group of four boys, childhood friends, whose sense of bonding and comradeship shatters as they struggle for power and control. The story's resolution offers no holistic level—the kind with which the novel opens—and makes it evident that the initial we-narration has been an attempt on the part of one of the boys, now much older, to simultaneously mask himself as part of the we-group, disperse his sense of guilt, and recreate this long-lost sense of belonging. *deadkidsongs* cannot be justifiably described as a communal we-narrative, even though the novel's first part is a first-person plural narrative situation with a small community as a speaker. Its aesthetic effect relies on the ambiguity of its we-voice and the tension between the plural reference on the surface and the strong sense of the implied "I" beneath it. The same applies to the short story "Parricide." Furthermore, these narratives do not establish a dominant narrative situation, and can thus be described as "multiperson narratives" (see also Richardson 1994) rather than we-narratives, communal or collective.

Sometimes, however, we-narratives combine references to "we" and "I" without becoming first-person or multiperson narratives. The case in point is Ferris's 2007 novel *Then We Came to the End*, where "the end" means a gradual and total disintegration of its office community: The office has ceased to exist because the advertising agency has been restructured under the pressure of an economic crisis. By the end of the novel, this leaves only the reader and the "I" of an unspecified narrative instance:

> And we would leave, eventually. Out to the parking lot, a few parting words. "Sure was good to see you again," we'd say. And with that, we'd get in our cars and open the windows and drive off, tapping the horn a final time. But for the moment, it was nice just to sit there together. We were the only two left. Just the two of us, you and me. (385)

In this final line, the communal "we" becomes a dual one: "I + you." However, one single I-reference in the very last sentence of an almost four-hundred-page novel consistently written in the first-person plural does not change the narrative situation into that of the first-person singular: Communal action, emotion, and speech throughout the book construct a strong "we" character narrator, and its distinct voice is still aesthetically effective in the final paragraph. A direct reference to the narratee as complicit in the story along with the one who narrates is not a revelation of the masked "I" narrator, but a metaleptic change of the character narrator's "we" to the authorial "we" of Ferris and his actual reader. The final line of the novel creates a local effect of suggesting the end of the office narrator, and with it, the end of its story: Ferris gives up the voice of the fictional we-narrator by exposing another communicative relationship, or a "feedback loop" (Phelan 2017, 6), between the author and his reader that has been underlying the fictional narrator's communication all along. In other words, this break in the dominant collective mode of the novel has no retrospective significance for the plural "we." The readers, arguably, treat it locally under what Phelan (2013) describes as conventionally accepted breaks because it is brief, positioned at the end of the narrative, and because it activates a referential possibility already inherent in the "we" pronoun—the reader-narratee can feel directly addressed throughout the book.[10] Since the contextual significance of the we-narrator and its group identity remains, this novel is a we-narrative in the sense defined in the introduction.

---

10. This is why a definition of we-narrative has to combine structural and contextual elements. I argue that this revelation of the "I" is also not enough to warrant calling *Then We Came to the End* a "pseudo we-narrative." Richardson (1994) calls certain multiperson narratives such as Ian McEwan's *Atonement* (which involves an alternation of the type I < > s/he) or Jorge Luis Borges's "The Shape of the Sword" and Audrey Niffenegger's *The Time Traveller's Wife* (I < > you) "pseudo third-person" and "pseudo second-person" narratives whose I-narrators only reveal themselves at the end. This is not the case for *Then We Came to the End* because the mention of the "I" does not suggest that this "I" has been narrating the whole story.

"Multiperson" and We-Narratives

As is clear by now, we-narratives are distinct from other narrative situations, even if these employ we-references extensively. But, because we-narrators often tell stories about individuals, the problem of the relationship between the collective and the individual levels of reference remains crucial for any theorization of a we-narrative. As Margolin observes, "not every narrative containing a [collective narrative agent] is a collective narrative," and even collective narratives "do not consist entirely of the story of their collective protagonist" (2000, 594). This is why a clear-cut distinction between a we-narrative and other narrative uses of the first-person plural pronoun can seem problematic at times, especially if a we-narrative mentions the pronoun "I" at some point. Any classification of we-narratives should therefore take into account, besides formal features, the contextual use of the "we" and its performative force. For example, there is a significant contextual difference between the uses of we-discourses in *Then We Came to the End, deadkidsongs,* "Parricide," and "That Will Be Fine" discussed above (chapter 2 elaborates on performative and indicative uses of "we"). Structurally, this difference is produced by a mixture of narrative situations: "Parricide" and *deadkidsongs* do not establish a dominant narrative situation, while "That Will Be Fine" and *Then We Came to the End* do and can be unreservedly classified as first-person singular and first-person plural narrative situations, respectively. Stanzel has already observed this type of dynamic in long narrative works:

> Each individual novel is, of course, a structured sequence of a number of modulations of these narrative situations, one usually dominating: it is this predominance that decides a novel's place in the typological circle. Occasionally a novel has been located in more than one place to indicate a particularly significant change of the narrative situation from one part to another (e.g. *Vanity Fair, Ulysses*). (1978, 253)

A useful designation for a narrative that combines different narrative situations and can be located on more than one position on Stanzel's Typological Circle has been suggested by Richardson in his 1994 article on multiperson narration. I adopt the term "multiperson narration" to discuss the interrelation between narrative voices in the plural and singular modes when neither of them is dominant in the narrative situation. Multiperson narration, in a broad sense, entails the conjunction, juxtaposition, and alternation of different persons and narrative modes, which, consequently, creates what Stanzel called a dynamization of narrative situation (1984, 63). An example of such alternation is the switching between first- and third-person pronouns with a consequent shift in narrative perspective (internal versus external),[11] as in, for example, Margaret Atwood's novel *The Edible Woman* (1980) or Margaret Drabble's *The Seven Sisters* (2003). I use "multiperson" to refer to a cluster of objectified narrators (i.e., those designated with a pronoun, or assigned a "person") within one narrative totality (e.g., a novel) and one narrative level.

Richardson identifies four major kinds of multiperson texts: "Works that systematically oscillate between different narrative positions, those that collapse apparently different types of narration into a single voice, works whose narration remains fundamentally ambiguous, and texts that employ narratorial stances that would be impossible in nonfictional discourse" (1994, 312). To streamline Richardson's classification, I suggest singling out two broad types of multiperson narratives: those that oscillate between narrative positions and that can be understood to have more than one narrator (e.g., Dorris's *A Yellow Raft in the Blue Water*), and those in which multiple pronouns are used to designate one and the same character or narrator-character—the latter group being what Richardson's article is chiefly concerned with. Any of the two groups can include "works whose narration remains fundamentally ambiguous," which is to say texts whose narrative instance is difficult or impossible to identify—provided it is important for the understanding of the text to do so (see Richardson 1994, 315).[12] As for narrators who are impossible outside of fiction, Richardson seems to refer here not to multiperson narratives per se, but to what he later calls "unnatural narration," which can again describe pronominal shifts of any type.

Oates's short story "Parricide" is, therefore, a multiperson narrative and a good example of alternations between *we < > I* within one and the same narrating instance. Another short story, "The Visitation" by Tom Whalen from the collection *Sudden Fiction* (1986), can serve as an example of different instances within one narrative level. By means of alternating communal (we) and individual (I) voices, the story describes the strange encounter of a small town with "deities." No one knows who they are, where they came from, or why they came. Accounts of the deities are confusing and can be read as the

---

11. Perspectival shifts, as a phenomenon related to multiperson narration, have been treated under the heading of "multiperspectivity" (V. Nünning and A. Nünning 2000, 13) as a form of mediacy "where one and the same issue is presented differently from two or more angles of perception or individual points of view." I only concentrate here on the category of person as related to the establishment of narrative situations and return to the issue of perspective in chapter 4.

12. That is, in the texts that have a "teller-character" (Stanzel 1981) or a "telling frame" (Fludernik 1996, 43–45, 51). Noncommunicational theories of narrative (Patron 2010) suggest that in some narrative texts the question of who is speaking is irrelevant.

ironic image of a threatening outsider: They are animal-like, flying creatures, or go around donning suits and bowlers, or physically differ from "us" by having "fingers, five per hand, thicker than ours" (141). The deities constantly vandalize the town and misbehave in various ways and the havoc they wreak is conveyed in very short, staccato paragraphs, typographically separated from each other into episodic clusters, which cannot be united into an account by one narrator (except, perhaps, as separate strands of the communal "we"). For example:

> We call a town meeting, but the wrathful deities show up as a woodwind ensemble and drown out our words with their reedy squeals.
>
> I climb up to the cupola on Town Hall and scream up into the sky meaningless syllables. After an hour or so I climb back down and go home. When I enter the kitchen, I see four of them sitting around my overturned refrigerator, feeding on its remains.
>
> We call on the parish priest and ask him what we can do.
>
> Have you tried reason? he says.
>
> We strap him with our belts to a chair, then deliver him up to them.
>
> Life in our village goes on.
>
> They enter my shop, three of them dressed in dark double-breasted suits with shiny bowlers. We're here to plunder, they say.
>
> I say, Well. (Whalen 1986, 142)

These voices do not suggest a single narrator (neither "I" nor "we") and, in fact, work against such unification in order to re-create on the level of form the sense of confusion and (interpretive) helplessness that the village experiences having. The story offers a meditation on what makes up a community by pitching together the strangers and the small town: The "deities" are uninvited intruders into "our" pace of life and they violate "our" most cherished distinction—private property—as they enter "our" houses and "my shop," walk on "our" lawns, or plunder "my books and objects" (142). Moreover, the story asks what is left of a community when the usual institutions and authorities, the town mayor and the parish priest, cannot restore the previous order. Not much, apparently, because when the intruders disappear, the community has been transformed: "We crumple on our knees to the pavement; we grin stupidly at one another; we begin to tear out each other's hair" (143). This peculiar text can be seen as a thematization of the ideological implications of pronouns: community ("we"), individuality and private property ("I"), outsiders ("they").

As I mentioned in the introduction, several existing approaches to we-narratives define them broadly in terms of a more or less consistent use of we-references by an explicit I-narrator. Thus, for example, Marcus writes:

> In using this term, I refer not only to narratives told wholly or mostly in the first-person plural, but also to narratives in which there are thematically significant shifts from "we" to other pronouns and vice versa. I avoid a more rigorous definition, since I claim that some of the most noteworthy ways of employing the first-person plural are best illustrated in texts that alternate between "we" and other forms of narration. (2008c, 2)

However, as I have argued in this chapter, such a broad approach may lead to a conflation of distinct narrative phenomena and obscure their structural and rhetorical significance. For example, describing we-narratives by comparing them to narration in other persons, Marcus observes: "Like first-person singular narration, 'we' narration is based on personal experience and is thus limited to the scope of human knowledge (in contrast with omniscient narration). 'We' narratives lack the objectivity, reliability, and veracity conventionally attributed to third-person narration" (2008c, 1–2). This comparison is problematic in several respects. First, it neglects the basic distinction between narration and narrative, generally understood as "process" versus "product."[13] "Narration" in the plural is a particular narrative technique or a feature of narrative discourse. It should not be confused with a full-blown we-*narrative* as a narrative in which one narrative situation—that of the first-person plural—is the dominant one. Thus, the distinction is between a type of narrative discourse and a type of narrative form. Consequently, most of the examples that Marcus covers in his article are instances of we-narration—they offer plenty of material for analysis, but they do so within the dynamic of the narrative situations in which they are used (mostly, first-person narratives), and thus often work differently from we-discourses in a fully realized we-narrative. Secondly, I argue that we-narration is very much *unlike* I-narration in that it is based on the collective experience of a collective body and thereby transcends the

---

13. Although the difference between the two terms is as problematic as, say, that between "content" and "form," their general usage has established certain differences in meaning. Even though the definitions of the terms as given by Gerald Prince in his *Dictionary of Narratology* (1988) reproduce some of their vagueness and overlap, "narration" can be primarily understood as "the production of a narrative; the recounting" (57). "Narrative," although inseparable from the process of its construction, primarily refers to the product or material object: It is a "product and process, object and act, structure and structuration" (58).

individual subject in the scope of its knowledge, including temporal and spatial limitations.

For these reasons, I suggest distinguishing between we-narrative and other uses of we-discourses in fiction without, however, ignoring narratives that combine we- and first-person narrative situations. This distinction proves highly productive for analyses of we-narration in texts like Whalen's "The Visitation" or Oates's "Parricide." When approaching texts like these, it is important not to reduce them to a single narrative situation, but rather to treat them as multiperson narratives. Among the texts that I consider in this book, Litt's novel *deadkidsongs* can also best be described as a multiperson narrative. I discuss this novel in detail in chapter 4 and comment here only on its structure: In *deadkidsongs,* various narrative situations (first-person plural, first-person singular, and a mixture of authorial and figural situations) are limited to separate parts and chapters of the novel. Neither of the situations dominates in the novel even though, at first, chapters in the first-person plural have the thematic significance of unifying all the voices of characters who, in other chapters, function as individual narrators. Within the context of the whole novel, however, the significance of these vocally disparate parts and chapters becomes apparent: Told by different characters who are all members of one group, they contribute to the sense of the group's disintegration, its internal power struggles, and the trauma it strives to suppress. Even we-narratives, where there is a clearly dominant narrative situation of the first-person plural, often contain separate chapters in, for example, the figural mode, in order to allow individual characters—whether group members or not—to speak for themselves. Oates's novel *Broke Heart Blues* thus gives voice to its protagonist, John Reddy Heart, who speaks for himself after the novel's communal narrator, much like in "A Rose for Emily," has offered its own—and hence one-sided—version of his crime (see chapter 5). Ferris's *Then We Came to the End* singles out the boss of the advertising agency—an outsider to the group of coworkers and hence the subject of gossip—in a separate chapter, a kind of intermission in which she voices her fears (in free indirect speech with internal focalization) about her battle with cancer, thereby individualizing what has previously been just another topic of speculation for the office we-narrator. Such examples in we-narratives are numerous. But, to reiterate, the fully developed we-narrative hinges on a collective subjectivity and establishes a dominant situation of narration to which other pronominal digressions are subordinated. In this way, it differs both from first-person narratives in the singular *and* from multiperson narratives.

As Stanzel observes, pronominal alternations may be motivated by content or form when they deliberately foreground the conventions or estrange the norms according to which the "narrative element person" is used (1984, 109). The case of "The Visitation" is one such example (of thematic, content-motivated alternations). Alternatively, pronominal shifts may have no obvious semantic load. This is the case for changes within a figural narrative situation or within an interior monologue (Stanzel 1984, 106–8). Within we-narratives, semantically *insignificant* shifts are usually those between the "we" and the third-person references to one of the characters about whom "we" speak. Often this character acquires a certain narratorial independence when the narration moves into her or his perspective, or into free indirect discourse. Another example of a structurally insignificant—but interpretively curious—shift is the ending of *Then We Came to the End* because it does not invalidate the communal stance of the novel on the whole. Obviously, the significance of this or that pronominal shift cannot be established by a definition and varies according to context. In order to address these various cases, a distinction between narrative situations and their multiperson combinations is necessary.

We-Narration: An "Unnatural" Technique?

My definition and approach to we-narratives must now be positioned in relation to the theories of "unnatural" narratives. According to Jan Alber and Rüdiger Heinze, "unnatural" narratology supplements the work of structuralist narratologists—specifically Roland Barthes, Gérard Genette, A. J. Greimas, Stanzel, and Tzvetan Todorov—by providing analytical tools that were previously unavailable in order to "describe the fact that many narratives deviate from real-world frames in a wide variety of different ways" (2011, 6). These deviations are then described as "unnatural" in several distinct ways. According to Alber, for example, "unnatural" elements in fiction include people (narrators and characters), scenarios, and temporal and spatial phenomena that are nonactualizable in the real world, or, in other words, physically, logically, or humanly impossible outside fiction (Alber, Nielsen, and Richardson 2013, 6). Nielsen adds to this list also acts of narration that would be impossible or implausible in real-world storytelling situations (6). Richardson considers those texts "unnatural" that deviate from "the mimetic conventions that govern conversational natural narratives, nonfictional works, and realistic works" (5). We-narrators, it might be argued, are "unnatural" if viewed under these criteria: In conversational storytelling, "we" cannot tell a story in unison; real-world narrators cannot know the transpersonal information that fictional we-narrators often offer; they cannot think or feel as a group, and so on.

However, beyond this constatation, the "unnatural" approach does not offer a productive analytical framework for we-narratives, and it continues to invite questions of whether it can offer that for fictional narratives in general. Much has been said since the popularization of the term in 2010 and, without reiterating the entirety of the debates (including my own previous contributions thereto), I shall summarize their key points and restrict more detailed comments to the footnotes.[14] To begin with the broader issues that arise from the above definitions of the "unnatural": In all of them, the term has a conflicted relation to mimesis, realism, and reality,[15] and is implicitly based on a semi-biological notion of naturalness of some narrative phenomena over others. This is contrary to the explicit claim by "unnatural" narratologists that they define the "unnatural" in antithesis to a sociolinguistic understanding of "natural" as derived from "what William Labov called conversational natural narratives" (Alber, Nielsen, and Richardson 2013, 3), and in dialogue with Fludernik's "natural narratology."[16] But sociolinguistics does not operate with the notion of naturalness of storytelling, and the term "natural narrative" has never been suggested by Labov. In fact, it was Fludernik who first suggested using it as a shorthand description of "**spontaneous** conversational storytelling" (1996, 13).[17] "Natural," in its original context in *Towards a "Natural"*

---

14. Since its inception in Alber et al. (2010), unnatural narratology has continued to struggle to define its subject matter: "unnatural" narrative. See, for example, debates in Alber et al. (2012) and Fludernik (2012) and, especially, the analytically and philosophically rigorous critique in Klauk and Köppe (2013), which the unnaturalists' response in Alber, Iversen, Nielsen, and Richardson (2013) does not actually refute. I have discussed further inconsistencies of the unnatural approach in several reviews (N. Bekhta 2013, 2019). For the most recent extensive debate about the approach, see the 2016 special issue of *Style* 50, no. 4.

15. Thus, we-narratives have also been linked to the "unnatural" via a conception of "anti-mimesis." For an explanation of the term, see Alber and Heinze (2011, 3–4). Although he originally suggested the term, Richardson has recently modified his formal conception of anti-mimesis and introduced a comparison to reality (Alber, Iversen, Nielsen, and Richardson 2013, 102). Moreover, once the term became adopted by other unnaturalists, it lost its specificity as a description of narrative form. Alber, for example, links it to "Plato's definition of mimesis as reproduction or 'imitation' of the empirical world" (2013, 450). In this sense, "the unnatural is only anti-mimetic . . . because physically, logically, or humanly impossible scenarios and events are clearly not imitations of the world as we know it" (450). See Klauk and Köppe (2013, 80–85) for a critique.

16. See Alber, Iversen, Nielsen, and Richardson (2013, 103–4); Nielsen (2013, 70–72). In the most recent article providing an overview of the developments in unnatural narratology, Richardson comments, once again, that "the word 'unnatural' has no extranarrative connotations, but is merely a narratological term derived from sociolinguistics" (2016, 393).

17. Aware of its metaphorical nature, Fludernik even places it in scare quotes. The impersonal way in which she introduces her term in *Towards a "Natural" Narratology* (1996) may be the source of the subsequent attributions of the phrase to Labov instead. I quote Fludernik's

Narratology, then, refers only to the *spontaneity of some* storytelling in oral contexts. Consequently, "unnatural" narratives would more properly mean nonspontaneous stories, which is to say *all* literary narratives.

Moreover, even within its opposition to narrative categories derived from analyses of conversational storytelling, "unnatural" narratology does not, in fact, deviate from the classical narratological tradition. As Per Krogh Hansen notes, "the outset for theorizing and studying narrative is less dependent on oral or conversational storytelling than on a more general understanding of verbal language" (2011, 164). In Todorov's and Genette's theories, derived from Saussurean linguistics,

> oral and conversational storytelling was not given primacy. Quite to the contrary: considerable efforts have been made to deanthropomorphize the concept of the narrator in this tradition and to disclose defamiliarizing techniques and strategies as a 'natural' inventory of narrative communication. In my opinion, the interest that 'unnatural narratology' claims to have in "unnatural, unconventional, and unrealistic elements of realism"—including narrative techniques such as omniscience, paralepsis, redundant telling—do not really differ from those of 'narratology proper' insofar as all of these concepts are derived from the latter. (Hansen 2011, 164)

Hansen's observation confirms my own: In one sense, unnatural narratology claims to break with the classical tradition, while at the same time exercising the very same tradition. It proposes to offer an alternative to classical narratology and calls for new interpretive approaches, but instead works with the established ones.[18] "Unnatural" frequently implies those features of narratives that produce defamiliarizing effects and narrative techniques that possess a sense of novelty (see Alber and Heinze 2011, 2). This notion thus competes

---

comment in full: "*Natural narrative* is a term that has come to define 'naturally occurring' storytelling in the linguistic literature of discourse analysis (Labov 1972). What will be called *natural narrative* in this book includes, mainly, spontaneous conversational storytelling, a term which would be more appropriate but is rather unwieldy. *Natural* narrative, in contradistinction to the wider area of *oral* narrative, comprises only spontaneous forms of (therefore conversational) storytelling" (13–14). Fludernik adds a clarification in her 2012 response to the "unnatural" narratologists: "Although Labov is generally credited with introducing the term *natural narrative* (see, for instance, Simpson [2004] 114 et passim), the text of Labov and Labov and Waletzky does not seem to contain the collocation" (368). Unfortunately, this has gone unnoticed in later publications on "unnatural" narratives.

18. For example, Alber (2013) and Nielsen (2013) draw extensively on the phenomenon of naturalization as defined by Culler (1975, 131–60) but rename its strategies under the heading of "unnaturalizing."

with the long-existing accounts of similar phenomena by Russian Formalists and structuralist narratologists, while also reproducing their limitations.[19]

Finally, as the target of attack from the unnaturalists, the "mimetic bias" (Alber, Nielsen, and Richardson 2013, 4) of classical narratology is also not as pervasive as their critique would suggest. For example, classifying animal narrators—or group narrators—as "physically impossible" (and hence "unnatural") does not undermine the analytical validity of the category of narrator. Such phenomena, although impossible in the real world, have already been naturalized and, subsequently, conventionalized in fictional texts and thus do not pose a theoretical problem for narrative comprehension and interpretation. The same applies to the logically possible in everyday communication and fiction. Logical and semantic impossibilities of communication viewed pragmatically do not and must not apply to narrative fiction as communication. In his *Narrative Discourse Revisited,* Genette (1988, 125) quotes Roland Barthes's remark—"I can't say 'I am dead'"—and goes on to prove that fictional narratives do not know such limitations. Homodiegetic narration with external focalization—as is the case with stories whose narrators are dead—is perfectly possible in the realm of fiction.

> For the question is not so much *in what sense* such propositions are "absurd" (a logical problem) but (1) is it *possible* to utter propositions that are absurd (in any sense whatsoever)—a question, I venture to say, that is *literary* and the answer to which is obviously positive . . . and (2) are such utterances, for the reader or the listener, in one way or another (which we should not be too quick to call "figurative"), acceptable, despite—or rather *taking into account* and thus, in a sense, *by virtue of*—their present anomalousness. (126)

Genette's remarks are applicable to a proposition of a plural nature: A we-voice that tells a story goes against linguistic logic and physical possibility, but is possible in fiction—indeed, in writing—and if its effects are anomalous or atypical, the collective voice might be all the more literarily or rhetorically successful for it. In other words, we *can* say "We are alive." Or even that "We know everything about everybody. We even know things that happen when we are not there; things that happen behind people's closed doors deep in the middle of the night. . . . The community is the owner of the story, and it can

---

19. Thus, "unnatural" narratology overlooks the same aspects of literary form as those neglected by the formalists: for example, the unity of "the intrinsic, thematic determinateness of genres" (Bakhtin and Medvedev 1978, 131) with their extrinsic function in concrete historical-social contexts, which is vital to a comprehensive understanding of literary change.

tell it the way it deems it fit" (Mda 1995, 12). Such possibilities are the quintes-sence of fiction, not its "unnatural" deviations.

Within the realm of "unnatural" narratology, however, we-narratives have been measured by "the degree to which they diverge from the poetics of real-ism" (Richardson 2006, 59), with realism eventually referring to mimesis (Richardson 2011), understood within this field as reproduction by fiction of the empirical world (Alber 2013, 450).[20] This points back to the comparison of the content of literary works with what is possible in the perceived reality, while failing to account for the phenomenon of literary narratives in their entirety, for example, in their status as works of art and products of sym-bolically significant human activity. Within narratology, a rhetorical approach would be helpful here, as, when it comes concretely to we-narrators, would a tripartite division, suggested by Phelan, of the elements of narrative texts into mimetic, synthetic, and thematic. Fictional character narrators can be said to function in three ways: "as representations of possible people (. . . their mimetic function), as representative of larger groups or ideas (their thematic functions), and as artificial constructs within the larger construct of the work (their synthetic functions)" (Phelan 2005, 12–13). We-narrators often have a convincing collective voice and a communal identity whose composition does not draw attention to itself or to its (lack of) realism, but rather enhances the reader's mimetic engagement with the collective subject it tries to create. A good indication of the success of the latter strategy are the reviews of and arti-cles on we-narratives that do not stop to wonder about the "we" who is telling the story, so "natural" does it seem—as is the case with numerous analyses of "A Rose for Emily." In another example, T. D. Max's (1999, n.pag.) review of Oates's we-novel *Broke Heart Blues* simply describes its suburban, persis-tently communal we-narrator as a "punctilious first-person narrator, a kind of demented class secretary," hinting already at its thematic function of being concerned with preserving communal memory. This is also what Fludernik alludes to when discussing the effects of unusual narratorial pronouns—all those that are not "I"—with the comment that "we" is "the most realistic and natural" kind among these (1996, 224). She continues: "*We* narrative is a fairly unproblematic case, or so it seems," being mostly either "an extended first-person narrative" or "I + you" narratives that "usually background the *we* for very 'realistic' reasons: If both the narrator and the addressee have shared the experience, there is little motivation to evoke it narratively except in passing"

---

20. "Mimesis" has become a term obscured by its numerous uses across narratology and literary theory in general (see Halliwell 2013). But the unnaturalists compound this obscurity by using it in different senses within a single field—a problem inherent in all existing definitions of the "unnatural," as, for example, Klauk and Köppe (2013, 85) diagnose.

(224). But many we-narratives also move beyond these unproblematic cases and foreground their synthetic elements, even going so far as to comment upon the nature of their communal or collective narrators. Some passages of we-narration might simply become a formal exercise for exploring the implications and limits of the technique, as is the case, for example, in *Many Pretty Toys* (1999), where the group narrator tries to truthfully document *all* of its members' opinions on the matter at hand. Even so, we-narratives function just like other narrative forms in that they freely combine mimetic, synthetic, and thematic functions of narration and create familiar or defamiliarizing effects.

These effects, as I have argued, can be successfully addressed via a combination of the classical narratological and rhetorical frameworks. Using the Stanzelian framework for the description of narrative types, I have thus suggested approaching we-narrative as a narrative situation that allows for a consideration of a specific type of plural narrator and the ensuing rhetorical effects of representing groups, communities, and collectives as characters and narrators. In the next chapter, I move on to the linguistic-philosophical aspects of the first-person plural as the originator of narrative voice. It is also in the linguistic peculiarity of "we" that its numerous narrative effects lie, from unremarkable to striking.

CHAPTER 2

We-Discourses

The We-Pronoun and Its Indicative and Performative Uses in Fiction

> Who was wittier, who had more savvy, who had sailed it out of the park. We all had the same prayer: *please let it be me.* Regardless of who that me was, he or she tried to be very discreet about it, but there was no denying it, they reigned victorious for a day while the rest of us returned to our desks to chew silently on our own spines. We had lost, and our dimwittedness made us vulnerable to low opinion, whispered denigrations, and the dread prospect of being next. . . . Nobody talks about it, nobody says a word, but the real engine running the place is the primal desire to kill. To be the best ad person in the building, to inspire jealousy, to defeat all the rest. The threat of layoffs just made it a more efficient machine. (Ferris 2007, 108–9)

In his office novel *Then We Came to the End,* Joshua Ferris constructs a communal narrating voice for a group of people working at an advertising agency in Chicago during an economic crisis at the end of the 1990s. Whenever this competitive, gossipy and, simultaneously, coherent and unanimous group narrator receives a new advertising project, proving who is most suited to work on it, which subgroup, which team, which copywriter, is a matter of life and death. The we-reference becomes strained with all the competing factions, as the passage above shows. On the one hand, "we all" have the same wish—to be the best in order to keep "our" jobs—and so, at first, the we-reference seems to include every single office worker in this agency. This unanimity is underscored by a comment that "me" does not matter. On the other hand, the pronominal shift to "they" in the next subclause reveals the opposite: Whenever "one of us" wins the new ad project, then their "me" matters. The narration turns into the third person and thereby one of "us" is excluded, however temporarily, from the scope of the we-reference: "*They* reigned victorious for a day while *the rest of us* returned to our desks." In this business, losing is collective, while winning is individual, especially under the fear of layoffs. Still, the victory is so fleeting and the competition so constant that the we-reference persists, soon again including the formerly excluded colleagues. The pronominal dynamic of this scene culminates in the penultimate sentence of the passage, with the impersonal subject reference: "The primal desire to kill" unites all of "us," winners and losers, individuals, teams, and the whole agency.

The we-pronoun, as has been noted by linguists and narratologists alike, has a complex referential scope. In one and the same context, it can be inclusive and exclusive, broad in scope and very narrow, applicable to the humanity on the whole, or limited to a concrete corporation, group, or individual. It can function as a means of constructing solidarity, as a statement of both belonging and exclusion, and as an ideologically charged evocation of commonality despite obvious differences. Or, it can be a neutral reference to multiple collective experiences that are part of people's social lives. And while everyday stories of shared experiences—of joint trips, accidents, celebrations, and so on—rarely raise objections to their communal form, the workings of a politically inflected "we" usually stand out. One may think of public resistance to certain political slogans during the 2016 US presidential elections ("We will make America great again"), to Angela Merkel's speech ("*Wir schaffen das*") during the 2015 refugee crisis in Germany, or to the right-wing mobilization of this pronoun during the Brexit referendum in 2016 ("We want our country back").[1] In these cases "we" has only really meant parts of the respective nations and served to painfully underline social divisions. Nevertheless, in all of these cases "we" has been successfully mobilized by political forces to secure considerable support.

---

1. Another telling example of such resistance is Costello's comment on uses of the first-person plural in journalism and speeches dedicated to the tenth anniversary of 9/11: "I know I'm not the only one made uncomfortable by the ready invocation of this public *We*. It seems at once abstract and presumptuous, and it plays to a dangerous human desire: to become part of a crowd, and to define oneself against *Them*. Does this 'we' have any real antecedent for an unbounded, diverse populace? Does it claim to speak for *me*? Whatever the founders may have meant by 'we, the people,' it rings hollow in the arena of contemporary politics and popular journalism" (2012, n.pag.).

The effects of the first-person plural in political speeches were studied in a 2013 empirical survey by Niklas Steffens and Alexander Haslam. Having analyzed the official campaign speeches of all prime ministerial candidates in Australian elections since 1901, they established that in 80 percent of the elections, successful candidates used more references to "we" and "us" than their losing opponents. Although, of course, the situation is far more complicated when one takes into account party programs and the social, political, and economic climate at the time, generally speaking, the we-reference is a powerful rhetorical tool. The evocation of "we" alone produces positive affective responses. When used in particular ways, it seems to construct communities and allegiances where there are few other connecting factors. It evokes the implicit dichotomy of "us versus them," which further provokes individuals to subconsciously align with "us" and dissociate from "them," who, in turn, are treated if not with suspicion, then with indifference or neutrality (see, e.g., Sapolsky 2017, 387–424). This referential, affective, and rhetorical complexity exists in fictional we-narratives too, which, as a narrative form, have been interpreted both as formally unremarkable and experimentally "unnatural."

In fiction the first-person plural may indeed be "the most realistic and natural" type of "odd" narratorial pronouns (Fludernik 1996, 224) because everyday stories are often told in the plural, and in them, the pronoun first presupposes an "I" and then others. That is why, when "we" is used in place of an I-narrator, its unusualness is less striking than, for example, that of second-person or invented pronouns. But the first-person plural is also the most "flexible, heterogeneous and ambiguous of all personal pronouns, since it is capable of designating all three speech roles as well as being uttered by single or multiple speakers" (Margolin 1996, 119). We-narrators are inherently unstable and may at any point in narrative exclude or include new characters, fictional narratees, or readers, as the brief opening example has already suggested. Furthermore, it is often hard to immediately distinguish whether we-narration is being used to speak for or about a group or to mask a singular speaker, thus opening up this technique to unreliability and manipulative narrative strategies.

In this chapter, I look at the ambiguity of the plural narrating voice and the multiplicity of its effects, which can be both unremarkable and unsettling. I examine the deictic qualities of "we" as a pronoun for potential causes of such ambiguity. Most important, this chapter also adds a linguistic-pragmatic context to the structural definition of we-narrative offered earlier, and formulates a differentiation between indicative and performative uses of "we" in fiction; this distinction underlies my definition of we-narrative and its analyses throughout the book. In essence, we-references by the narrator are found in two distinct situations in narrative fiction.[2] An indicative, or straightforward, we-reference has the structure of "I + somebody else." It is the "we" of the first-person narrative, where the homodiegetic I-narrator talks about her belonging to various groups, or it is part of the authorial narrative, where the heterodiegetic narrator addresses herself and narratees. A performative "we," by contrast, is a reference by an unspecified entity that creates a group subject and a plural narrating instance, and that defines the first-person *plural* narrative situation. To demonstrate how this distinction comes about, I first give a short overview of we-discourses in fiction and nonfiction and discuss the linguistic-philosophical possibility of pluralizing the "I." This anticipates some of the problems that a plural narrator poses to the established models of narrative communication discussed in detail in chapter 3. I then conclude with examples of indicative and performative uses of "we."

Types of We-Discourses: From Everyday Contexts to Lyrical Personas and Plural Narrators

We-discourses are widely used in all kinds of fictional and nonfictional contexts, which have been usefully summarized by Margolin (1996, 116). To begin with *nonfiction,* the non-narrative "we"[3] abounds in political, educational, academic, and business contexts where different kinds of speeches and company reports are given, declarations made, negotiations held, or petitions issued—all of which are designed to represent a collective agency of some sort, be it a political party or a group of academics working on a common project. This loose grouping also includes what might be termed ritual uses of "we" in collective praying or chanting. Nonfictional narratives with extensive uses of we-reference, too, form a significant part of everyday storytelling and are, in most cases, stories of the past activities of small groups (e.g., friends who have had an adventure together or a couple who has just returned from a holiday), though they are also popular in interviews, museum settings, constructions of corporate identity, and so on. These types of discourses most often use the we-reference in what I suggest describing as the indicative sense, meaning that they refer to a single speaker together with some actual, projected, or imagined group.

---

2. As for the cases in between, which I mentioned in chapter 1, they can be said to oscillate between the indicative and the performative "we" to create particular effects.

3. I use "it"/"itself"/"which" rather than "we"/"ourselves"/"who" when speaking about the first-person plural pronoun in this chapter in the abstract sense of a linguistic category.

For the purposes of this short overview, I also divide *literary and fictional uses* of "we" into those found in non-narrative as well as narrative contexts. "We" often figures in lyric poetry, especially in poetry with a strong communal, social function, as Bonnie Costello (2017) demonstrates. The plural reference appears in songs (e.g., revolutionary hymns of solidarity or protest), and in the monologues and speeches of the chorus in Greek drama. These forms often make their way into prose narratives as well. Margaret Atwood's novel *The Penelopiad* (2005) offers an example of a playful appropriation of a we-chorus. *The Penelopiad* can be considered an alternative take on the events of *The Odyssey* from a female perspective. Penelope, the wife of Odysseus, and twelve maids, hanged by Odysseus for sleeping with Penelope's suitors, recount the epic story as they experienced it. Chapters of Penelope's self-reflexive narratorial monologue alternate with songs performed by the maids.[4] The twelve maids play the part of the chorus to Penelope's first-person narrating and so their collective voice, usual for a chorus, does not draw attention to itself as a synthetic narrative element. To give an example:

The Chorus Line: Dreamboats, A Ballad

Sleep is the only rest we get;
It's then we are at peace:
We do not have to mop the floor
And wipe away the grease.
We are not chased around the hall
And tumbled in the dirt
By every dimwit nobleman
Who wants a slice of skirt.
And when we sleep we like to dream;
We dream we are at sea,
We sail the waves in golden boats,
So happy clean and free. (125)

The chorus's function in *The Penelopiad* is to give voice to women who were even more marginalized than Penelope: In their songs, the twelve maids describe the hardships of exploitation and their daily routines, make fun of Odysseus, comment on Penelope's story, parody epic songs of praise for noble-

---

4. The maids' songs are occasionally playfully complemented by other genres: a lament (Atwood 2005, 13), a drama (147), a lecture (163), and a trial transcript (175). Even in the trial mode, the maids act as a single entity, being collectively addressed and defending themselves as a group.

men, and more. The chorus chapters function as intermissions: As in other multiperson narratives, they do not have direct diegetic links to, nor influence on, the progression of Penelope's narration. Nevertheless, the maids' perspective thematically contributes to the general impulse of Penelope's story and thus provides a fuller picture of injustice, oppression, and exploitation.[5] This particular use of a we-voice by victims to address their oppressors or to speak about causes of their demise seems to be a recurrent strategy: In David Peace's multiperson novel *Occupied City* (2010), "we" refers to the twelve victims of the infamous 1948 bank robbery in Tokyo where the robber, posing as a doctor, injected the bank customers and employees with cyanide; in Otsuka's *The Buddha in the Attic,* discussed in this chapter and chapter 3, the plural voice becomes an instrument for narrating the destinies of female immigrants and their exploiters.

Finally, in *fictional narratives* "we" is often used in the same indicative manner as in nonfictional ones. Full-blown we-narratives are relatively rare—that is, narratives that strive to create a collective *narrative* voice, formally distinct from lyrical or indicative we-discourses. Thus, drawing on the nonfictional uses of "we," Fludernik describes the fictional "we" in terms of "natural" storytelling pronouns, in contrast to the truly experimental pronominal strategies ("you," "one," or invented pronouns). Compared to the "highly odd" literary you-narrative, a fictional "we" often comes across as formally mundane because "*we* narratives, both inclusive (*I* + *you*) and exclusive (*I* + *he/she/ they*), are quite common in real-life storytelling. Couples tell of their experiences hiking, setting up house, managing unemployment or disease; soldiers, students, pupils, office colleagues and members of choirs, chess clubs, sports competitions, football teams and so on and so forth—all tell stories about their various shared experiences" (Fludernik 2011, 114).[6] However, fiction also offers a possibility that Fludernik does not consider: The possibility of a we-voice that is neither inclusive nor exclusive, in the sense that its structure is not that of "I + somebody," but rather of a collectivity, of a "we (+/− others)." Indeed, I would like to argue that there is a crucial difference between this performative we-mode and the indicative or, as Fludernik calls them, "natural" cases. The difference lies in the subjectivity that a fully collective we-reference constructs

5. A strikingly similar motif figures also in the short story "The History of Girls" by Ayşe Papatya Bucak (2016), where the fully collective "we" of sisterhood, telling a story of what it is like to be a girl in contemporary (Turkish) society, transforms into an "I" when only one girl of the group is left alive.

6. See also Richardson: "Unlike second person narratives that are 'unnatural' from the outset—that is, that do not exist in 'natural narrative'—first person plural texts are typically directed to a much wider audience and do not immediately call attention to themselves as artificial constructs possible only in literature" (2006, 37).

and that, as J. M. Bernstein points out in a different context, is "a subjectivity that is not privative and exclusive, a 'we speak' which neither collapses into many exclusive subjectivities nor pretends to the elimination of all subjectivity from narrative" (1984, 257). In the case of a couple telling a holiday story or a football fan relating how "we" won the game yesterday, the "I" of the individual subject is very much present. In a performative "we," this "I" is erased and a collective voice is created.

A distinction between oral and written narratives underlies all of the groupings above. Written nonfictional narratives can, theoretically, create a sense of a truly collective, indiscriminate voice, which I have been describing as the voice of fictional we-narratives. But oral stories that use "we" have a harder time completely dissociating this "we" from the individual who speaks it. In general, it is my observation that when it comes to typical uses of we-discourses, nonfictional and oral contexts more readily afford an indicative "we," while written fictional narratives tend toward performative "we." But in all of the above contexts, the function of the first-person plural pronoun is similar in one respect: By the sheer power of its plural reference, "we" communicates information about group membership and thus performs a general discursive function of creating a sense of belonging and difference ("we" versus "they"):

> The use of WE pronouns is intrinsically connected to the linguistic establishment of social groups. Speakers define explicitly and publicly social groups vis à vis their interlocutors by using WE pronouns. At the same time, they state their membership to these groups. This is the prototypical use of WE pronouns. They are therefore per se a strong means to establish and reinforce social identities. (Helmbrecht 2002, 42)

As Johannes Helmbrecht suggests here, "we"—used prototypically—establishes various social groups, articulating a community and a collective identity. At the same time, such use covers only a fraction of all referential possibilities. To put it even in more technical terms, in prototypical nonfictional uses of "we," the most common situation of reference of the first-person plural is a singular subject of enunciation ("I") that speaks about and/or on behalf of one or more individuals who are physically or implicitly present and whose actions and mental states are manifested in the discourse of this subject (see Margolin 2000, 592; Rivarola 1984, 206). In small groups, such a speaker may even represent a position discussed beforehand, when each member of the we-group had a chance to express their opinions and beliefs individually, or when the speaker could elicit them in other ways. Nonprototypical types of we-reference are those in which either no collectivity exists, or the speaker does not belong to the collectivity (see Helmbrecht 2002, 44–45). These types, without any attempt at an exhaustive typology, can be loosely grouped as follows:

1. *Pseudo-inclusive "we"*: The first-person plural pronoun is used to refer to an individual either in (1.1) a so-called act of "plural autodesignation" (Rivarola 1984, 206), which, depending on the pragmatic reasons for its use, can be further classified into the traditional rhetorical forms of *pluralis majestatis, pluralis modestatis,* and *pluralis auctoris*; or as (1.2) a *nursery we,* which, strictly speaking, is a reference solely to the addressee, not to the speaker. Generally, these uses of "we" may be described in terms of a pseudo-inclusive reference as they strive to express modesty, suggest a shared point of view between the hearer and the speaker, avoid responsibility for an undesired state of affairs caused by the speaker, or imply the speaker's symbolic solidarity with the hearer when the former is in a superior position with respect to the latter (see Haverkate 1984, 88).

2. *Desired "we"*: "We" is used not to establish a group but to "express an emotional or a social connection of the speaker to a group without referring to the speaker or without including the speaker in the group of individuals referred to" (Helmbrecht 2002, 44). In other words, "we" is used to express a desired belonging to a group.

At this point, some elaboration is needed on the particular cases that compose the above groups. "We" of the plural autodesignation is based on two oppositions: It will be either an amplified "more massive, more solemn, and less defined" royal "we" or "a broader and more diffuse expression: . . . the 'we' of the author or orator" (Benveniste 1971c, 203). The nursery "we," on the other hand, "refers to a single addressee connotating a certain relationship of care between speaker and hearer" (Helmbrecht 2002, 34). This connotation, however, is not unambiguous and implies a certain power and patronizing superiority on the part of the speaker, being similar in this respect to *pluralis majestatis*. (Think, for example, of the tone and implications of a doctor's "How are we feeling today?" or a babysitter's "Aren't we a sweet little thing?") *Pluralis majestatis,* expressing "institutional power or superiority of the speaker compared to addressee" (Helmbrecht 2002, 34), refers solely to the addresser, while at the same time bearing connotations of plurality—of "an emperor being the summation and representative of all the subjects" (R. Brown and Gilman 1960, 255). *Pluralis auctoris,* or epistolary plural, typically includes both the addresser (the author or the narrator) and the addressee and may serve to suggest a (wished for) shared point of view between the author and her readers, or else a modest or strategic retreat behind the less personal "we." The hortatory use of "we" usually works in a positive manner, as in an inclusive suggestion to a friend with whom you share an office: "Let's go outside and eat lunch in the park" sounds more appropriate and less coercive than "I want you to come with me for lunch in the park." The hortatory "we" minimizes "the social distance between speaker and hearer" or masks the speaker's imposition (Helmbrecht 2002, 45). An example of a desired "we" would be a football fan's assertion that "We won the game yesterday" (as opposed to, e.g., "Borussia Dortmund won the game yesterday"). Such a statement is emotionally non-neutral and expresses the speaker's closeness to or *symbolic membership* in the "we" group that did the playing and the winning.

Curiously, these implications of the first-person plural pronoun are often made explicit in we-narratives. For example, in the novel *deadkidsongs,* when one member of the we-group, Paul (who goes by the code name for rank "019734"), is being punished for misconduct by the rest of the group, this brings about a self-reflexive comment on the use of "we" by the we-narrator:

> Andrew said, "I hope you understand why we had to put you through that, 019734. It was vital."
> Paul replied, "Completely, sir."
> We all noticed what Andrew had said, "we had to", not "I had to": we. This was the final part of the humiliation. For, on this occasion, Paul was excluded from the "we" that usually contained him. By his use of the word "we", Andrew was implying the existence of two categories: the trustworthy, and the untrustworthy. (Litt 2001, 74)

Using the we-reference, Andrew—the group leader—thus insults Paul by marking him out as an untrustworthy group member or perhaps even as a former group member who must now regain trust and acceptance. While "we" offers belonging and protection, the singular "you" suggests vulnerability when singled out from "us." And even though by this point in the novel the rest of the boys already have their doubts about Andrew's leadership, in this situation they seem to be content with blending in as part of this new group, formed by Andrew's use of "we."

As the following case studies show, written narratives, factual and fictional alike, extend the list of nonprototypical uses of "we" and include we-references that are plural, as in the examples from the two types above, but that do not originate with a single speaker—unlike in types (1) and (2). In other words, we must distinguish *a third group of non-prototypical uses* of the first-person plural in which "we" is uttered collectively: Such a collective "we" designates the existence of a group subject and originates from a collective speaker. In this possibility lies a crucial difference between indicative and performative uses of "we"—a possibility offered in we-narratives, I argue, but withheld in other narrative situations, even if they occasionally use we-discourses.

Deictic Features of the First-Person Plural Pronoun

The pronoun "we," as is clear by now, can be used with reference to various groups and in various contexts, even by radically opposing political parties addressing one and the same nation during elections. The many referential possibilities and rhetorical effects discussed above are possible not the least because of the semantic emptiness of the "we": Just like other pronouns and deictic elements[7] of language, it does not refer to a concept or an individual and does not denominate any lexical content-bearing entity (Benveniste 1971b, 226). While, for example, there are linguistic concepts of "group" or "community" that can be defined or described, as I attempted to do in the previous chapter, and to which individual uses of the words group or community refer, there are no such semantically definable concepts for the personal pronouns. "I" refers to anyone who says it. Pronouns and other deictic words function as signposts of sorts: They acquire meaning by directing attention to the object of reference, by pointing it out, rather than by describing it, and are thus dependent on spatial, temporal, and social contexts.[8] "We" can mean anyone.

In the narratological analyses I have discussed so far, however, "we" has rarely been considered to mean a group-as-speaker. I believe the reasons for this lie in the strong influence of enunciative linguistics and the philosophy of language on narratological approaches to fiction, and in the remainder of this chapter I spell out some of their underlying premises, suggesting an alternative structure of meaning for the fictional "we." Speaking about the mean-

---

7. Such as pronouns, spatial and temporal adverbs, and some demonstratives.

8. See, for example, E. Brown (2006, 131); Hanks (2008, 99); Fillmore (1998, 59). Also see Fludernik (1991). Identifying its referent by "pointing it out" is the "deictic proper" usage of the pronoun, which in specialized literature is distinguished from its "phoric" uses (e.g., anaphoric and cataphoric, as well as references to things outside the discourse). Unlike pointing to the referent directly, a phoric pronominal usage "provides an index to some part of the discourse in which it occurs; it 'corefers' rather than refers" (E. Brown 2006, 131); for example, it could refer to a noun phrase that has already been introduced (anaphoric use) or anticipate a noun phrase that will provide the pronoun with the necessary meaning (cataphoric use). As the deictic/phoric distinction is not overly relevant to the rest of my analysis, I will forgo a more detailed description.

ing of personal pronouns, Benveniste observes how "*I* is the individual who utters the present instance of discourse containing the linguistic instance *I*" (1971a, 218). In other words, it is only in the enunciative situation, in speech, that the abstract *linguistic* element "I" can acquire meaning, that is, during the conversion of language into discourse. The functions of "I" are not, however, limited to its role of designating its speaker: "I" refers to itself, being simultaneously the referent and the referee. Furthermore, it presupposes an addressee, a "you." "I" and "you" are defined on the basis of their deictic proximity and, based on their involvement in communication, are distinguished from the "nonperson" of the third-person pronoun.[9] The situation of address, of dialogue, is what gives meaning to all three persons.[10] The first-person singular plays a key role in this system of deictic coordinates since it is the starting point in the system, its *deictic center,* a *zero point* (Bühler 1990, 116 ff.). The rest of the personal pronouns occupy non-zero points, and their meaning and reference, besides changing according to context, is also modeled around the pronoun of the first person.[11] In this system, it follows, there is no place for a plural deictic center of "we" since it by default refers back to its "I": the "we" comes into being after the "I" has been established.

Similarly, the communicative situation in literary narrative has been modeled on the roles of the three persons, with the zero-point position of the first-person pronoun assigned to the narrator. And, arguably, this is why we-narrators are readily interpreted as covert first-person narrators. According to Gerald Prince, "there is at least one narrator in any narrative and this narrator may or may not be explicitly designated by an I" (1982, 8). The explicit designation obviously occurs in first-person narratives. In cases where the

---

9. Benveniste calls the third person a nonperson because it is outside communication; it is spoken *of,* and it is the only one by which a thing is verbally predicated (1971c, 197–99). The third person, according to Benveniste, lacks the "personal element" of denomination that the first and the second persons have. Plus, it is the only possibility of expressing impersonal/"objective" statements and, most important, the only possibility of expressing "[an instance] of discourse not meant to refer to [itself] but to predicate the process of someone or something outside the instance itself" (Benveniste 1971a, 221). In narratology, these connotations of the third person continue to influence descriptions of third-person narration as the most "objective" mode of narration.

10. In the linguistics of enunciation, persons are defined "in terms of their communicative role in any given speech event, that is, as role bearers. The first person singular is understood as the locutionary role (speaker); the second person, singular or plural, as the allocuted role (addressee, the one spoken to); and the third person, singular or plural, as the delocuted role, the one spoken of" (Margolin 1996, 116). See also Dieltjens and Heynderickx (2007, 233). These functions, however, can be and are modified in interesting ways in fiction.

11. See Fillmore (1971, 1998); Fludernik (2011, 102). The zero point has also been described by the term "origo," that is, "the speaker ('I'), place ('here') and time of utterance ('now')" (Stockwell 2002, 43).

"I" of the narrator is seemingly absent from the narration, there are still what Prince calls "signs of the *I*," that is, traces of the originating center of the narrative discourse. These signs include references to the narratee, the use of "we" that does not designate characters in quoted speech or narratees and, hence, refers to the narrator, and all other deictics indicative of the perceptual, relational, and spatiotemporal location of the narrator. Curiously, Prince suggests that "we" is a *sign* of the (first-person) narrator, not the explicit narrating instance itself. Even in an investigation of first-person plural narratives, Margolin (1996, 123) similarly claims that the narrating voice is always an "I." It follows, then, that in a situation of communication, the we-narrator's perspective on narrated events is always partly individual, and when it comes to "mental factors, such as the beliefs, attitudes, internal states" of other group members (Margolin 2001, 246), the we-narrator can only narrate what she has inferred: "Any 'we felt,' 'we thought,' 'it occurred to us' statement . . . is internally heterogeneous, based as it is on the individual speaker's immediate knowledge of his/her own psyche, and on (defeasible) hypotheses formed by this 'we' sayer regarding his/her coagents" (246). Margolin's and other narratological approaches to we-narrators seem to implicitly draw on Benveniste's (1971b) observation that there is no possibility of the pluralization of the "I" into "I + I" and that "we" is only conceivable as "I + others." In other words, the plural of "I" is only possible via an addition of "you" or someone else; it is not possible to utter a "we" in which many "I"s are present simultaneously. Only the third person "admits of a true plural" (Benveniste 1971b, 204).

In a nutshell, then, models of fictional narration have been organized around the figure of the narrator who can *only* be designated by the first-person singular (see Genette 1988, 97), just as pronominal persons and deictic categories are organized around the "I." What happens, then, if the deictic zero point is occupied by a plurality? How does it influence the reception and interpretation of a narrative that employs plural narration? I argue that—at least—in a fictional situation of communication, in collective we-narratives, the reconstruction of such a singular originator of discourse is often impossible and interpretively fruitless. Full-blown we-narratives with performative we-references do not imply a reference to an "I," which presumably speaks for or on behalf of the we-group, unlike indicative we-references, where the "I" is more or less easily reconstructible. If the discourse sets out only with a "we" and never ties it to an "I," into what can this "we" be translated? Potentially, into a virtually endless combination of referential possibilities. "We" comprises various numbers of referents, with varying types of relations and hierarchies between them built upon inclusion and exclusion. Moreover, "the combinations are endless as each *we*-component can be divided into two or

more new components" (Dieltjens and Heynderickx 2007, 239).[12] This makes
the first-person plural pronoun the most referentially complex person category, "the quintessential model of referential instability," as Dawn Fulton
(2003, 1106) observes. Translating such a complex speaker position into any
combination of pronouns other than "we" may amount to an act of speculation.[13] In we-narratives, the use of the first-person plural points to a plurality,
but it is a matter of characterization and interpretation to discern the composition of such a plurality, and more often than not, "we" do not easily accept
unambiguous ascriptions, let alone provide lists of "our" members.

In any case, with or without a member list, we-voices retain a degree of
unusualness in the speaker position because, linguistically speaking, there
cannot be a full-blown plural voice in the first person. In order to recognize
it in fiction, then, one needs to discern its rhetorical and aesthetic possibility.
For personal pronouns, "the condition of existence is the ability to speak: *I*
exists because it speaks, *we* does not exist because it does not speak" (Rivarola 1984, 202, my translation). "We" cannot exist as an enunciating subject
because it cannot have a voice, that is, it cannot physically produce utterances. Even on occasions where all "I"-members that compose the "we" speak
in unison, like during collective chanting, "we" is, rather, an amplification of
"I," a diffusion of its limits but not a "multiplication of identical objects," as
Benveniste puts it, because "there cannot be 'we' except by starting with 'I,'
and this 'I' dominates the 'non-I' element by means of its transcendent quality. The presence of 'I' is constitutive of 'we'" (1971c, 202). Similarly, Jespersen
in *The Philosophy of Grammar* (1958) calls the first-person plural "the plural
of approximation":

> The most important instance of the plural of approximation is *we*, which
> means I + one or more not-I's. **It follows from the definition of the first
> person that it is only thinkable in the singular,** as it means the speaker in
> this particular instance. Even when a body of men, in response to "Who will

---

12. "We" either equals "I" and someone else or it equals another group plus someone else.
In both cases, "someone else" and "group" have a vast number of possible configurations and,
with respect to the three traditional roles in communication (Sender, Receiver, Other), there
are twenty-seven theoretically possible combinations (Dieltjens and Heynderickx 2007, 236).
"We" can also mean only "you" or "they" when used manipulatively or mitigatingly.

13. Especially if we also consider the fact that, in English, the "we" pronoun's morphological structure does not tell much about its composition: Neither the inclusive/exclusive category,
which in other languages functions as the instrument for the speaker-addressee distinction, nor
the categories of number (dual we, trial we, we, many, etc.) and gender are distinguishable in
English.

join me?" answer "We all will," it means in the mouth of each speaker nothing but "I will and all the others will (I presume)." (192)

In other words, when someone says "We will join you" or "We felt happy," this
someone—in a straightforward communicative situation—is expressing her
own desire or state and presumes that other members of her group share it;
"we" thus refers to "I + others."[14] However, in fiction, if the discursive context
encourages only a plural reference, as in many we-narratives, then the uttered
"we" transcends, in some sense, the mere "I" and creates a collectivity, a collective narrative agent, and thus a possibility for this "we" to have a voice. This
possibility is what the fictional narrative "we" has in common with the non-
narrative "we" of, say, poetry, and it expands the range of the nonprototypical
uses of the first-person plural pronoun. This possibility, as discussed in the
next section, is also the basis for a distinction between two uses of "we" in fiction: A we-reference with an implicit or explicit "I" and a "we" as a collectivity,
which creates a pluralized, multiplied "I." The former is a feature of the first-
person singular narrative situation, and the latter creates a narrative situation
of first-person plural.

Indicative and Performative Uses of "We" in Fiction: A Linguistic-Pragmatic Definition of We-Narrative

To capture the distinction between the two narrative situations, I have suggested borrowing a set of terms from theoretical grammar and speech act
theory to differentiate between indicative and performative uses of the personal pronoun "we": The indicative "we" comprises the prototypical and two
types of nonprototypical we-references in fiction, while performative we-uses
express something other than a statement about a certain group, namely a verbal action of constructing a collective subject.[15] In *Narrative Discourse* (1980),
Genette metaphorically extends the categories of the verb (mood and tense)
to describe the features of narrative discourse in general. I suggest a similarly

---

14. Unless, of course, this "we" is of the pseudo-inclusive kind, as when "I" do not share
the group's desire but feel obliged to comply, or when "we" is used to only mean "you," excluding "me."

15. The indicative "we" can also be described by declarative or constative terms, as they
circumscribe similar linguistic or discursive phenomena. I choose the former because of its
more immediate commonsensical association with the verb "to indicate" that something is.
Similarly, "performative" may refer to an illocutionary act, but it also has a wider currency in
literary and cultural studies and hence, hopefully, its connotations are more understandable.

metaphorical use of linguistic terms here to describe the modalities of various narrative uses of the we-pronoun.[16]

Under the indicative "we" I have grouped the usage of the first-person plural pronoun in an individual speaker's reference to herself and another person or group to which she belongs or with which she associates herself—both situationally, that is, at the moment of speaking, or more generally. That is, such a "we" is used in the context of a *constatation* or statement. In this manner, "we" indicates the existence of a we-group: The speaker together with addressees and/or members of the group to which this speaker belongs. Use of the indicative "we" does not transcend the "I" (for example, by multiplying it, to use Benveniste's phrase) and thus does not create a plural narrative voice—in the sense of a voice of a structurally communal or collective narrator. Such we-references are the ones used by I-narrators in first-person or authorial narrative situations (in Stanzel's sense): in Faulkner's "That Will Be Fine," for instance, or in the short story "We Didn't" (1994) by Stuart Dybek. "We Didn't" is mentioned as a we-narrative in several bibliographies (see, e.g., Fludernik 2011). However, this tale of sexual frustration is a man's monologue addressed to a woman about how many times, on what occasions, and at which locations "we didn't" (have sex), and the use of the dual "we" in this first-person narration is only due to the fact that the speaker needs to address himself and the woman as a couple. This mode of address in the story is persistent, but remains indicative. It highlights the obsessive frustration of the narrator with the relationship (via comparisons between "us" and "others") and contributes to the bitter tone of the monologue, but this "we" does not create a sense of a collective subject, a joint character position or experience.

The performative "we," on the other hand, creates a more complex reference: It expresses something that is imagined or projected, performatively creating something that did not exist before.[17] That is to say, performative we-narration creates a group character narrator. The performative force of such a "we," I argue, erases the implication of a singular speaker who might utter it and constructs a collective storytelling voice. Such we-references create plu-

---

16. This convention of using linguistic categories for descriptions of narrative precedes Genette, of course, with, for example, Tzvetan Todorov's modal poetics and A. J. Greimas's suggestion to approach narrative modeling as if it were an individual sentence. Fredric Jameson, similarly, picks up the latter suggestion to talk of "narrative modalizations—the subjunctive, the optative, the imperative, and the like," which can describe the registers in which deep narrative structures are actualized (2001, 151). The indicative mode, for example, describes narrative realism.

17. This argument goes contrary to Margolin's (2001, 244) observation that the speech acts of the we-narrator (for Margolin, a singular member of the we-group) are primarily constative and it is the "we" in poetry that has performative power.

ral narrators in the fullest sense. They have two salient features: First, they never reveal an "I" or even hint at the possibility of a singular individual who speaks for the group; second, the narration often—although not necessarily—approaches a narrative mode that Phelan has termed "lyric progression" (2005, 10; discussed in detail in chapter 3). An example of a we-narrative with a performative "we" that creates a plural, communal narrator is Ferris's novel *Then We Came to the End* (2007). Its opening situation of narration, where "we" offer a description of "ourselves" in general terms, is recurrent throughout the novel. It begins as follows:

> We were fractious and overpaid. Our mornings lacked promise. At least those of us who smoked had something to look forward to at ten-fifteen. Most of us liked most everyone, a few of us hated specific individuals, one or two people loved everyone and everything. Those who loved everyone were unanimously reviled. We loved free bagels in the morning. They happened all too infrequently. Our benefits were astonishing in comprehensiveness and quality of care. Sometimes we questioned whether they were worth it. We thought moving to India might be better, or going back to nursing school. (3)

This passage introduces the novel's plural narrator-protagonist—a group of coworkers at an advertising agency. Rather than voicing a fully homogeneous group, "we" move between general statements that are true for all group members, such as "We were fractious and overpaid," and particularizations true for parts of the group ("most of us," "a few of us," "one or two people," the latter being the reference most detached from the group). This communal narrator also voices individual thoughts or dreams in what might be described as a free indirect we-mode: "Sometimes we questioned"; "We thought moving to India might be better." As the we-narration progresses in this manner, a convention of communal reference is established and the lack of "I" is not perceivable. The we-reference, used consistently by a community as narrator and experiencer, turns the office into a character and establishes the peculiar authority of the narrative voice, which is at once personal and authorial, subjectively individual and generally true. This narrator defines the narrative situation of *Then We Came to the End* as one of first-person *plural*.

Another crucial, if insufficient as a structural marker, feature that distinguishes Ferris's novel from, say, Dybek's or Oates's short stories, is the consistency and duration of use of the performative "we": Its fully collective nature only becomes detectable over time, through repetition. We-narration's initial effect is, arguably, that of the indicative "we," and it only acquires its performa-

tive force within a larger portion of a narrative. For example, the openings of
(a) Ferris's novel, (b) Faulkner's "That Will Be Fine," and (c) Oates's "Parricide"
might seem the same when it comes to pronominal usage: (a) "We were fractious and overpaid. Our mornings lacked promise. At least those of us who
smoked had something to look forward to at ten-fifteen"; (b) "We could hear
the water running into the tub. We looked at the presents scattered over the
bed where mamma had wrapped them in the colored paper, with our names
on them"; (c) "He is sitting at a long, ungainly table, his thin arms awkwardly
folded. As we file into the room he shifts uncomfortably." However, in the
course of the following pages the situations of narration change dramatically
in each of these three texts, as I have shown.

Fulton comments on the mechanism of the performative creation of a collective speaker (and the formation of solidarity) as follows: "By definition [the
first person plural pronoun] gathers subjectivities together and allows them to
speak as one. **Repeated use** of the pronoun reinforces the idea of solidarity, as
each verb, each sentence marked by the first person plural suggests common
thought and common action" (2003, 1106). We-locutions not only work pro-
actively, performatively creating present and future unity, but also imply a pre-
existing we-group: "In order to speak as one and identify itself as a group, in
other words, the *we* assumes a prior union through which this common voice
is articulated" (1106). For the creation of we-narrator this means that even
though the we-reference might begin in an indicative context, its repeated and
consistent use not only creates a collective narrator character as the narrative
progresses but also retrospectively marks this narrative as a we-narrative from
start to finish.[18] Thus, on the one hand, a quantitative argument cannot define
a we-narrative: It is not the frequency of occurrence of this or that pronoun
but the relationship between the narrator and the narrated, as well as the type
of narrator, that defines a narrative situation, as Stanzel's (1984, 49) work has
persuasively demonstrated. On the other hand, however, this relationship can
only become visible through the duration and consistency of the collective
"we," making them intrinsic features of a we-narrative.

---

18. Let me refer again to the ending of *Then We Came to the End*, which offers a good
example of the reverse. The office "we," having eventually disintegrated due to layoffs, meets five
years later for an improvised reunion and, as the night progresses, fewer of "us" stick around
until the final two sentences of the novel read, "We were the only two left. Just the two of us,
you and me" (385). This revelation of the dual "we" of the narrator and the narratee, however,
comes unexpectedly, since nothing in the nearly four hundred pages of the novel has suggested
that the narratee is one of "us"—quite the contrary. Thus, the dual "we" produces a local effect
of mild delight for the previously excluded narratee (and, perhaps, for the reader) of being—
finally!—included into the group, but it does not retroactively undo the collectiveness of the
we-narrator in the novel.

One more example may be useful here. In her novella *The Buddha in the Attic* (2011), Otsuka describes the situation of Japanese immigrant women in the US in the early 1900s by using a particularized we-voice similar to Ferris's ("all of us," "one of us," "some of us"). Through a formulaic and repeated use of the we-voice, even in descriptions of individual group members, she thus prompts the reader to engage not with the particular events of "our" story, but with the general condition and exploitation of women immigrants in the domestic and social spheres. Such a focus is created with the help of a lyric mode of progression, and so I shall return to this novella in the next chapter, which discusses lyric progression in we-narratives in general. But for now, one paragraph from *The Buddha* will be enough to demonstrate the performative force of a certain type of repeated we-reference. For example, this is how the novel describes the women's married life and their relationships with their husbands:

> One of us blamed them for everything and wished they were dead. One of us blamed them for everything and wished that she were dead. Others of us learned to live without thinking of them at all. . . . We put away our mirrors. We stopped combing our hair. We forgot about makeup. *Whenever I powder my nose it just looks like frost on a mountain.* We forgot about Buddha. We forgot about God. . . . We cooked for them. We cleaned for them. We helped them chop wood. But it was not we who were cooking and cleaning and chopping, it was somebody else. And often our husbands did not even notice we'd disappeared. (36–37)

Such a collective voice allows Otsuka to carry out a two-fold task: Her novella sets out to shed light on the life of Japanese immigrant women in the US, but the focus soon shifts from the misfortunes of the women to the ethnic minority in general. On the one hand, Otsuka tells the tragic life story of Japanese women who travel to the US as "picture brides." The individual stories of these women presumably yield themselves to a certain amount of generalization— so alike are they, despite their differences—and can be told in a more or less homogeneous collective voice. Individual remarks figure as corroborations of such homogeneity, via particularizations ("one of us . . . ," "some of us . . .") and the quoted speech or thoughts of some of the women—usually limited to a single sentence or line. On the other hand, toward the end of the novel she makes use of the unifying quality of the performative we-voice to thematize the disappearance of the women's individualities and the effacement of the whole community in the context of the economic and racial discrimination against immigrants in early twentieth-century America.

As always, there are borderline cases. The performative "we" is, after all, created on the basis of the indicative "we," and the latter is often not as straightforward as the above examples might suggest. Think of the implications of *pluralis majestatis* or the ambiguity of the authorial "we." Often its "indications" are not entirely clear. Helmbrecht, for example, speaks of the "anaphoric side of first person plural pronouns," which means that, generally, it is "not possible to start some conversation with *we* without a previous introduction of the members of this group" (2002, 31–32). That is, it is not possible for the addressee of such an utterance to establish the referent of the "we" and, hence, its meaning. Most fictional we-discourses, however, begin with a cataphoric use of "we" (i.e., with forward reference) and take their time before revealing the reference class of the first-person plural pronoun. Faulkner's opening in "That Will Be Fine" is a case in point, no matter how briefly he delays the identification of the I-narrator and his nanny Rosie. A more interesting case is Oates's "Parricide," discussed in chapter 1, which introduces a group of medical students, refers to them as "we," and then singles out only one of them after a certain sense of group unity has been established; "I" then hides once more behind the safety of group anonymity. The first transition from "we" to "I" is marked more strongly than in "That Will Be Fine" because Oates withholds the disclosure of the I-speaker for a longer stretch of text while, at the same time, consolidating the we-group. Moving between the collective and the individual perspectives, texts like these make explicit the tension inherent in the we-voice between the group and the individual and show that the process of constructing a collective "we" is gradual.

As I hope to have made clear, the distinction between uses of we-discourse is not grammatical but contextual. The opening sentences of Faulkner's story and of Ferris's novel can both be read as indicative. Yet, as the text progresses, the latter acquires a performative mode. Consequently, Faulkner's story is a typical first-person narrative, whereas Ferris's novel is what I propose to call a we-narrative. This distinction between the indicative and performative uses of "we" explains the reasons for two noted effects of we-narration: It has been described both as unremarkable and as odd or playful. As Richardson observes, we-narratives "do not immediately call attention to themselves as artificial constructs possible only in literature," but at the same time they "routinely (if at times barely perceptibly) make themselves strange and . . . produce unlikely or impossible kinds of telling" (2006, 37). In other words, there is a fine line between the two effects, as one mode may swiftly develop into the other.

CHAPTER 3

Plural Narrators

Collective Voices, Lyric Progression,
and Direct Speech by Groups

> We spoke to them in snatches, each of us add-
> ing a sentence to a communal conversation.
>
> —Jeffrey Eugenides, *The Virgin Suicides*

THIS CHAPTER deals with the key element of the first-person *plural* narrative situation: its group narrator. When "we" are said to be speaking, as in the epigraph from *The Virgin Suicides* above, it usually means that members of a (situational) group are speaking in snatches and thus constructing a communal conversation or a story. But, as is clear by now, my interest lies in a different kind of "we," conceivable in written narratives: a narrating voice that is truly plural—indiscriminate and unanimous. Within the established models of narration, with their strong ties to enunciative-linguistic conceptions of communication, such plural narrators cannot be easily accommodated. Since the subject of enunciation is by definition an "I," any we-narrator is usually viewed as an I-narrator in disguise or, at least, is measured by the standards of the singular voice. However, this established analytical apparatus is currently under revision,[1] and in this chapter I aim to contribute to its reconceptualization by discussing we-narrators in modified terms. My main focus, however, is on the peculiarities of we-narration itself: on the relation between collective and individual characters and voices, on lyric progression as a distinctive quality of

---

1. See Patron and Nicholls (2013, 244–46). For debates about narrative communication, see Phelan (2011, 57, 59); Richardson (2011b, 24–25); Walsh (2010, 35–36). For the notion of non-communicative narrative, see Fludernik (1994b). For rethinking of the author's role, see Walsh (2007, 2010); Patron (2010); and Margolin (2011)—especially the discussion under Margolin's publication.

many we-narratives, and on techniques for representing direct speech of the many at once. The main case studies for this chapter are Julie Otsuka's novella *The Buddha in the Attic* (2011) and Susan Sontag's short story "Baby" (1978). I also use supporting examples from the we-narrative part of *deadkidsongs* and from *Then We Came to the End,* my continual points of reference throughout this book because the former offers one of the most interesting experiments with narrative voice (in my corpus of multiperson and we-narratives) and the latter is the paradigmatic we-narrative in the novelistic genre.

A Pragmatic Rhetorical Approach to the Possibility of a Plural Narrator

First, some preliminary theoretical considerations.[2] Arguably, one classical conception of the narrator continues to exert its influence on current discussions of narration by a collective "we." Broadly speaking, this conception is based on two premises: The narrator as a (1) always-present and (2) always-singular speaker. Both run into problems when narration in the plural is to be described and classified. Speaking to the first premise, many prominent narratologists, including Genette, dismiss "narrative without a narrator, the utterance without an uttering" as a "pure illusion" (1988, 101).[3] Similarly, Shlomith Rimmon-Kenan emphasizes that both the narrator, as a "higher

---

2. So much has been written and said about the narrator over the past few decades that I shall only focus on two premises relevant to my discussion of we-narrators. Among the recent publications on the narrator, see Walsh (1997); for an overview of the Genettian classification of the narrator, its critique, and a suggestion for a solution, see Walsh (2010); see also Köppe and Stühring (2011) for a summary of the classical theory of the narrator and the assumptions it is founded upon, including a critique thereof, as well as Patron (2011). In Ukrainian, Ivan Bekhta has published an extensive investigation of narrator's discourse in Anglophone fiction, *Дискурс наратора в англомовній прозі* (2004; see also I. Bekhta 2013). In French, Sylvie Patron's *Le Narrateur: Introduction à la théorie narrative* (2009) approaches the problem of the narrator from the standpoint of poetic, or noncommunicational, theory of narrative fiction. For a debate in the German context, see Birke and Köppe's edited volume *Author and Narrator: Transdisciplinary Contributions to a Narratological Debate* (2015). An insightful analysis of the communication model is offered by Harry E. Shaw (2005, 301–2) who observes that in practice, the communication diagram is not as symmetrical as it seems, with agents of transmission—especially the narrator—afforded more weight than the audience. For an inquiry into types and roles of narrative audiences see Phelan (1994, 1996) and Rabinowitz (1977).

3. "Utterance" is recast as "statement" (*énoncé*) in Seymour Chatman's model (1975, 309), where it refers to the narrative discourse on the whole. Narrative discourse is "the means by which the content is communicated, the set of actual narrative 'statements'" (295) and thus presupposes an utterer (the narrator) and a listener (the narratee), who may be explicit or not, but is indispensable to the narrative transmission.

authority," and the corresponding narratee are "constitutive, not just optional, factors in narrative communication" (2008, 89). While this is the case in the very literal sense that every oral narrative is uttered by someone and every written one composed by someone, the situation is trickier when it comes to intratextual speakers. Whenever we-narratives, for example, shift between we-narrators and single focal characters, temporarily denying the controlling authority of the collective narrator—as in the passage from *deadkidsongs* discussed below—this cannot be easily reconciled within a pan-narrator model unless the model generates explanatory categories of covert or nondramatized fictional tellers. The second premise, crucial for my present purposes, establishes the conception of the narrator as the literal subject of enunciation and hence a singular "I": "The narrator can be in his narrative (like every subject of an enunciating in his enunciated statement) *only* in the 'first person'" (Genette 1980, 244).[4] Didier Coste stresses the same point: "Any person used in an utterance presupposes a first person against and with which it makes sense, so that the enunciating 'I,' unknowable in its act, is however always represented in any text; and any receiver must determine his position in relation to it" (1989, 175). In other words, and in accordance with the enunciative-linguistic theories discussed in the previous chapter, "I" is viewed as the deictic center of a narrative communicative situation that produces all other persons, including "we," in relation to itself.

In recent narratological investigations of we-narration, this framework is literalized. For example, approaching we-narratives within his conception of anti-mimetic storytelling, Richardson observes that "according to conventions that have governed literary fiction since romanticism, the 'we' speaker cannot know the private thoughts" of other characters (2015, 202), as is the case in, for example, Joseph Conrad's *The Nigger of the "Narcissus"* (1899). This implies that the we-narrator is to be seen as "I + others," where the "I" is constrained by certain limitations as a real-world speaker—a convention of recent literary theory, perhaps, but not of fiction. "Unnatural" narratology in general rests on the conception of a humanlike singular narrator prompting the development of such counter-concepts as "unnatural acts of narration," "unnatural voices," or the narrator's "impossible knowledge." The implication with all of these is that whenever first-person narrators are described as "unnatural," there exists a backdrop of supposedly "natural" fictional narrators, fully governed by human limitations: Once dramatized—that is, present as characters in the storyworld—they must not know what is happening in two places

---

4. See also Prince (1982, 7–10).

at the same time, must not narrate what they have not witnessed or quote extended dialogues and stories from other characters,[5] and so on. Above all, such assumptions automatically problematize narrating communities or other amorphous first-person narrators. While Richardson, in his earlier publications, acknowledged, in line with Genette, that omniscient first-person narration is not so much a material or psychological impossibility as a technique of "textual coherence and narrative tonality" (Genette qtd. in Richardson 2009, 154), his subsequent work goes on to identify plural narrators as "unnatural" phenomena when compared to the possibilities of a nonfictional world.

And, while current analyses of unusual narrative voices would benefit from a revisiting of the classical conception of the narrator—dismissed all too easily in "unnatural" narratological debates—a more flexible understanding of the narrator's aesthetic function would benefit both. However, this category proves difficult to modify or challenge—despite consistent attempts (see the first footnote to this chapter). This is partly due to the narrator's theoretical function: Having emerged to distinguish the "I" of the real author from the "I" of the fictional character around the 1950s (particularly in so-called third-person narratives; see Stanzel 1984, 81), the narrator came to be the signature feature of fictionality as such; any radical modification to the narrator—denying its ubiquity, for example—therefore shakes the foundations of dominant conceptions of the literary narrative. The established theories of narrative communication understand it as transmission[6] and depend on the narrator

---

5. Consider, for example, a reading of an excerpt from *The Golden Ass* by Apuleius, which Nielsen classifies as "unnatural" and highly problematic because, being a first-person narrative, it contains a "very elaborate story of Cupid and Psyche related by an old woman" (2011, 74) that the narrator hears and claims he will not remember—and yet the full story is here, in front of the reader, as part of the narrator's account. However, such an "unnaturalizing" approach forgets that complex narration embedded verbatim within another first-person narrative is a technique very common in the history of literature, and that the classical concept of the narrator accommodates this strategy. A similar example to *The Golden Ass* is analyzed by Coste (1989, 170–71): In Guy de Maupassant's short story "Allouma," a first-person narrator is introduced only in order to introduce a second-degree narrator, who then proceeds to tell a book-length story. Such asymmetrical embeddings do not foreground the "unnatural" qualities of the narrator, but are a habitual structural device employed to achieve certain effects. One such effect is to create the "raw, uninterpreted reality" (171) of what is being told, which, in turn, creates the illusion of direct, unmediated access to the story.

6. Chatman's (1978, 151) Narrative Communication Diagram and Rimmon-Kenan's (2008) explanation, among many other publications, provide concise and clear summaries of this conception of narrative communication. See also Shaw (2005) for an overview of the communication diagram and debates around its categories. One modification to the diagram has been suggested by Phelan (2011, 2017: chapter 1), who argues for the inclusion of characters as narrating agents. Chatman's model remains a helpful heuristic, but "we should replace the belief that it contains some immutable truth about narrative" with a realization that there are also other types of narrative communication that it cannot describe (Phelan 2017, 19). Similarly,

to distinguish between fiction (in the sense of a report of imaginary events by a fictional narrator) and nonfiction (a report of true events by an empirical person, an author). As Klauk observes: "In the extreme case the presumption that there must be a [singular, NB] narrator telling a certain narration rests on theoretical reasons alone, since the text carries no clues that point to a [singular, NB] narrator" (2011, 40). Positing a universally present *fictional* narrator has functioned as "a kind of inaugural step inside the frame of fiction, the fictionality of which is henceforth held in abeyance" (Walsh 2007, 69), thus releasing "the author from any accountability for the 'facts' of fictional narrative" (74) and, at the same time, allowing for a consideration of the reader's ethical and emotional engagement with fictional characters and events as if with real people and situations.

It would thus seem that fictionality is the main reason for the indispensability of a certain conception of the narrator in the established model (the fictional narrator being a marker of fictional narrative)[7] and the model would benefit from the addition of the author category, if only for the sake of making visible the constant conflation of the actual author and the fictional narrator when it comes to the act of narrative representation and the representation itself.[8] As early as in 1979, Stanzel had to clarify this confusion in his *Theory*

---

there are other types of narrators than the seemingly universal type that Genettian narratology "endowed . . . with properties traditionally attributed to the narrator-character of first-person fictional narratives" (Patron 2011, 329). See Walsh (2007, 86) for another radical critique of the view of narration as transmission.

7. This is not the place for an extensive discussion of the problem of fictionality. For my argument, it suffices to point out that fictionality can be more productively treated as a contextual rather than textual quality. See Walsh (2007, 45): "The distinction between fiction and nonfiction rests upon the rhetorical use to which a narrative is put, which is to say the kind of interpretive response it invites in being presented as one or the other." As Köppe and Stühring (2011) show, pan-narrator approaches rely on the narrator to explain the nature of fictionality rather than the workings of a given fictional narrative: by upholding the literal view of narratives as speech acts, for example, which presupposes an utterer who, in the case of fictional narratives, has to be a fictional narrator (63), or by maintaining that narrators are "indispensable for the fiction because it is their voice that creates the fiction in the first place" (67).

8. The relation of the narrator category to the author functions has been a long-standing point of debate, connected to the changing conceptions of fiction since the beginning of the twentieth century. In 1989 Coste summarized the following issues: On the one hand, the distinction between the two is clear and "the author would be responsible for the whole text, using an intermediate specialized instance—the narrator—to tell (within the text)" (166). On the other hand, conflation of the narrator and the author still happens in theoretical discourses when "(1) the narrator is said to be an abstraction, but he *has* a function, or better a 'mission' or task; our theorists speak of 'him' as if he were a human being or perhaps a spirit, without a personality, but still capable of good and ill will, success and failure, authority and interpretation; (2) *the* narrator is viewed singly in principle, even though 'he' may end up subdivided or multiplied" (166). A notable exception to the first point is Mieke Bal (1985, 119): "I shall refer to the narrator as *it*, however odd this may seem."

of Narrative by stressing that the narrator has to be treated as a "representa-tive[ ] of the **rendered** mediacy of the narrative and [has] nothing directly to do with the production of the work, with the act which generates the fictional world (plot, scene, characters *and* narrator) as fictional images" (1984, 17). Stanzel's category of narrative situation, including its element of "person," only describes the "rendered mediacy" (1984, 21; i.e., *gestaltete Mittelbarkeit,* Stan-zel 1991, 37) of a given narrative text, which is to say, its form.[9] The difference between the act and the form has been variously called "the deep structure of a narrative work"—or "spirit of narration" (Kayser via Thomas Mann), "nar-rative function" (Hamburger), "implied author" (Booth), just "author"—and the "surface structure" (Stanzel 1984, 15). And further:

> In every word of the printed page of a novel the narrative function leaves its trace, "written by *someone.*" The process of production, the genesis of a nar-rative text (deep structure) must, however, as stated above, be distinguished from the process of transmission, "a tale that has been told" (surface struc-ture). It is not legitimate to treat these two statements as parallel. (20)

And yet their conflation still informs recent narratological work.[10]

With these considerations in mind, it is now possible to qualify Genette's and Coste's postulates above as to the singularity of the enunciating subject: They apply not to the fictional narrator but to the author (the narrative func-tion, etc.) as the ultimate producer of the fictional narrative act. (Although I do not intend this claim to be categorical—one still has to consider texts

---

9. Stanzel's use of *Mittelbarkeit* comes from his interest in the ability of fiction to present the world as experienced—mediated—through various perspectives, which are not necessarily those of the author alone or even at all. I refer to experience in broad terms, such as, as Jameson formulated it, "an inchoate yet original subjective substance which is then shaped and named, and in effect given form, by pre-existing social and collective categories" (2017, xiii). Experience is any aspect of reality processed by a human mind—processed, for example, in an inextricable unity of form and content with the help of narrative as a socially available structuration prin-ciple. Narrative, among other symbolic forms, shapes and is shaped by experience.

10. See Aczel's (1998, 491–92) arguments against optional-narrator theories. See also Palm-er's approach, in a different context, to characters as "people in novels," which endows fictional constructs with the real-world agency: "Fictional mind-reading tends to involve characters, often in moments of crisis, who are **self-consciously using** complex theory of mind to try to interpret the opaque intentions and motives of another" (2011, 210). See, in the discussion of we-discourses, Fludernik's (2018, 173, 176) reference to fictional instances as "the speakers **and writers** of *we*-narratives." At the same time, the usefulness of the author category becomes clear when talking about the fluid boundary between authorial and narratorial (in contemporary sense) voices in nineteenth-century fiction where "narrator personae . . . hover on the bound-aries of the fictional world; at key moments they step into the fiction and seem to become part of it" (Fludernik 2011, 120).

authored by a collective.) The author, as the singular subject of enunciation, is distinct from the represented narrating "I," the latter being the subject of the utterance, or the *énoncé*. In other words, the "I" of narrative fiction does not relate indexically to the author's "I," just as the narrative "we" does not. In enunciative terms, then, the question of who is speaking when it comes to we-narrators can be resolved in *intra*narrative terms: The speaker is a fictional entity represented in the narrative discourse (which makes it unnecessary to explain the "we" in terms of actual enunciating possibilities), a narrating group constructed by the author and by the narrative text in plural terms.

Recently, Walsh has called attention to these issues in rhetorical terms: Narrative representation is a real-world communicative gesture, a rhetorical act (on the part of the author) that may or may not take the form of narrative transmission (2010, 35).[11] The performance of this real-world communicative gesture "in the case of fictional narrative, is offered as fictive rather than informative, and creates, rather than transmits, all subordinate levels of narration" (35). Fictionality is thus detached from the narrator, being a contextual marker, and the narrator can be approached as a properly fictional character that can take all sorts of shapes. Sylvie Patron, going further, has suggested explaining experimental narrative forms that are not structured as if transmitting a story by the narrator to the narratee within the "deep structure" or the logic of the rhetorical act itself. In her analysis of narration in the experimental, fragmented novel *Pedro Páramo* by Juan Rulfo, Patron concludes that "the only adequate explanation for the formal peculiarities of the extracts in question is as choices made by the author for technical or artistic reasons" (2010, 263). In line with Stanzel and Walsh, Patron distinguishes between "the content of the fictional representation" (the characters and the events, the narrator, if there is one) and "the means employed to help construct this representation (language, style, the composition of the text on different levels)" (267). She argues that "in certain fictional narratives nobody speaks—or more precisely, the question ['who speaks?'] is not asked since it is not pertinent" (254). In certain cases, there is no intrafictional originator of the narrative voice, and hence there is no point in constructing a hidden character who has "really" produced this narrative.[12] In my view, however, this is not to say that

---

11. A counterview that inverts this hierarchy between the representation and transmission can be found in, for example, Lintvelt's *Essai de typologie narrative*: "The compulsory constitutive task of the narrator is to fulfill the *narrative function,* called *representative function* by Dolezel. This function is always combined with the *control function* [*function de contrôle ou de régie*], since the narrator controls the structure of the text in the sense that he is able to quote the discourse of the actors" (24–25, qtd. in Coste 1989, 165).

12. As Aczel rightly remarks: "The issue here is at least partly terminological. If one chooses to restrict the term 'narrator' to an identifiable teller persona, then there ostensibly

narrative communication is canceled out if there is no identifiable intrafictional speaker: The general communicative act of narrative representation, the Platonic diegesis (the voice of the poet, or authorial storyteller), remains.[13] To slightly modify this argument: If there is a group of speakers whose identity is that of a transgenerational town community like in "A Rose for Emily," there is no further theoretical need to look for clues about a singular, "actual" speaker behind this community. In rhetorical terms, in we-narratives "Who speaks?" can be answered within the frame of mimesis (the poet speaking as if someone else): a mimetic narrating instance (a collective or communal character-narrator) represented by the diegesis. And while the mimetic narrating instance can also be described in the more conventional terms of character narrator, I am interested in the usefulness of the notion of diegesis in this Platonic distinction, as discussed in Walsh (2010), and its potential to describe the complex communicative dynamics of we-narratives in which first-person plural narrators briefly disappear or combine with the third-person voices of reflector characters in curious ways.

In sum, although coming from distinct theoretical movements,[14] Patron and Walsh both speak to the necessity that narratology consider the author

---

are narratorless narratives" (1998, 492). But if one retains the narrator category for something other than the designation of an identifiable teller, then it is for reasons of addressing the issue of fictionality. Curiously, in his earlier work on we-narrative, Richardson arrived at a similar conclusion, commenting on earlier critics of Conrad's use of various narrative voices in *The Nigger of the "Narcissus"*: "We need to ask, 'What is the narration doing now?' rather than, 'Who is speaking here?'" (2006, 42).

13. It should be noted that while I am looking for alternative conceptions of narrative communication, I do not find it productive to deny narrative *as* communication altogether, since this would unnecessarily limit the available approaches, such as those of rhetorical theories. One can view literary narrative as a form of communication in at least two senses: (1) In the broadest sense of narrative as a form of institutionalized human interaction, a meaning-sharing act (Walsh 2007, 111), and (2) in a more specific, narratological sense as the interaction within and through a narrative in "a feedback loop among authorial agency, textual phenomena, and reader response" (Phelan qtd. in Herman et al. 2012, 30). It seems safe to say that in the first sense narrative is *always* a communication: Stories, after all, "do not emerge circumstantially out of phenomena: they exist as stories by virtue of being articulated" (Walsh 2007, 87). Thus, following the rhetorical strand of narratology, I treat narrative as a "rhetorical action," a communicative event "in which an author addresses an audience for some purposes" (Herman et al. 2012, 56).

14. In fact, their theories seem to differ only regarding their conception of narrative communication. Since Patron views narration in narrow terms as transmission where "one narrates something that exists, phenomenally or discursively, prior to the act of narration" (2017, n.pag.), authors cannot be narrators. Walsh, on the contrary, claims that "the narrator is always either a character who narrates or the author. There is no intermediate position. The author of a fiction can adopt one of two strategies: To narrate a representation or to represent a narration" (1997, 505). For Walsh, narrative fiction *always* is a communicative act and thus always has a narrator, but, as "certain 'narrators' are outside representation" (2007, 174n1), it is legitimate to talk of

in a "poetic sense" (rather than biographical) as "the actual instance of the production of a narrative" (Patron 2011, 329), since "fictional representation is an authorial activity" (Walsh 1997, 511). Bringing the category of the author into narratological models usefully addresses the roles and functions that logically belong to the creator of the text (e.g., the control function) and not to its creation, the fictional narrator. It grounds fictionality in the orientation of an authorial rhetorical act and allows us to approach to a literary text as an aesthetic totality, even if its narrators are fragmented, disappearing, or contradictory. It makes possible an examination of a narrative (with its style, themes, and symbols) as a historically and culturally situated literary work.[15] It must be noted again that the issue of the author's role is pertinent to a conceptualization of narrative communication, but not to the establishment of *the* meaning of a narrative.[16] For an analysis of we-narratives, the usefulness of the author category lies in the simple possibility it opens up: Ultimately, the author is the producer of fictional statements, the source of the fictionality of a narrative, and its unifying agent—which, of course, would not be possible without the reader's participation and the broader context of conventions. The author's rhetorical act constructs the we-voice for some (aesthetic, political, or other) purpose, and the we-narrator, consequently, does not have to bear the role of an "impossible enunciator." The we-narrator can be treated as a represented, that is intrafictional, agent on a par with non-narrating characters, embedded impersonal discourses, and other elements of narrative that all contribute to the text's meaning and effect. In other words, an approach to we-narratives that includes the author in the narrative communication model removes the largely irrelevant questions of how a group can physically speak as one, of how a fictional character can know something that is unknowable within the limitations of one human mind, and so on. Of course, there can be narratives that put forward such questions, but if the text does not justify asking them, they are merely false

---

authors as the originators of fictional communicative acts. At the same time, the reception and interpretation of such acts does not have to rely on "the idealized intentionality of the 'implied author,'" nor on "the idea that fiction should be then approached as a communication of authorial intentions" (Walsh 2007, 131).

15. See also Stanzel's (1984, 74) considerations of the author vis-à-vis the narrative style, as well as Patron's (2011, 330–31) discussion of the merits of rethinking the enunciative analysis of narratives from the position of the author.

16. There is a similar caveat to the deep/surface structure distinction in Stanzel: "The narrative strategies of the surface structure are, of course, connected to the deeper levels of the narrative text via language and its norms, but they are not totally determined by it. The mediacy of presentation of the narrative text provides latitude for the author in which he can design an appropriate form for the transmission of each story" (1984, 20).

interpretive problems and the creations of theory rather than of the narratives themselves.

Collective and Individual Voices in We-narratives

The narrative situation of the first-person plural is much more complex than the above focus on the plural narrator may have suggested. We-narrators, despite being the dominant feature of this narrative situation, often recede into the background when the discursive acts of individual characters—internally focalized passages, interior monologues, and so on—are represented. This again brings up the analytical question of who is speaking in such passages where the we-narrator cannot plausibly be speaking. Generally, in we-narratives, a community or other collectivity tells the story as if it were transmitted, that is, re-created from past events within this community, perhaps over generations. In other words, we-narration is often structured as a narrative transmission. For example, the we-narrator in Oates's *Broke Heart Blues* talks to "our" narratees about past events in the town as "we" know them to have happened decades before "our" telling. In Stanzel's terms, this we-narrator belongs to the storyworld of the narrated characters, to their realm of existence (it is homodiegetic, in Genette's term). Nevertheless, constant shifts between collective we-narrators and singular characters, as well as we-narrators' varying scopes of knowledge of and access to the storyworld, complicate the existing taxonomy. We-narration frequently gives way to other modes (e.g., to heterodiegetic narration with a covert narrator or reflector mode), while eventually embedding or otherwise reincorporating such digressions to its dominating authority.

A curious concise example of such vocal complexity can be found in *deadkidsongs,* a multiperson novel whose first part is written in the first-person plural. I shall discuss the novel's structure in detail in the next chapter when focusing on the question of diegetic levels in we-narratives, but a short summary of its plot is appropriate here. The action of *deadkidsongs* takes place during the 1970s in Great Britain where four friends, Matthew, Andrew, Peter, and Paul—or, as they refer to themselves, Gang—spend their time play-acting war, training to defend Britain against the "Russkis" (Litt 2001, 12). The first part of the novel is narrated collectively by all four boys as a we-narrator, followed by four chapters in each individual boy's voice; there are also third-person, heterodiegetic sections about each of them. When Matthew dies suddenly of meningitis, the boys' war game spins out of control. They decide to put their military skills to use to avenge their friend, who died because of his grandparents' negligence (or so the boys think), and aim to actually kill the grandparents. The fulfillment of this plan coincides with an escalating rivalry between Andrew and Paul over the leadership of Gang. Ultimately, Andrew, having abandoned Gang, carries out the plan on his own: He kills both the grandparents and Matthew's sister; having tortured them and mutilated their corpses, he then takes his own life. This is one version of the story; the novel also offers an alternative ending, where the war does indeed take place and the "Russkis" invade, but its implausibility within the novel's structure only reinforces a third, implied version of what happened. This third reading suggests that Paul is in fact both the masked I-narrator and the murderer, and that the whole story—which is presented in the form of a manuscript—is his indirect confession before he himself commits suicide decades after the events described.

The novel consists of an intricate web of voices and embedded narratives, with the opening we-narration having a considerable influence on the rest. In the first part of *deadkidsongs,* "we" are the narrator-protagonist and the focalizer, but, as is usual in full-blown we-narratives, "our" narration competes with situations in which "our" members are on their own, unobserved by "us." Such shifts are usually executed smoothly, and there is minimal interference of the collective teller mode in the passages written in the reflector mode of individual characters—as will be clear in the examples from *Then We Came to the End* and *Ways of Dying* in the next chapter. The following excerpt (1), however, demonstrates a more complicated relationship:[17]

> The day had grown even hotter, outside the confines of our gorse haven. As **we walked** past The Prom, **we saw** a group of younger boys having a game of French cricket on the school playing-fields. **The desire** to join them **was strong in all of us,** but **we resisted** it. Once **we came out** onto the road, Paul indicated that he had to get home before his father. . . .
>
> Paul nodded, then turned and started to walk slowly **away from us.**
>
> As soon as he was **out of our sight,** however, he started to run, as fast as he possibly could. He dodged off the tarmac road, full of pot-holes, making his way along the short-cut, a narrow lane between scrotty hedges.
>
> He sprinted all the way home. (Litt 2001, 77)

Here "we" narrate "our" collective actions (walking, seeing) and shared feelings (desire to join and resisting). Halfway into the passage, however, Paul is

---

17. To be more specific: This is a complication for a narratologist. In an actual reading situation, arguably, the structural unusualness of some parts of this quote will be overlooked—it will be subsumed by what Phelan calls "the dominant system of probability" of a given narrative (2017, 47–49). I shall return to this issue in chapter 5.

singled out. All four boys are singled out from time to time, but Paul plays an increasingly special role in this part of the novel as a we-member who questions "our" unity, although never directly. The incident in the above example adds to a developing sense of the group's disintegration: "Our" unity is still intact when one of "us" is temporarily singled out, but it shatters when such splits become deeper and more frequent. At one point, the novel even comments on this self-reflexively: "Of course we know, as it was later proven, that any individual absence, of the permanent sort, not Paul's temporary incarceration, meant a total change to all Gang-Members" (50). The way Paul's departure in the above passage is described may be interpreted as one of the first synthetic (*sensu* Phelan) signs of the imminent split in Gang. It also complicates the relation between narration and focalization: "We" narrate what "we" no longer see.

The we-narrator's single members often act or talk (in direct speech) on their own, independently of the we-narration, and often their individual thoughts are presented in a manner typical of heterodiegetic narration. This happens as a combination of various forms of mediacy: The narrated storyworld is presented via "our" narration and perspective, but some parts of it are also presented through the perspectives of individual characters. In the example above, however, as the narration moves from the homodiegetic "we" to a more heterodiegetic one in the next section of the novel, it remains conspicuously focalized: "We" observe Paul as he walks slowly away from "us" and then breaks free from "our" narratorial control and group influence as he runs out of "our" sight. The first-person plural pronoun figures once more in the following section, which then turns into the strongly reflectorized figural narrative situation centered on Paul. Through this transition, the we-narrator arguably has all the features of a heterodiegetic narrator who becomes covert at such points in the narrative when characters act as reflector figures. As Stanzel observes: Direct rendering of the content of a character's consciousness "takes place in the absence of a personalized narrator," which creates for the reader an effect of unmediated insight into that character's thoughts and feelings (1984, 107). It is, to stress again, a transition characteristic of heterodiegetic narration. After the last sentence of the quote above, the new section of *deadkidsongs* opens as follows (2):

> Once home, Paul entered the cottage as stealthily as he could. Like all of us, he was an experienced creeper-about. His mother was in the kitchen, standing at the sink. Paul slunk by very quietly. As he did, he noticed that, although his mother's hands were up to the wrists in the washing-up water, she wasn't doing any washing-up. In fact, all she was doing was staring

straight out over the lawn. Paul thought he might have heard her sob, but he was too concerned with getting into the bathroom to pay it much attention. He managed the stairs with little difficulty. (Litt 2001, 78)

Paul's actions after he leaves "us" and goes home are narrated completely from his perspective: how he sneaks into the house so that his mother doesn't see his dirty clothes, how he registers but doesn't react to his mother being upset. The same applies to the later telling of how he plays with his genitals while taking a bath, his concerns about looking too much like a girl, about whose father is best, and if he can be a Gang leader. The rest of this section is focalized entirely through Paul, and besides the phrase "like all of us" in the second sentence, nothing indicates that the we-narrator is related to the scene in any way. Paul's thoughts and actions are far too private to be plausibly accommodated as something "we" as Gang narrate for thematic and structural reasons. Thematically, the image of the we-narrator as a character so far has been that of a group concerned with making "our" adventures epic in preparation for a glorious war. It is only in private, unbeknown to the rest of the group, that the boys can admit their various weaknesses or nonmilitary concerns. Stylistically, there is no indication of the we-narrator's idiom, either, as Paul's thoughts gradually acquire a new tone. Still, like the transition in passage (1), this section is marked by the we-narrator's intrusion: "Like all of us." Thus, on the one hand, narrated events that concern only Paul do not form part of "our" narratorial idiom or perspective, but they are—minimally—still tied to "our" heterodiegetic presence.

In analytical terms, the homodiegetic we-narrator in the first passage (1) either disappears mid-sentence or is able to narrate that Paul started running when he was "out of our sight" and report what he saw on the road and did at home. Similarly, in the second passage (2), the we-narrator's comment on Paul's stealth skills functions as a remainder of the waning control that "we" have over Paul and can be described as the homodiegetic narrator's transformation into a heterodiegetic one, which subsequently becomes covert. The analytical problem for a classical narrator-centered approach emerges again here. One of its premises, as Walsh summarizes, has been to "allow the narrative to be read as something known rather than something imagined, something reported as fact rather than something told as fiction" (1997, 499).[18] The narrator must know something in order to be able to narrate it. To rationalize the we-narrator's knowledge of other characters' minds and events the narrator itself has not witnessed—and thus to save the integrity of the classical

---

18. For example, Genette (1980, 241) and Stanzel (1984, 17).

model—one could propose several explanations for the passage above: The homodiegetic narrator's omniscience is literal ("we" are superhuman, tele-pathic, or otherwise in possession of superior cognitive abilities); the narra-tor acquired knowledge of the events after the fact (Paul told "us" for some reason); unreliability ("we" are following Paul without saying so); "we" are imagining what Paul was doing when he left. None of these explanations, I would argue, suggests itself to the empirical reader: They all invite purely ana-lytical speculations that the narrative itself does not interpretively encourage. Paul's running away from "us" is not narrated as imagined, but rather as what "really happened," and there are no signs that "we" are unreliable at this point. Paul's secretive plans to take over the leadership of the group do not invite the conclusion that he later told "us" what happened—and it would be strange to share such an insignificant action or such private details with the rest of the group in any case. Neither can these transitions be analyzed in terms of the broad knowledge possibilities of the we-narrator: In *deadkidsongs*, "our" joint knowledge and actions are usually contrasted with those of each of the four boys on their own. This is contrary to the progression of, for example, *Then We Came to the End,* where individual perspectives contribute to a cumula-tive we-perspective.

There is no analytical necessity to resolve this mixing of narrations and perspectives, however, by, for example, attempting to subsume the multiplicity of voices under a single narrator. As I have suggested above, these and simi-lar passages are better approached from a pragmatic rhetorical stance, within which omniscience becomes a quality of imagination: "The reader is not obliged to hypothesize a narrator who really is omniscient within the terms of a given fiction because the authorial imaginative act doesn't merely initiate a fiction, but pervades it" (Walsh 1997, 499). Fictional information does not need to be presented as known rather than as imagined. Thus, the question here really is not about knowledge and who can narrate it, but about what the above combination of narrative modes achieves in the broader framework of the rhetorical communicative act *deadkidsongs,* or about what significance these technical choices have for interpretation. In other words, questions of "who narrates" in the sense of an overarching narrative instance are easily resolved with recourse to the author: Ultimately, she or he is the originator of all discourses in a given narrative, the extra-/heterodiegetic narrator. This is not to say, however, that narration happens in the author's own voice, as it were, but that we are dealing with his act of narrative representation under the regime of fictionality that, in some cases, is structured in diegetic terms (i.e., without an objectified, fictional narrating instance) and, in other cases, in mimetic terms (i.e., in the voices of character narrators). In the example from *deadkidsongs*, this means that we are dealing with a rhetorically motivated transition from one mode of mediacy (narration, by the we-narrator) to another (presentation, through the reflector-character Paul), which, in the process, alters the status of the we-narrator and removes it, temporally, from the page.

It may be tempting to fall back on the pan-narrator theory by arguing that the homodiegetic we-narrator turns into a covert, heterodiegetic one, but this theory's implications for the conception of fictionality strain its limits. While in passage (2) "we" do not and cannot narrate Paul's private activities, positing another *intratextual* but absent narratorial figure who presents Paul's day is only necessary if the source of all narrative utterances must be located within the narrative text itself—that is, in accordance with the classical model of narrative communication. I believe, however, that a pragmatic approach, which allows for any element of narrative representation to be modified or eliminated as the author sees fit, is more beneficial for the description of the effects of directness (as in nonmediacy through the we-narrator, or any narrator) that are created in example (2) via the transition into a fully reflectorized mode.

Within this latter approach, the ubiquitous presence of the fictional narrator is redescribed as a ubiquitous presence of narrative representation in various modes (*sensu* Stanzel), with or without *fictional* teller figures. Or, indeed, it is redescribed within the Platonic dyad of diegesis and mimesis, as Walsh (2010) suggests. By reviving Plato's distinction between the poet's own voice (diegesis, a matter of information) and the poet's speaking in the voice of the character (mimesis, a matter of imitation), Walsh teases out a functional distinction between the levels of fictive representation. Diegesis describes a narrative instance, or "voice as instance" (48), as part of a rhetorical act offered under "the real-world communicative regime of fictionality" (41). Diegetic voice is not objectified as a fictional character (or a fictional narrator) and covers the narrative *object*: narrative information that is offered to the reader, rhetorical means with which the author chooses to structure the information, and so on.[19] Mimesis refers to the ways in which the acts of narration repre-

---

19. In other words, diegetic voice describes the same narrative instance as a nondramatized narrator. However, the nondramatized narrator is a category complicit in the untenable conception of narrative fiction that postulates that every fictional narrative must have a fictional narrator (for a more detailed discussion of why it is untenable, see Köppe and Stühring 2011, 63). The category of the diegetic voice, instead, while attending to the fact that every narrative *does have* a narrator—it is told by someone on some occasion and for some purpose, as the rhetorical definition goes—also attends to the aesthetic complexity of fictional narratives and to their status as symbolic acts within a framework of relations between their authors and readers. Fictional narratives can be said to be ultimately narrated by their authors (which is to say, there can be no noncommunicative narratives), but these narratives are also composed and stylized

sented by diegesis are structured. Mimetic voice, or "voice as idiom" (49), is objectified as a character and covers the discursive or narrative *subject*:[20] It is a matter of rhetorical effects, it characterizes the fictional narrative instance, and is a source of the reader's ethical engagement with the narrator as a character. In the case of we-narratives, this means that the plural narrating voice belongs to the level of mimesis: A collectivity is represented as a speaker, characterized by a distinct voice as idiom, and is a character in the given storyworld. Importantly, the distinction between instance and idiom is analytical and not absolute (49) and applies to all narrative situations, depending on the rhetorical emphasis one brings to the analysis of a given voice aspect: In voice as instance, the emphasis falls on the representational act; in voice as idiom, on an object of representation.[21] Or, in other words, "a narrative told by a character, considered as idiom, contributes to the job of characterization; considered as instance, it contributes to the job of narration" (49). Both senses of voice are applicable to the represented narrative instance of the we-narrator: Its diegetic aspect invites the reader to consider the significance of the narrated (events), and the mimetic aspect invites an ethical evaluation of the character narrator.

Within this analytical framework, it becomes possible to interpret narration and change of perspectives mid-sentence in *deadkidsongs* by attending to the act of representation on the whole, or diegesis: that is, by asking how it advances our understanding of the novel and what significance this change has for the we-narrator, Paul, and the narrative progression. Arguably, Litt has the we-narrator narrate this piece of information to introduce a contrast between "our" control over narration and over the rest of the scene and Paul's literal (in the fictional world) and figurative escape (from the narrator's control) and in order to highlight Paul's special status. The narration is partly

according to the available forms, aesthetic, personal or political programs, and so on (which is to say, an analytical model should make it possible to acknowledge local erasure of voices, intermittent figures, and other techniques and effects).

20. See I. Bekhta (2004) on character being a "discursive person," realized in a text as a structure of discourses (232).

21. To avoid confusion, however, in cases of "pure" diegesis when the voice is not objectified as any character (e.g., in authorial narrative), the "diegetic idiom" is best described not as mimesis, but as the author's style. See Daniel Hartley: Style in Walsh's sense "is the idiom of diegesis, the non-character narrator: It is as close as one can come to the author's own voice under the 'regime of fictionality'" (2016, 89). Walsh also distinguishes voice as interpellation, the third, peculiar type of voice that refers to the representational subject position created by the narration. It covers the (narrow) sense of focalization as well as the (broader) implied ideological subject position of the discourse with which the reader imaginatively aligns herself (Walsh 2010, 53). I omit it in the present discussion.

mimetic (i.e., we-narrator as a character) and partly diegetic (the technique of delinking narration from the we-narrator for rhetorical effect and the subsequent mediation of the world through Paul's mind, without a mimetic narrating instance). The "we" in the above passage is not only backgrounded for the duration of the narration about Paul that follows; it positively disappears. Rather than struggling to devise an analytical explanation that would "save" a narrator who is absent from a scene, one can approach the disappearing narrator as a representational issue and not as the literal source of narrative discourse. The narrator does not require "continuity of being" (Walsh 1997, 507) because it is ontologically subordinate to language as a means of representation. In the passages above, the specific rhetorical effects are created by means of such an "intermittent narrating character" (507), which is combined with other modes of narrative representation.

In a nutshell, the logic of communicative exchange—where fictional narration is considered within the framework of a transmission (e.g., Genette 1988, 16) that originates in the necessarily fictional enunciator—cannot frame fiction on the whole and, if sustained, produces a misunderstanding of the nature of fictionality (Köppe and Stühring 2011; Patron 2010; Walsh 2007, 2010). The fictionality function of the narrator is one of the reasons for postulating ubiquitous, covert and overt singular narrators where, for example, narratives suggest collective voices—intermittent and amorphous or fully dramatized as characters. A popular alternative take on we-narratives, suggested by "unnatural" approaches working *ex negativo*, often mystifies experimental or unconventional narrative voices, creating an array of false interpretive and analytical problems. In this section, I have offered a practical examination of the recent rhetorical-pragmatic theories of narrative that explicitly situate fictional narrators within the rhetorical representational act as a whole. These theories, I believe, provide a productive refreshment of the existing models without completely invalidating them. In what follows I adopt this pragmatic rhetorical framework for my analyses.

Lyric Progression and the Representation of Direct Speech in We-Narratives

I have already discussed several salient features of we-narration that are rooted in the plural narrator, a collectivity at the center of enunciation. As noted in chapter 2, the performative "we" distinguishes we-*narration* from other uses of we-*discourses* in fiction and contributes to the creation of a fully fledged we-narrator. Other factors in this process include the absence of an I-speaker and repetitions, over prolonged stretches of the narrative, of we-utterances that describe collective actions, as well as shared emotions and other mental states. I shall now explore one more characteristic of we-narration: If the we-narrator narrates about "ourselves" rather than someone else, then the narration often assumes a mode of lyric progression (curiously, witness narration by the we-narrator often gains a voyeuristic quality, of which more in chapter 4). I adopt the term "lyric progression" from Phelan (2005, 10) to suggest that a fully developed collective voice in we-narrative is also distinguishable from singular first-person narrators by a certain degree of lyricality. One important consequence of lyric progression in we-narratives is the dissolution of the character-narrator, since this type of narration places more emphasis on the condition or state of larger-scale groups, for the expression of which a certain nebulousness of the we-narrator's identity is necessary. Otsuka's novella *The Buddha in the Attic* (2011) and Sontag's short story "Baby" (1978) are both convincing candidates for the paradigmatic example of a we-narrative with lyric progression. Indeed, we-narratives can serve as a good testing ground for an investigation of this type of progression in general.[22]

Narrative progression, as Phelan describes it, is "the synthesis of the narrative's internal logic, as it unfolds from beginning through middle to end, with the developing interests and responses of the audience to that unfolding" (2005, 19). The "unfolding" refers to the introduction and complication of instabilities, conflicts in the story, and tensions in the discourse (e.g., unreliability) that sustain the reader's interest in the narrative, evoke certain ethical responses, and are either resolved at the narrative's end or resist resolution. In this respect, the mechanisms of progression of the lyric narrative are distinctive, especially when it comes to the development of a protagonist-centered plot, the role of the narrator, and the reader's involvement with the narrative. A narrative progresses lyrically if:

(1) The character narrator does not undergo any substantial change within the temporal frame of the main action; instead, the text focuses on revealing

---

22. Lyricality is not, of course, a universal feature of we-narratives, but it is a common one. Of the narratives analyzed in this book, only "A Rose for Emily" and *deadkidsongs* are exceptions to this tendency. I shall not enter into the distinction between narrative and lyric in more detail here. In the context of types of progression, the meaning of "lyric" rests on a difference between types of responses and readerly engagement with lyrical and narrative kinds of texts; see Phelan (1996, 31). Additionally, there are distinctive conventions that the readers bring to the reading of lyric and narrative: "It would be misleading to argue that the 'text itself' is the sole basis upon which we will experience the poem as lyric rather than as narrative" (35).

the dimensions of the character narrator's current situation. (2) The dominant tense of the narrative is the present . . . . In other words, revelations about "what happened" are made not for their own sake but in the service of explaining "what is." (3) The implied author invites the authorial audience to enter sympathetically into the character narrator's perspective but does not ask us to render an ethical judgement of that perspective or of the character narrator. (Phelan 2005, 158)

In other words, unlike typically narrative texts, a lyrical narrative does not place its main focus on the unfolding of a plot and thus does not draw the reader's attention to the character's actions or the events described. It focuses, rather, "on the underlying value structure" of the narrative (159). The reader is thus invited to assume the role of a participant (rather than observer or judge) who would adopt or understand the speaker's perspective rather than evaluate it. If narrative is "somebody telling somebody else on some occasion for some purpose that something happened" (161), then lyric narrative is either "(1) somebody telling somebody else (who may or may not be present to the speaker) or even himself or herself on some occasion for some purpose that something is—a situation, an emotion, a perception, an attitude, a belief," or (2) this speaker is telling "about his or her meditations on something" (162). Similarly, we-narratives that progress lyrically focus not on the narrated events themselves, but on what these events say about the situation of the narrating community. The ethical judgments and perspectives of the narrators in *The Buddha in the Attic* and "Baby," for example, are postponed or substituted by a different kind of ethical engagement with the narrative: Readers "enter" into the perspectival position offered by the text and engage with what "we" experience rather than ethically analyzing these experiences. Thus, for example, the question of whether or not "Baby"'s collective narrator is crazy does not strike the reader as central.

The actual progression of a narrative is, of course, more complicated than any theoretical generalization can account for. Sometimes the lyric narrative focuses on the past, including changes of characters or situations over time; sometimes the reader's judgment of characters and their actions is involved; and so on. Nevertheless, like with narrative situations, one can speak here of a dominant mode that then subordinates other modes and defines the narrative progression. Stanzel, emphasizing the constant modifications in narrative situations in a novel, "from chapter to chapter or from paragraph to paragraph" (1984, 46), notes that only if it is possible to determine a predominant narrative situation in a novel can that novel be described in terms of this situation, for example, "the authorial novel" (46–47). This resonates with the Formalist concept of the dominant,[23] which Roman Jakobson defines as "the focusing component of a work of art: It rules, determines, and transforms the remaining components. It is the dominant which guarantees the integrity of the structure" (1987, 41). In the case of narrative progression, the relevant components are the plot dynamics (characters, events, and their interconnections), the narratorial dynamics (the "how" of the telling and its perspective), and the readerly dynamics (such as the reader's various interests, judgments, and ethical responses).[24] If the dominant orientation of a narrative is to tell how something is or what a character or narrator thinks or feels about something, then these components may be said to be subordinated to such an overarching orientation, and the narrative progresses lyrically.

In we-narratives lyric progression has one further important consequence: It leads to a higher degree of amorphousness (or to a near-complete dissolution) of the narrator as character. In "Baby," the dual "we" refers to a couple, possibly parents, who alternatingly attend individual and joint therapy sessions. Due to several techniques, which I shall discuss below, the "we" referring to the two parents soon dissolves into a composite voice of parenthood, a chorus of worries and fears for a child. This voice ultimately breaks down into a call to an authority figure (the doctor, in this case) to save "our" Baby, and the ending becomes a cry of emotion and pain rather than a resolution of the story's complication. Similarly, in Otsuka's *The Buddha in the Attic*, lyric progression transforms an already vaguely characterized we-narrator (a group of Japanese picture brides) to encompass all Japanese female immigrants to the US in the 1900s, all of the immigrant community, and, finally, all of American society as well. Descriptions of the process and consequences of immigration do not serve to make some related further point: The events of the plot are narrated in order for the reader to see what immigrant life "is." I shall begin with a closer examination of Otsuka's novella and then move on to "Baby."

Julie Otsuka's *The Buddha in the Attic*

The we-narrator in *The Buddha in the Attic*—initially—consists of a group of women who are traveling to the US as "mail-order" or "picture brides." Marriage between male Japanese contract workers—who, for various rea-

---

23. I am grateful to Jim Phelan for this reference.

24. For a detailed discussion of narrative progression, see Phelan and Rabinowitz in Herman et al. (2012, 57–83).

sons, could not return home from Hawaii or the continental US—and women in Japan became a recognized practice "during the first two decades of the twentieth century, when Japanese men, hoping to form a class of independent farmers and producers, developed the notion of establishing a permanent settlement" (Tanaka 2004, 115–16). Legally forbidden from marrying American women and with no money for the trip back to Japan, Japanese immigrants married women from Japan "at distance" after a brief exchange of photographs and background information. As Kei Tanaka notes:

> During the peak period between 1908 and 1920 until the abolition of picture marriage by the Japanese government, it is estimated that over 10,000 picture brides entered the United States. Although they constituted only about one quarter of the immigrant female population, in a symbolic sense, picture brides came to represent the entire population of Japanese immigrant women. (116)

In her novella, Otsuka (2011) develops precisely this symbol: Her we-narrator functions less as a collective *character* of a picture bride, a specific community, or a settlement, and more as a collective *image* of female Japanese immigrants in the US in the early twentieth century. She prompts the reader to engage not so much with "our" actions and what was happening to "us"—these are mostly variations of the same grim reality of "we were deceived," "we suffered," "we were exploited"—but with the general condition of oppression and exploitation first of women immigrants, and later of the whole of immigrant community.

Otsuka thus invites the reader to participate in the narrated events (rather than observe them) and to identify with a highly marginalized position: an immigrant woman of color. For this purpose, Otsuka's choice of narrative voice and perspective subtly changes over the course of the story: To successfully function as a subject position for the reader, the initial racialized and gendered perspective has to become more general, and thus the we-voice gradually includes all Japanese immigrants, female and male, and, in a final move, all Americans. This expansion—without a change of pronoun—transforms the theme of the novella from the fate of immigrant women to that of the shadow existence, disappearance, oppression, and exploitation of subaltern communities in general. Such a reading of the first-person plural voice as that of the oppressed is supported by the novella's choice of epigraph from Ecclesiastes 44:8–9 about those "who are perished, as though they had never been," and by the ending, in which the American community ponders the disappearance of the Japanese and of the fading of their once coexistent community: "All we know is that the Japanese are out there somewhere, in one place or another, and we shall probably not meet them again in this world" (129). The use of precisely the *first-person* (plural) to give voice to the marginalized is a bold move: By the time of the referential reversal, when the Japanese communities become referred to as "they," the reader has already grown accustomed to experiencing the storyworld through "their" first-person voice and perspective. The third-person reference to the Japanese settlements comes across as an unexpected and forceful distancing, thus inviting the reader to speculate on the arbitrary nature of divisions into "us" versus "them."

The generalization of the we-reference and its reversal happens in several stages. First, the narrative is divided into thematic sections that serve as transformations of collections of singular events into markers of life stages. *The Buddha in the Attic* starts with the women traveling on the boat to the US to meet their new husbands for the first time ("Come, Japanese!"); it then describes the "wedding night" with the husbands ("First Night"), the settling down in American communities, extreme poverty, work, and exploitation bordering on slavery ("Whites"), experiences of pregnancy and childbirth ("Babies"), and then the disappointment of the children growing up Americanized ("The Children"). In the chapter "Traitors," the story takes a new turn when the status of the whole Japanese community changes at the start of WWII. "Our" husbands are being taken away (presumably after the attack on Pearl Harbor) as potential enemy allies and, finally, whole families are forcibly resettled ("Last Day"). This progression of the plot may come across as a typically narrative one—a life story—but the collective narration generalizes what otherwise would have been personal experiences and events, encouraging readers to dwell less on the development of an individual's life than on the significance of shared circumstances for an entire community. In the final chapter of the novella, "A Disappearance," a reversal in perspective happens as the American community, referred to earlier only as "they" and through "our" perspective, is given a collective we-voice to ponder the fates of the Japanese they had never noticed until the day whole settlements were forcibly interned.

Thus, even though the novella's structure suggests that the character narrator undergoes a number of changes throughout the story, these changes are subordinated to the dominant, lyrical orientation toward telling about various dimensions of immigration. This is partly due to the way the changes are narrated. On the scale of individual paragraphs, the narrating voice in *The*

Buddha in the Attic proceeds according to a pattern that repeats itself in each paragraph in each chapter: The we-narrator starts by setting a topic for the following passage with a generalized statement, which is then particularized by listing what "one of us," "some of us," or "others of us" did or thought. Every now and then a piece of direct speech or thought is given (marked out from the rest of the text by italics). This move also serves to make more versatile the otherwise potentially monotonous generalizations. Consider, for example, the following passage from the chapter "Come, Japanese!":

> On the boat we carried with us in our trunks all the things we would need for our new lives: white silk kimonos for our wedding night, colorful kimonos for everyday wear, plain cotton kimonos for when we grew old, calligraphy brushes, . . . smooth black stones from the river that ran behind our house, a lock of hair from a boy we had once touched, and loved, and promised to write, even though we knew we never would, silver mirrors given to us by our mothers, whose last words still rang in our ears. *You will see: Women are weak but mothers are strong.* (9–10)

The first sentence of the paragraph describes a fact that holds true for all of "us," and then the particularizations follow, which, nevertheless, can still be read as collectively true until even more individual notes appear. The statements that one of "us" lived near the river, one of "us" left a boy she loved, and that to one of "us" a mother gave a piece of advice and a silver mirror are much more specific than those about kimonos and what "we" carried in "our" trunks. The gradual individualization thus paves the way for the line of direct speech that, strikingly, ends the paragraph. Still, these things and memories are described as if belonging to a collectivity and, due to the force of the repetition of the descriptive structures, their particular nature does not acquire importance. What is emphasized is the fact that these things and memories carry the sentiment shared by all of "us" without exception: "We" are not going to the US of "our" own will; the pain of leaving home together with the fear of what awaits "us" is immense.

Moving through the description of individual fates and living conditions, the we-narrator does not discriminate between them and does not utter any evaluations or comments. Nonfocalized, these passages of enumeration become a collective picture of a life of hardship. The following paragraph, for example, proceeds by listing places "we" live: "Home was a cot in one of their bunkhouses at the Fair Ranch in Yolo. Home was a long tent beneath a leafy plum tree at Kettleman's. Home was a wooden shanty in Camp no. 7" (24).

Such repetitive structures contribute to the performative force of the "we"; moreover, the collective reference is maintained even if "we" are obviously talking about individual cases:

> **Some of us** worked as cooks in their [American, NB] labor camps, and **some of us** as dishwashers, and ruined our delicate hands. **Others of us** were brought out to their remote interior valleys to work as sharecroppers on their lands. **Perhaps our husband** had rented twenty acres from a man named Caldwell, who owned thousands of acres in the heart of the southern San Joaquin Valley, and every year **we paid** Mr. Caldwell sixty percent of our yield. (33–34)

This passage lists the different places and jobs in which some or other of "us" ended up. The collective mode does not cease, even when in the third sentence only one of "us" is mentioned. To maintain the collective reference and generalizing sense, a particular woman's situation opens with an uncertain "perhaps," though it ends with a very specific description of Mr. Caldwell and San Joaquin Valley. Even though it is her husband who rents land from Caldwell, he is referred to as "our husband." Thus, by the end of the sentence the we-reference to the woman and her husband who had to pay 60 percent of their yield every year loses its specific reference to a particular family and becomes a more allegorical image of all of "us" having to pay exorbitant interest to "our" exploiters.

This example again demonstrates one of the salient features of a collective we-narrative—the alternation between the individual and the collective: "Both individual and collective levels exist concurrently and are irreducible to each other, so that [there is] an unresolved tension between the two" (Margolin 2000, 592). This tension will be at its most visible in the following discussion of direct speech and then of collective focalization in chapter 4. Progressing by distributing its elements between the we-group and its individual members, *The Buddha in the Attic* creates a collective voice and an image of a life of an immigrant community while, at the same time, keeping the individual specificities of its members in sight. It is by a joint, common reference to these seemingly individual conditions that the we-narrator's collective identity is constructed as one of a group with shared goals, attitudes, perspectives, and so on. Generally, we-narrators as characters possess what Hicks describes as "the sense of the group as a group" (1974, 28). At the same time, we-narratives usually avoid investing narrative authority only in transpersonal, institutionally defined we-groups, which would efface "the specific individuals who embody it at any given point in time" (Margolin 2001, 247). They thus move between the individual and the collective voices, as Otsuka's text and *deadkidsongs* do. But, of course, there are also exceptions, as the following section shows.

Susan Sontag's "Baby"

> But once we decided to visit the doctor, we began to hurry, to fret. We . . . anticipated questions the doctor would ask and rehearsed our answers carefully. It seemed vital to agree on the answers even if we weren't sure they were correct. Doctors lose interest in people who contradict each other.
>
> —Don DeLillo, *White Noise*

Sontag's short story "Baby" from the collection *I, etcetera* (1978) is not a typical narrative: It does not satisfy the expectations of character and plot development, and, moreover, it does not fit the description of narrative as "report." Like "A Rose for Emily," this story problematizes the issues of the narrator's identity, knowledge, and reliability. Just as in *The Buddha in the Attic*, in "Baby" the telling is performed by a "we" whose identity becomes exceedingly nebulous throughout the course of the narrative because its referents expand. But, unlike in Otsuka's and Faulkner's texts, in Sontag's short story "we" talk *exclusively* through direct speech and therefore, technically, cannot be called a narrator in the classical sense; here narration occurs through character dialogue, and "we" function primarily as a character.[25] This representation of the direct speech of a group character makes particularly visible the tension, inherent to any we-narrative, between the individual and collective levels. In *The Buddha*, direct speech is scarce and a privilege of individual group members whose remarks are quoted by the we-narrator, thus disrupting the monotonous transpersonal we-voice. In "Baby," direct speech is the only means of telling the story. Usually, we-narratives are situated in between these extremes: "We" do not normally speak directly (but narrate), and it is

---

25. Classically, character dialogue has been dismissed from the narrative canvass as an "alien" element (see Stanzel 1984, 63–68): Narration happens through narrative sentences and report, and as for dialogue—it serves other means. However, Phelan (2011, 2017: chapter 9), among others, has convincingly demonstrated how narration also occurs through character dialogue.

the singled-out members of the we-group who get to speak, exchange dialogue, and voice the we-group directly.

Besides being a good case study for direct speech of the many, Sontag's story also advances the possibilities of lyric progression in we-narratives: With the help of lyricality, the story demonstrably transforms the dual, indicative we-reference into a collective we-voice. However, the lyrical quality and narration via direct speech make a summary of "Baby" quite difficult, as the question of what happened is subsumed by the description of what is. The story's opening paragraph unambiguously states that there is a problem:

> What we decided, doctor, was that it would be best to lay our problems before a really competent professional person. God knows, we've tried to do the best we could. But sometimes a person has to admit defeat. So we decided to talk to you. But we thought it would be better not to come together. If one of us could come Monday, Wednesday, and Friday, and the other on Tuesday, Thursday, and Saturday, that way you could get both of our points of view. (147)

An initial interpretive response to this information might lead a reader to expect a story about a couple in therapy—perhaps experiencing problems in their marriage—and to form initial judgments of this couple as somewhat brown-nosing (telling the doctor he is "a really competent professional"), but also bossy (announcing how they should arrange their sessions) and controlling (admitting defeat is a bit shameful and that talking to the professional is "our" last resort). Nevertheless, these expectations are not confirmed, and as the one-sided dialogue continues, it becomes increasingly difficult to project a coherent narrative and to continue constructing the characters or even their storyworld. The problem turns out to be related to their baby, not to their marriage, and the initial sense of control that the couple projects turns out to be a coping mechanism. The narrative-building cues gradually construct a lyrical we-voice with a focus on grief, epitomized by the couple in therapy as they struggle to cope with the death of their only son, who may have died as a result of their actions. At least, this is one plausible interpretation (in, perhaps, Sontag's own sense of interpretation as a means of showing what the text is, rather than what it means).

The story takes the form of a transcript of patient-doctor conversations—without the voice of the doctor who, presumably, asks the questions and often interrupts the responses. This has two immediate effects. First, the reader occasionally feels directly addressed. Second, because the voice of the doctor is not "audible," the reader has to infer that to which the couple responds and why they are being interrupted (as there are no apparent reasons in their statements). Consider the following dialogue:

> At the beginning, you can imagine, we felt very sure of ourselves. With a good income, a house with no mortgage, membership in three—
>
> Sometimes. Sure. Doesn't every couple? But they blow over. Then we usually celebrate by seeing a movie. We used to take in the plays at the Forum, too. But we don't have much time for that any more.
>
> Oh, we dote on him. After all, when you have an—
>
> Pretty regularly. Once, twice a week. Thank God, there's nothing wrong with that side of things.
>
> No, it was the group that suggested we consult you. We're not claiming all the credit for ourselves. But probably we would have thought of it anyway.
>
> All right, sure. We do. But what's wrong with that? We really get along very well, considering the difference in our educational backgrounds.
>
> Perhaps our problem seems ridiculous to you.
>
> No, no, we didn't mean it that way.
>
> All right.
>
> That door? (148)

This ends the first meeting of the couple with the doctor and, again, leaves more questions than answers. Were they well-off, but not anymore? What happened? Perhaps they celebrate making up after quarrels by going to the movies, but why do they have no time for the theater now? Who is "he"? What "side of things" exactly do they have in mind? Who is "the group"? To what do they concede in the remark about educational backgrounds and why do they think it might be wrong? Did they offend the doctor, and did he tell them to leave? Quite a few remarks throughout the story either remain unintelligible to the reader or open up a whole range of equally justifiable interpretations. In the quoted passage, it is still possible to infer potential questions to the couple's answers by activating the stereotypical portrayal of couples in therapy (quarreling, disagreeing, being sexually active). But if nothing else in the text corroborates such assumptions, the reader has to keep postponing her construction and judgments of this character, as these would be based on uncertain inferences.

Such partial dialogue and fragments of information nevertheless offer a narrative promise because the very structure of this short story suggests a temporal progression: It is arranged into segments headed by the day of the week on which the session took place. In their annotated bibliography of Sontag's works, Leland Poague and Kathy A. Parsons summarize the story's temporal development as follows:

> For the first two weeks (assuming they are sequential), one parent comes Monday, Wednesday, and Friday, the other Tuesday, Thursday, and Saturday. In the third week, the sessions are "doubled"; there are two entries for Monday, Tuesday, Wednesday, and Thursday. In the subsequent Friday entry, one parent tells the doctor that they can no longer afford double sessions; in the last entry, "Saturday," a reference is made to the previous session, indicating that a kind of doubling continued, one parent having had two sessions in a row. (2000, 69–70)

While the structure is fairly clear (although note that a small part of it is still based on an assumption), the temporal change is largely only schematic, one day not being too different from the other as the couple struggle to spell out their problem. The gender and identities of the characters behind the "we," their names, ages, jobs, and alike remain unspecified. The son is also always referred to as "Baby," which makes it impossible to establish his age. Even if the reader begins to seek stereotypical indications of the gender of the parent in the transcript of their discussions during the first week's individual sessions, all speculations are confounded in the subsequent section, when the sessions are doubled, and there is neither any indication as to who comes when nor any regularities in the speech. The only identity the text allows its reader to assume for its characters is a dual one: parents. Parts of their interview still focus on "us" as a couple, describing "our" relationship or "our" views on topics such as family and upbringing, but most of it describes Baby's looks, habits, health, events at school, work, sex life, and more unusual details such as the fact that he kept a chemistry lab, two ducks, and six chickens, or that he laughed at exactly 4:00 a.m. each morning. These details get progressively stranger (e.g., that he is poisoning "us") as "we" continue to mix them with mundane comments on how raising children is an art (Sontag 1978, 158). "Baby" does not encourage mimetic engagement with the parents, and the parents' characterizations of Baby are too insufficient or contradictory for the reader to sympathize or otherwise emotionally or ethically engage with him, either. What the reader receives in the partial and fragmentary manner of a transcribed conversation is an erratic, associative array of comments and topics that the parents pursue.

Such a chronological arrangement recalls "A Rose for Emily," whose temporal logic is also driven by the narrator's associative reminisces. (Associa-

tive chronology figures in *The Virgin Suicides* and *Broke Heart Blues* as well.)
Unlike in full-blown narratives, where, as Phelan observes, "the logic of story
is the logic of connected events" until they find resolution, in lyric narratives,

> the logic of event gives way to the logic of revelation and exploration of
> a character's emotions and attitudes in a particular situation. The move-
> ment from beginning to end typically follows the movement of the speak-
> er's thoughts, but these thoughts are not typically a review of his or her
> identity and situation. Instead, as the speaker's thoughts follow their appar-
> ently autonomous direction, the author finds a way to convey to the reader
> a rounded awareness of the speaker's character and situation. (2005, 173)

Structured in such an associative and lyrical manner, "Baby" subordinates
the rudimentary description of life events by the couple to an exploration of
their traumatized mind: Why are they at the doctor's? What is it that they are
struggling to express? Even with the doctor's guiding (but inaudible) questions, there seems to be little coherence in the associative flow of their telling:
Baby's age shifts, along with his occupation, interests, physique, eating habits,
and so on. As the contradictions escalate, "we" mention cutting Baby's foot off
so that he doesn't run away and him hiding a gun in his closet. The final session turns into a plea that the doctor tell Baby "he's not going to live forever"
(182), mixed with various pop-culture references, demands, and advice for
Baby—or for any child of any age, for that matter—and concludes with the
question, "Oh God, doctor, why did our Baby have to die?" (184). The final
question puts the focus back on the couple and their potential tragedy, but
the plea itself points to a more universal experience of raising a child. By the
end of the story, the peculiar we-voice transcends the dual "we" of a couple
and, in doing so, erases the divisions between female and male and mother
and father, producing an image of parenthood drowned in a routine of daily
disagreements, happy moments, and TV, *as well as* overwhelmed by trauma.

The summary above is not an interpretation in a conventional sense, not
an extrapolation of the trauma of parenthood as the platitude of a symbolic
reading—it is a mere description of the last point in "Baby's" progression
towards abstraction. If Sontag's observations in "Against Interpretation" are
applicable to her own fictions, then "Baby" is an exercise in what she deems
to be the best kind of contemporary art—that which resists interpretation of
content by either making its content blatantly clear (pop art) or absent and
obscure (abstract painting). It thus collapses the division between content and
form, asking the critic to "dissolve[ ] considerations of content into those of

form" (Sontag 1966, 12) and to show *"how it is what it is,* even *that it is what it is,* rather than to show *what it means"* (14). Lacking plot, "Baby" foregrounds its lyricality and the transformations of the we-voice, and so my attempt has been to show how these transformations progress from the indicative "we," of a couple conventionally talking about their lives, to a collective one, representing a more general sentiment, all the way to a dissolution of any specific reference into an idea in the final pages of the short story.

The transformation of the indicative "we" is gradual and relies on several factors. First, although each parent initially attends the session alone, their voice is consistently plural: "We decided, doctor," "We can afford it," "We're thinking of moving," "We'll try to find out tomorrow," "How are we going to manage for a whole day without you?," "We do keep fit," "We don't smoke," "We didn't want to go at the end of the last session," and so on. The we-reference is the only available self-reference and, by the sheer force of repetition, it extends far beyond its indicative use in the description of collective actions or shared opinions and becomes what I term the performative "we." Second, the doctor's clearly personal questions are always answered with the collective "we," and the information shared at individual sessions is later referred to in the plural as well: "Laurie died. The duck. Remember? We told you" (Sontag 1978, 167). This piece of information is revealed during the first week, when the parents' sessions alternate, such that it is possible to establish that Baby's two ducks were first mentioned by, say, Parent B, whereas Laurie's death is later referred to by Parent A, with the remark "We told you." This violates the implicit confidentiality of the sessions—Parent A was not the one who told the doctor about the ducks—and adds to the peculiar transpersonal narration, knowledge, and perspective that the short story creates.

"Baby" thus establishes a continuity between the consciousnesses of each of the parents, and so its we-narrator cannot be read as simply two individual voices contributing to a collective story on a higher level of interpretation. "We" in "Baby" seem to have followed a piece of advice quoted in the epigraph to this section, taken from Don DeLillo's *White Noise* (2011): They speak as if they have rehearsed their answers so as to be able to fake a semblance of coherence, agreement, and sanity when answering the doctor's questions. At the same time as a continuity of the characters' consciousness is established, "our" conversations with the doctor regularly offer mutually exclusive pieces of information about Baby, undermining this continuity. The final question provides a crucial clue for the interpretation, but it is still not enough to arrive at a determinate, rounded story. Ultimately, it is impossible to decide how Baby died, whether the parents had anything to do with his death, or whether their menacing remarks about cutting off his limbs are the result of a traumatized imagination. In a final blow to my attempts at interpretation-as-translation here, Sontag's text also contradicts its own emotional escalation, explicitly asking whether or not the story seems plausible:

> We had to cut Baby's right hand off. It was the only way. He kept playing with himself.
>
> We made a little wheelchair for Baby. And a bed with sides, so he doesn't fall out.
>
> We had to cut his left foot off, because he tried to run away again. . . .
>
> Do you believe everything we tell you, doctor? (179–80)

*

It should also be noted that the use of "we" in certain cases of lyrical narratives—which can only tendentiously be described as narratives in the first place—does not produce a collective speaker or character. These noncollective uses of "we" occur when the first-person plural pronoun functions as a "common/generic person" (Jespersen 1958, 215), an "all-persons" "we," and a "no-person" simultaneously, as in the generic phrases "As we all know, ..." A case in point is Atwood's short piece "We Want It All," which, not being an example of a we-narrative as such, is a good example for the generic use of "we." It opens as follows:

> What we want of course is the same old story. The trees pushing out their leaves, fluttering them, shucking them off, the water thrashing around in the oceans, the tweedling of the birds, the unfurling of the slugs, the worms vacuuming dirt. The zinnias and their pungent slow explosions. We want it all to go on and go on again, the same thing each year, monotonous and amazing, just as if we were still behaving ourselves, living in tents, raising sheep, slitting their throats for God's benefit, refusing to invent plastics. (Atwood 1994, 154)

Establishing the referential meaning of "we" in this text is not necessary, unlike in other nonlyrical and narrative-lyrical contexts. Its "we," as becomes clear in the context of the text as a whole, does not establish any narratorial agency and does not acquire the performative force of a collectivity. The text becomes, rather, a musing on the state of ecology, on threats to our existence as humans for which we have only ourselves to blame, and nostalgia for an idealized pre-industrial way of life combined with an insatiable need for progress.

Direct Speech of We-Narrators

The Buddha in the Attic and "Baby" make use of direct speech in very different ways. Otsuka's text is a good example of how we-narration is usually combined with the occasionally quoted direct speech of individual members of the we-group. It is quite exceptional for an entire we-narrative to be structured in the form of direct speech, as "Baby" is. Direct speech by we-narrators is rare and the "we" of a full-blown plural narrator usually includes a group larger than two people. The problem here, as Margolin phrases it, is "how can one activate and preserve the direct discourse features when the speech of many is concerned?" (2000, 602). For if "we" were, for example, to engage in a dialogue, this would demand a particularization of only one or several members speaking on behalf of the whole group, a differentiation between who is asking and who is responding, and so on. This would undermine "our" enunciative unity. On the other hand, if "our" speech is presented exclusively in a diegetic summary, no group-internal differences are preserved, and the narration can very soon become monotonous:

> The only case in which direct discourse features can be preserved on the collective level is that of a group speaking, praying, chanting, and so on, in unison, with everybody uttering exactly the same words at the same time—for example, "They all cried out as one person: '. . .'" But the range of group speech activities as coordinated social activities is infinitely wider and includes such complex activities as discussing and debating, questioning and querying, where individual speakers employ entirely different words, so that one cannot report that the group as a unit uttered this or that phrase. (Margolin 2000, 603)

Can a we-narrative, then, represent these various group speech activities without being constantly limited to a collective, totalizing perspective that eschews any differences between individual utterances? Margolin lists some potential solutions: a summary by a narrating instance (i.e., a global group perspective such as "we promised," "we discussed"); a verbatim quotation of jointly produced written discourses; or direct tagged discourse, utterances by named individual members of the group.[26] What usually occurs in we-narratives is a combination of summary with passages in which only some of "us" speak directly (direct tagged discourse), as if voicing what is on "our" communal mind. This direct discourse is usually quoted by the we-narrator, or, as in the curious example from Ferris's *Then We Came to the End,* appropriated into "our" narration as free indirect speech.

Then We Came to the End is characterized by narrative progression, and so I draw on it here to give an example of direct speech in nonlyrical we-narratives. In this novel, "our" narration is combined with dialogues between individual characters (usually those that do not belong to the we-group) and "our" narrative comments on what has been said in the dialogue, which sometimes appropriates the content of a quoted conversation into "our" free indirect speech. Consider the following passage in which, during a "double-meeting," Karen tells "our" boss, Joe, that she has an advertising concept (both Karen and Joe are outsiders to "our" group):

> We looked at her with our chins floating in our coffee cups. **Hold up! we wanted to shout. You can't have concepts. We haven't even double met yet!** "What's your idea?" asked Joe.
> **Her idea? We'll tell you her idea, Joe. To slaughter. . . .**
> "It surprises me that you have concepts already, Karen," said Larry Novotny. Karen and Larry didn't get on so well. "It really surprises me."
> "Initiative," Karen said smugly.
> "I don't want to speak for anybody else," Larry added, "but to be honest, **it really surprises the hell out of all of us.**" (109)

"We" are physically present at the scene, but "we" do not speak up "ourselves" ("we" only "wanted to shout"). "We" comment on the dialogue between Karen and Joe in "our" narration—with her presentation she wants to slaughter "us," her rivals—but "our" dislike for the situation is voiced directly only by a singled-out group member, Larry. He functions as a spokesperson for "our" group in this situation, thus making possible the direct speech of the "we" without making the we-narrator of this particular novel suddenly less realistic by having the group, for example, comically speak in unison. In *The Buddha in the Attic,* the situation was similar, as the summarizing narration of the we-narrator was punctuated by occasional insertions of untagged utterances of

26. See Margolin (2000, 603–4) for an exhaustive list. Here I am interested specifically in singling out those techniques that characterize a we-narrative, rather than covering all possibilities.

direct discourse by "our" individual members. In *Then We Came to the End*, however, the purpose of direct speech is different from both Otsuka's novel and Sontag's short story: Ferris's novel, even though it slides into the mode of lyric progression toward the very end, progresses narratively with a focus on the we-narrator as a character in an established storyworld, which means that the we-character often interacts with other, individual characters in various daily situations.

Importantly, when "we" speak through one of "our" members, this may be said to briefly transform the performative "we" into an indicative one. "We" in direct speech, in other words, loses some of its emphatic collective power and illocutionary force, as in the example above, because the we-reference implies three possibilities: (1) "all of us" and Larry as one of "us"; (2) only "some of us" (including Larry) as a smaller and identifiable group present at the meeting; and (3) Larry, not being one of "us," who uses the we-reference indicatively. If an individual speaker speaks *on behalf of* the group, then "his utterance possesses the status of group or collective speech act," and "the 'we' designates both topic entity and originator of the discourse" (Margolin 2000, 599). But single spokespeople can also create a more ambiguous situation, when they are not authorized to speak on behalf of the group but only speak *about* it. Speaking about the group (i.e., using the we-reference indicatively) does not exert collective authority and collective communicative intent and thus becomes an individual character's speech, not the channel for the we-narrator's utterance. Larry's comment, however, has the status of a group speech act because it is clear from the narrator's discourse that the group shares his sentiment and, from the broader context of the narrative, it is clear that Larry is "one of us." Overall, in a we-narrative the direct speech of individual characters (who belong to the we-narrator group) offers another means of foregrounding the collective nature of the narrator, if these characters are empowered to speak on behalf of the we-group and the content of the direct speech utterances is incorporated into the surrounding discourse of the we-narrator.

Consider one final extended example, where "we" visit "our" boss, Lynn Manson, in the hospital when "we" find out she has cancer. One of "us," Jim Jackers, suggests giving an ad presentation to cheer her up:

It was **hard to distance ourselves from him** inside Lynn's hospital room **when he announced that "we" had a presentation** for her. Lynn herself looked at him from her ocean of bed with an expression somewhere between surprise and skepticism. **We all held our breath** for fear of what inappropriate preamble might escape Jim's mouth. He reminded her of what the pro bono project had **once asked of us**—to present the breast cancer patient with something funny in her hour of need. For the first time in his life, he didn't call it the "pro boner" project.

"And so without further ado," he said, **with embarrassing grandiosity,** as he unzipped the black portfolio and pulled out the first ad. **What choice did we have but to stick around?** . . .

We watched Lynn's face for some sort of reaction. "Let me have a closer look," she said. Jim handed the ad to her. She took it and we felt no different than we did when sitting in her office waiting for her to assess and judge and deliver her verdict on real ads. . . .

She continued to smile as she thanked us. **We said our good-byes. We told her to feel better.** Out in the hallway, we encountered more nurses and medical equipment. **We said we thought she liked them. We asked Joe if he agreed. We said we nailed it, didn't we, Joe? Didn't we nail it?** We walked together down the hall. We were a full car heading down the elevator.

"Do you really think she liked those ads, Joe?" **asked Marcia.** "Or do you think she was smiling because of how atrocious they were?" (Ferris 2007, 350–53)

Jim is one of "us" and Joe is an outsider, like Lynn, who belongs to "our" management. But here Jim uses a we-reference without being authorized to do so—hence the distancing quotes in "our" report of what he said: "He announced that 'we' had a presentation." It was his idea to revive the ad project, and "we" have been dragged into it. In other words, there is no consensus that would allow Jim to use the we-reference to speak on behalf of all of "us" at the beginning of this passage, even though "we" admit that this ad campaign was "asked of us"—no quotes around the "we" in this passage, even though it is still part of Jim's discourse. Nevertheless, towards the end of the scene, having gotten excited about Lynn's positive reaction to the ads, "we" accept Jim's idea *post factum* and now all seek confirmation from Joe. "Our" reactions are presented as summaries of what was said out loud in that situation: "We said our good-byes," "We told her to feel better," "We said we thought she liked them," and so on. The direct speech in the last line comes from Marcia, one of "us," and expresses what's on all of "our" minds (it also serves as an opening for the subsequent dialogue among just some of "us"). What is also curious about this passage is "our" physical embodiment: Since "we" are in a hospital room and fit into the elevator, this location limits "our" scope and gives a hint about the size of the group, making this office "we" more concrete—but only for a while. Collective action and feelings, again, contribute to its characterization: "We" hold "our" breath and are embarrassed because of Jim, "we" are tensely watching Lynn for her reaction, "we" are relieved and excited about "our" success. And then "we" even engage into a conversation without losing the group reference—via free indirect discourse and the quoted speech of individual group members. Such are the techniques that turn a group into a character narrator.

*

Throughout this chapter, I have discussed various theoretical repercussions of groups acting as a character narrator. The versatility of techniques, discussed above, that make we-narration possible can be fully acknowledged within the pragmatic rhetorical framework laid out in the first part of this chapter. What such a framework of interpretation "in the plural" brings to the table is (a) a more flexible conception of the narrator as a character and an element of the narrative (but not its ultimate designer and organizer), which permits (b) an inclusion of character dialogue as means of narration, and (c) a better understanding of techniques and strategies of narration that hinge on the group nature of the narrator. Moving on from this general theoretical interest, the chapter then considered narrative progression of we-narratives and possibilities of direct speech for we-narrators.

CHAPTER 4

Plural Perspective

Group Ethos, Narrators-Voyeurs, and Diegetic Levels

This was how we saw the world. The four of us.

—Toby Litt, *deadkidsongs*

NARRATION ALWAYS involves perspectival choices, whether anchored in a seemingly neutral spatiotemporal location or more subjectively aligned with characters or narrators. This is a trivial point, admittedly, but less trivial is the question of whether and how a group focalizer influences these techniques. Group characters express all sorts of internal states, shared beliefs, attitudes, and emotions, just like singular characters do. They have been viewed as expressions of a collective mind or, if taken not as a collective but as an aggregation of discernible individuals, an "intermental mind" (Palmer 2005). We-narrators, as characters, thus exhibit their own perspectives (in the sense of A. Nünning 2001) and can function as focalizers.

Although the terminological debate is still ongoing, for the sake of convenience I use the term "focalization" to refer to questions of how the perception of the fictional world is arranged (e.g., in spatiotemporal coordinates) and the term "perspective" to refer to the related issues of the subjectivity of the perceiver. My main contention, based on this distinction, is that in spatiotemporal terms focalization in we-narratives essentially functions according to the same principles as singular first-person narratives. The two narrative situations differ in the issue of perspective, such as the kinds of control plural focalizers exert on the reader's apperception of the fictional reality and how they regulate access to various aspects of the storyworld. Whenever a focal point is located within the we-community or other collectivity, it contributes to an expression of this group's ethos, or even of a particular form of life (see N. Bekhta 2015)—rather than of a mind or consciousness, as would be the case with singular focalizers.

The extended context for this chapter's epigraph should clarify what I mean. *deadkidsongs* (Litt 2001) opens as follows, focalized through the we-narrator:

> When **we looked upwards** we **saw beneath us** a sky of rosebushes, gravel paths, equipment and thick, healthy, but slightly too-dry grass. . . . The ground **above us**, on the other hand, was blue, blue as the deep end of a very wide swimming pool. . . . **At the horizon,** a rough line of oak trees was interrupted half-way along by the leap of pylons and wires.
>
> **This was how we saw the world.** The four of us. Gang. Not The Gang. Just Gang. Andrew, Matthew, Paul and Peter. Hanging upside-down from the highest branches of the tallest spruce in Andrew's father's garden.
>
> "Can you see them yet?" asked **Peter,** who dangled on the lowest branch.
>
> "No," said **Matthew.** "Shut up." . . .
>
> "Well?" asked **Andrew.**
>
> "I can't see anything," said **Matthew.** "No, wait a minute. It's a blue pram, isn't it?"
>
> "Yes," said **Paul.** "With silver wheels."
>
> By now **we** could **all** see, but Matthew shouted out anyway. "He's in the lead! He's in the lead! Look, he's in the lead!"
>
> We cheered loudly. The luck of hanging upside-down had worked. (9–15)

These paragraphs orient the reader according to "our" physical location: "We" are hanging upside-down from the tree, observing a pram race, and describe what is above, below, and in front of "us." Nothing peculiar happens until "we" introduce "our" members: Four boys are mentioned by name and none refers to himself as "I," the speaker. This plural reference is consolidated ("we could all see") as the narration progresses over the next pages, with "we" speaking about "ourselves" and about each of the Gang members in turn. Such references produce a certain discomfort in the reader since she wishes to know which of the four is "actually" talking.[1] The narrator's account suggests the possibility of one speaker (which is not the case for most full-blown we-narrators)

---

1. At least, it has consistently caused this discomfort in my very modest empirical selection of colleagues, conference attendees, and friends. Unlike the majority of we-narratives considered in this book, the overarching effect of *deadkidsongs* arguably hinges on the reader's desire to discover who is actually telling the story. This is partly because, unlike other we-narratives, this novel introduces *all* the members of its relatively small we-group.

but never discloses it, creating a defamiliarizing effect. The collective focalization in this passage, however, remains unproblematic and produces a spatio-temporal anchor point for the reader within Gang.

The collective nature of the we-narrator more explicitly influences narrative perspective when it comes to interactions between the we-group and the characters about whom "we" narrate. (Similarly to how such interactions influence direct speech, as discussed in the previous chapter.) The following example from *Then We Came to the End* illustrates what "we" can and cannot know through the ascription of mental states. Usually, the thoughts and perceptions of individual members of the we-group, who are often singled out by the narrator, are presented as a matter of fact: That is, the transition from "our" perspective to the internal state of another character is not marked as hypothetical or otherwise problematic. The mental processes of in-group characters can be portrayed without complications—"we" know them because they are "us." The situation is different when the narration focuses on non-group members. In this case, "we" only speculate as to what "they" might be thinking or feeling. One such outsider is "our" boss, Lynn:

> When she left, **no doubt she realized** how little she knew about the individual lives of the people who worked for her, how impossible it was to get to know them despite little efforts here and there, and **she probably also felt** the slightest, just the very smallest discomfort **for how it seemed** Carl [one of "us," NB] had hugged her for an uncommonly long time, as he had hugged so many of us during those berserk and unpredictable days. (Ferris 2007, 141–42)

The we-narrator refers to the feelings of someone outside the group as hypothetical, projecting "our" understanding of Lynn's thoughts about "us." Curiously, this paragraph is immediately followed by a transition to another individual character's perception, but this time with no hypothetical caveats since Tom Mota is one of "us": "**When Tom Mota saw** Carl's blacked-out windows, **he knew** the day had come and gone when he should have said something to someone about what he knew. **He didn't want to** say anything. **First of all, another man's business was none of his own**" (142). This passage, focalized through Tom, moves toward reflectorized third-person narration about this character—a typical technique for we-narratives that allows for seamless transitions between "our" narration and diegetic (in Walsh's sense) passages concerning individual characters, without the burden of keeping the we-narrator in sight at all times. It is worth noting again how a similar transition from "our" narration and focalization to Paul's perception and diegetic narration in a passage from *deadkidsongs* cited earlier (see chapter 3) was executed in a different manner that marked the transition's significance. In that case, Gang's (the we-narrator's) relation to its particular member did not suggest a tension-free combination of perspectives, as in *Then We Came to the End*, but a struggle between them that manifested itself on the structural level. I shall return to what I call the *narrative freedom* of individual characters from the we-narrator's idiom in a later section of this chapter, but for now it should be clear that focalization in we-narratives can take various forms, resembling those in narratives with heterodiegetic narrators (when it comes to omniscience about group members) as well as with homodiegetic ones (when it comes to strangers and "our" limitations as characters involved in the storyworld). This similarity, however, does not mean that we-narrators can be classified as both hetero- and homodiegetic—this would defeat the purpose of Genette's category without clarifying the peculiar status of we-narrators. As I stated in my definition of we-narrative, for most intents and purposes we-narrators are homodiegetic narrators, although this category does not quite capture the peculiarity of narrating groups. In the following, I shall look into an alternative approach.

I focus here on three points: On (1) the plural perspective as an expression of group ethos, (2) the voyeuristic qualities of communal perspective, and (3) the relationship between plural and singular focalizers. Shifts between the narrator's perspective and internal focalization via individual characters occur often and easily—something first-person narrative would perhaps struggle to execute plausibly. This perspectival dynamic of we-narratives problematizes the distinctions of person and level. Perspective is also tightly connected to questions of the narrator's knowledge, but knowledge leads into another heated topic—unreliability—so I defer most of this discussion until chapter 5 to be able to concentrate on the above three points in detail here. When it comes to we-narratives, collective focalization has been discussed by Margolin (2001) and Richardson (2009); in this chapter, I develop some of their points while contesting others. For examples, I draw briefly on *Then We Came to the End*, "A Rose for Emily," and *The Virgin Suicides*, though *deadkidsongs* remains the chapter's primary point of reference.

We-Narrators as Focalizers

The scope and meaning of the concepts of perspective and focalization, as is the case with several crucial narratological terms, are difficult to pin down. Being a favorite subject of debate, Genette's "focalization" is sometimes used as a more narrowly defined version of "perspective," although Stanzel (1984,

114) views the two terms as synonyms.[2] Burkhard Niederhoff, in defining the two terms for *The Living Handbook of Narratology,* uses virtually the same formulations.[3] In the glossary to *New Perspectives on Narrative Perspective,* Willie van Peer and Seymour Chatman define focalization as "**the perceptual centre** from which the events in the story are presented" (2001, 357). Almost identically, perspective is "**the location** from which events in a story are presented to the reader" (358). The center or location are to be understood both literally and figuratively as "the spatiotemporal coordinates of an agent or observer" and as "the norms, attitudes, and values held by such an agent or observer" (358).[4] These spatial-ethical concepts imply, of course, varying levels of restriction and access to the storyworld. In Stanzel's formulation, perspective "involves the control of the process of apperception which the reader performs in order to obtain a concrete perceptual image of the fictional reality" (1984, 111). As Manfred Jahn clarifies: "Apperception is a person's (hence, a narrative agent's) specific way of understanding a percept in terms of previous experience, knowledge and preference. Apperception becomes recognizable when I realize that somebody sees X as Y where I see X as Z" (2012, 5). This understanding of perspective with an orientation toward the reader's and fictional agent's apperception of the fictional reality resonates well with the rhetorical interest in the ethics of narrative. But an overlap in the many senses of focalization and perception is unavoidable, it seems, especially if one considers that a character-focalizer's perspective is necessarily limited in scope by that character's ontological status, as well as influenced by their subjectivities and agendas.

---

2. Genette uses "focalization" as a more abstract term than "vision" or "point of view" to refer to the "focus of narration" (1980, 189), a focal point in discourse disconnected from the narrator that also covers the thoughts and perceptions of the character. For an overview of the debates around the concept, see Phelan (2005, 110–19). See also a discussion on the website of *the living handbook of narratology* in response to Niederhoff's article on focalization.

3. "Focalization . . . may be defined as a selection or restriction of narrative information in relation to the experience and knowledge of the narrator, the characters or other, more hypothetical entities in the storyworld" (Niederhoff 2011a) and "Perspective . . . may be defined as the way the representation of the story is influenced by the position, personality and values of the narrator, the characters and, possibly, other, more hypothetical entities in the storyworld" (Niederhoff 2011b). The overlap between "experience and knowledge" and "position, personality and values" contribute to the vagueness of this distinction.

4. This last sense of focalization/perspective is most prominent in Brigit Neumann and Ansgar Nünning's approach: "Focalization . . . encompasses all perceptive, cognitive and emotional elements within the consciousness of the narrator or the characters. It includes processes such as thinking, feeling and remembering, in addition to sensory perception" (2008, 31). Focalization, as the norms and values that condition a given perception, is also sometimes understood in ideological terms, but, as Walsh convincingly demonstrates, this "more abstract, ideological construction of a subject position" (2010, 56), which he calls "interpellation," should be distinguished from focalization.

Therefore, my analyses below are motivated by Phelan's pragmatic approach to the issue that "focalization is not a complicated matter of the relation between narrators' vision and knowledge and characters' vision and knowledge but as a straightforward question of who perceives" (2001, 63). Focalization can be treated pertaining to the question "Whose perception orients the narrative text?" or "Whose subjectivity orients the narrative text?" (Jahn 2012, 5 and 8), and its identification and description are often a matter of interpretation. Rather than struggling to refine distinctions between perspective and various forms of focalization, I follow J. H. Miller (2005, 125) in arguing that it is more pressing to demonstrate how these phenomena function in a narrative text (specifically, in we-narrative), using focalization roughly to refer to spatiotemporal orientation and perspective to cover issues related to the perceiver.

The perceptions and, relatedly, knowledge of we-narrators have been described as problematic, especially if "we" narrate the thoughts and feelings of other characters. This tendency, as I have argued, is a consequence of the erroneous assumption—explicit or implicit—that we-narrative (or instances of we-narration) is similar to or the same as first-person narrative (or I-narrators using we-references). Marcus, for example, argues that both situations are "based on personal experience and [are] thus limited to the scope of human knowledge (in contrast with omniscient narration)" (2008c, 1). From the standpoint of a first-person novel and under the limitations of a first-person singular narrator, Richardson describes the broad perspective of we-narrators as transgressive, problematic, and otherwise abnormal: They possess "knowledge that they cannot normally have acquired" (2009, 144). For example, when "we" narrate an individual character's thoughts and feelings, and focalization moves from the collective (i.e., external with respect to an individual) to that of individual characters (i.e., internal), this is "something of course a first person narrator, singular or plural, is not supposed to be able to do" (145). Similarly, Margolin writes:

> Collective observation statements of the "we saw" or "we noticed" variety are once again a hybrid of the "we" sayer's own immediate sense experiences and of the presumed experiences ascribed to the cofocalizers by the speaker on the basis of their public actions and statements. After all, one can no more directly know what and how much someone else sees or hears than one can know what they think or feel. (2001, 246)

That is, one certainly cannot know what others think or feel and so, similarly, one cannot know how they perceive the world. This is because, for Margolin, there has to be a single utterer of the "we." Hence any collective statements and focalizations are compared to what the individual may know and what she can infer or assume about co-members of her group. In my view, this may well be true of nonfictional we-discourses, but is unnecessarily limiting when applied to fiction. For literary we-discourses, this is rather a description of a strategy of naturalization—one reason why we-narrations do not immediately strike readers as odd, as many theorists have observed. To the degree that the folk-psychological practices of ascribing feelings and thoughts to others are something we routinely do in everyday life, such ascriptions do not stand out in fiction. Moreover, we-narrators often overtly thematize these cognitive processes.

The collective scope of focalization, however, cannot be compared to that of individual I-narrators as it transcends any personal experience. I contend that collective focalization and knowledge should be treated under the conditions of we-narrative and not as extensions of a first-person narrative situation. The limitations of the I-narrator do not extend to the plural narrator. What follows from this is the simple observation that a focal point can be located with(in) a group in the case of a we-narrator just as it can in the "I" of a singular narrator-focalizer, but unlike I-narrators, the group will have broader perspectival and epistemological possibilities. This is not, of course, to say that we-focalization is completely unproblematic. On the contrary, the situation of collective focalization is more nuanced than either the extremes of "unnatural" or structurally unproblematic can describe.

As focalizers, we-narrators, of course, express emotions, opinions, and judgments pertinent to the narrated situation—even if only implicitly. These are often expressed in a generalized manner, as in this example from *Then We Came to the End*: "**We had no idea** Joe carried with him the reformer's spirit. **We had mixed feelings** about reformers. **Some of us thought** they were noble, and likely to change nothing. **Others were** outright hostile" (Ferris 2007, 89–90). Expressing the group's impressions about a company meeting, "we" make "our" thoughts and feelings known—either as generally true (all of "us" "had no idea" or "had mixed feelings") or in a particularized manner ("some of us," "others"). Once assigned to the we-group as their originator, these comments do not necessarily become transgressive in the senses that Richardson mentions. The following excerpt from the opening of Jeffrey Eugenides's novel *The Virgin Suicides* (1994) describes the morning on which the last of the Lisbon girls committed suicide and the paramedics, by now well-known in the neighborhood, arrive at the Lisbon family home:

> They got out of the EMS truck, as usual moving much too slowly in our opinion, and the fat one said under his breath, "This ain't TV, folks, this is how fast we go." He was carrying the heavy respirator and cardiac unit past

the bushes that had grown monstrous and over the erupting lawn, tame and immaculate thirteen months earlier when the trouble began. (3)

Similarly to *deadkidsongs,* "we" (a group of boys) are observing a scene, evaluating the state of the lawn—which locates the narrator as physically present at the scene—and the speed of the paramedics, commenting on things either explicitly ("much too slowly in our opinion") or indirectly ("monstrous bushes" and "erupting lawn"). Curiously, the paramedic addresses the observers as "folks," which suggests that at that moment "we" includes not only the group of boys, who usually compose this we-narrator, but also other people from the neighborhood who witness the drama. The comment about the lawn is the first clue toward the characterization of the suburban "we" in this novel: Their obsession with keeping lawns neat reveals the mind-set of a comfortably middle-class community.

The changing perspective of the we-narrator when it comes to the lawn in front of the Lisbon family's house is instructive about norms and values of this community. It functions as a signal of "our" changing attitudes toward them in general: First, when one of their daughters attempts to kill herself, they are the neighbors in need of "our" help; later on, an embarrassment or even a threat to "our" own lawns (i.e., the ways and values of "our" community). At first, "we" try to help the Lisbons keep their yard tidy, but they completely ignore "our" gesture of goodwill. In fall, "we" all rake the leaves "in military ranks, heaping piles in the street. Different families used different methods. . . . We all did our part. Afterward, the scrubbed grass, like thoroughly brushed hair, gave us a pleasure we felt all the way to our bowels" (Eugenides 1994, 91). But the Lisbons ignore this communal ritual, separating themselves from "us": "As weeks passed, their leaves remained. When they blew onto other people's lawns there was grumbling. 'These aren't *my* leaves,' Mr. Amberson said, stuffing them into a can" (92). It is the neglect of the lawn and the house that attracts the reporters whose newspapers did not care to report Cecilia's suicide "because of its sheer prosaicness" (93). When Cecilia is buried during the cemetery workers' strike, which "we" have ignored until now because "we didn't think it affected us" (36), "we" see the strike almost as an assault on American values: "Inside [the cemetery, NB], neglect resulting from the strike was obvious"; "plastic American flags abused by rain"; "The grass hadn't been cut in nearly seven weeks. Mourners stood ankle-deep as the pallbearers carried out the coffin" (38). How "we" see the lawn reveals a great deal about "our" communal values as the collective perspective becomes an expression of this community's ethos (unlike with I-narrators, where it is more readily connected to issues of consciousness).

Richardson describes "collective focalization" or "we-perspective" as a depiction of similar or shared thoughts "as if they were part of a single mind" (2009, 145). The "single mind" of the collective narrator resonates with Alan Palmer's theory of intermental thinking and social minds in fiction, which thus merits a brief digression. In an early article on the topic, Palmer, observing that fiction constructs minds, concludes that "much of the mental functioning that occurs in novels is done by large organizations, small groups, work colleagues, friends, families, couples, and other intermental units" (2005, 427). Relying on theories of distributed cognition and folk psychology, Palmer's approach offers a cognitive-narratological explanation of the possibility of group narrators knowing the thoughts of many characters that compose them—the very possibility that Richardson questions. However, from this observation, Palmer proceeds to the radical claim that such "units" possess minds of their own, "actually and literally" (427) and so, for example, the town of Middlemarch can be treated as a conscious entity, even without it being dramatized as a we-narrator or other group character. Later, introducing the idea of social mind into his theory, Palmer treats as "minds" both social aspects of an individual mind (2011, 211) and groups as such (223; see also Alders 2015, 113).

The conflation of categories that results when *social mind* is transferred into a narratological context makes it somewhat difficult to use this phrase as a description of mental aspects of we-narrators: On the one hand, all human minds are social in some sense, but on the other, these minds acquire particular properties—*in addition* to their general "social mindedness"—when functioning as part of a group in the we-mode (see Tuomela 2013, 18). To be able to distinguish between the two modes, I- and we-mode, I think it is necessary to talk about groups as groups rather than minds. Otherwise, "social mind" in analyses of fiction risks reproducing some of the problems of the narrator category discussed in chapter 3: It runs into trouble as long as its causes and effects are inversed. Just as any fictional narrator is a represented character and not a literal originator of narrative, so fictional minds are products and effects of fictional representation, not the minds of "people . . . who are self-consciously using complex theory of mind to try to interpret the opaque intentions and motives of another" (Palmer 2011, 210). Generally, cognitive theories of fictional social minds have yet to add to analyses of we-narratives.[5] However, as I write these lines, new work is emerging on the

---

5. For example, Richardson's (2015) use of "social mind" for talking about we-narratives seems to be entirely interchangeable with "focalization," which he uses to describe the same phenomena in the 2009 version of the 2015 article; see also Alber's (2015) use of "mind" and "mind interaction" inspired by Palmer's notion. For an extensive debate over the usefulness of

intersection between we-narratives and other collective forms of fiction and phenomenology and philosophy of mind, offering promising inquiries into we-perspectives and shared experiences of human and post-human minds as they find expression in narrative form (see Caracciolo 2018 and forthcoming; Gallotti and Lyne 2019).

Arguably, a more accurate description of how the mental functioning of *we-narrators* is represented *in fiction* comes via a metaphorical understanding of group mind (sometimes also called collective mind, or even collective soul) that circulates in sociology, social psychology, and philosophy of sociality. Since social groups are commonly treated as entities or persons, they are habitually described in terms of intentionality and agency, but as Tuomela observes, "this is partly metaphorical since the intentional framework of agents and persons conceptually and factually includes, for example, their perceptions, sensations and qualitative experiences, and emotions—thus, features that group persons in the full sense do not properly have. For instance, groups do not blush when ashamed" (2013, 16). Similarly, groups may be described as having a thought ("We all thought that . . ."), but it would be a stretch to claim that there is a mind between group members in any literal sense, doing that thinking.

> The upshot is that a group cannot *really* think, want, etc., and is not *really* normatively responsible and capable of making normative agreements, although it is highly useful for people to *view* them as having these capabilities. Thus, we extrinsically attribute wants, beliefs, etc., as well as responsibility to certain kinds of groups. In this sense, the "person-aspect" of groups is functionally and thus predictively useful *collective artifact*. (Tuomela 2013, 16)

In other words, group agents (and, to transfer this to narratology, group characters) exist only functionally, through their individual members acting, thinking, and so on under the collectivity condition and in a we-mode (as discussed in the introduction). But since progroup individual thinking combines to produce group thought (opinion and so on), it is useful to treat the group as if a person itself. Metaphorical personhood is one of group's "collective artifacts," or full-blown group notions, such as group beliefs and social institutions. It is in this sense that I talk about ascriptions of mental states to

---

the category, see the special 2011 issue of *Style* 45, no. 2 and especially contributions by Jahn, Caroll, Kafalenos, Hogan, and Page.

we-narrators, rather than suggesting that group characters construct a literal (fictional) mind.

In a nutshell, expressions of mental states and perspectives originating within the narrating we-group contribute to an expression of the group's ethos (certain constitutive beliefs, values, goals, and norms).[6] Ethos is what then creates an image of this group as a character: gossipy office workers in *Then We Came to the End*, whose chief goal is to keep their jobs; infatuated teenagers turning into a middle-class suburban community in *The Virgin Suicides*, concerned with preserving their comfortable way of life; or adolescent boys obsessed with violence, patriotism, and war in *deadkidsongs*. In the latter novel, to give a concrete example, playing army games during the Cold War becomes increasingly perverse when, in the absence of real enemies, the boys start viewing their pacifist families as traitors or planning military-scale revenge for being grounded. Another, more concentrated example of the group's perspective-as-ethos is the highly militarized world view that structures the group hierarchies in *deadkidsongs*:

> The highest up the tree was Andrew, because we all agreed that he had the best father. Then came Paul, whose father was a teacher. Then Matthew, whose father, as well as whose mother, was dead. Last and lowest of all was Peter, whose father came home late every day except Friday.
>
> We had a command structure, because Gang had to have a command structure. But there was no other and no better reason for it than that. Andrew was Sergeant. Matthew, Sub-Lieutenant. Paul and Peter Corporals. Yet between us there were no innate inferiorities. (Or none at this time apparent.) Each had his skills, each his points of refusal. . . .
>
> We dressed efficiently, in a way that prepared us for every eventuality. Especially, War. (Litt 2001, 10)

The boys love war (note the pious capitalization, "War") and military discipline, constantly training for a battle with the "Commies," among other things. They rank themselves by the role model of the cruelest father (Andrew's father beats his wife and son) because "denial of love" (52) is what makes one strong. Militarism marks the idiom of this we-narrator as well: "[Paul] urged strongly

---

6. I use "ethos" in a general sense of a body of practice of a group. This use ties in with my earlier discussion of how communities and other collectivities come into being and see themselves as one. "Group ethos" thus stands somewhat apart from how Liesbeth Korthals Altes approaches this notion in its specific rhetorical sense in her book *Ethos and Narrative Interpretation: The Negotiation of Values in Fiction* (2014), while looking into ascription of values such as sincerity, reliability, or authority to authors and fictional characters and their function in the process of literary interpretation.

that we take revenge upon his father with the utmost haste. Andrew assured him that plans were already in hand" (77). Such a perspective on the world exerts a very strong influence on each of the boys, even if they, individually, may have different views (as the reader finds out later), and justifies the otherwise arbitrary distinctions on which the abuse of the weaker boys by the stronger ones is based. This ethos is what holds their group together.

We-Narrators as Voyeurs

When the we-narrator's focus moves from itself as a community to an individual story, turning the narrator into an observer, its collective focalization very often establishes compulsive situations of observation or spying, and we-narrators come to function as voyeurs. I do not suggest that *all* witness we-narrators acquire this role. It is when "our" gaze is consistently directed toward the nonconformist individual(s), without "us" being privy to their thoughts, that the voyeuristic focalization can occur. The particular affinity between this effect of external focalization and we-narrators arguably comes from the conflict structure of stories that *communal* we-narrators typically tell: These are often stories about individuals who, for whatever reason, stand apart from "us" or who are complete outsiders in "our" communities. This situation, as I discussed in chapter 1, is partly conditioned by the nature of communities themselves: Outsiders and boundaries make communities visible (see A. Cohen 1985, 13), and so a story about a community would most likely mention them in some way. Communities must also constantly negotiate their boundaries and try to contain under their shared ethos individual views, desires, or actions. Such negotiation involves monitoring for disruption, which may lead to obsessive observation.

External focalization establishes a voyeuristic atmosphere, for example, in Oates's *Broke Heart Blues* (2000), where "we" narrate about an alleged sixteen-year-old killer, John Reddy Heart, who becomes the center of attention, mystifications, and unbounded infatuation for his whole school and town. I shall have more to say about the novel in relation to unreliability in chapter 5, but for now let me quote two examples of its we-narrator's watching. The constitution of the we-narrator in this novel fluctuates from chapter to chapter, but it seems to stay within the group of John's peers. First, the girls investigate his new address, after John comes back to town after a one-year imprisonment (note how the direct speech of the many is presented):

> John Reddy was home! We jostled one another leaning over to peer up
> at his lighted window on the third, top floor of the building. Or what we

believed to be John Reddy's window. "Is that it? Are you sure?" "Of course I am sure! Don't be ridiculous." "Who's being ridiculous? That's an insult." "Shhh! *Look.*" We stared, breathless. We saw that the blind at that window had been pulled down carelessly and hung crooked. . . . Anxiously we studied the blind. . . . (11)

Then the boys watch the girls, who "we" know are infatuated by John:

We watched, a haphazard and unknowing trapezoid of (male, yearning) observers, one of us from a second-floor window of the school, another from the parking lot and the third as he was leaving the building at the rear, as the girls in maroon gym shorts and dazzling-white T-shirts ran, clutching hands. . . . It was John Reddy Heart toward whom those girls were running, we knew. Yet we were resigned, not bitter; philosophical, not raging with testosterone jealousy. (284)

Fluctuation in who composes the "we" (from girls only to boys only to everyone in town) are clearly marked by the chapter divisions, and so *Broke Heart Blues* can offer multiple gendered perspectives on the story as it progresses. This novel, where the observers and the observed are usually connected via a sexual fantasy or a relationship, strongly recalls the voyeuristic obsession that runs through *The Virgin Suicides* in which the Lisbon family and, specifically, five Lisbon girls, catch the eye and hearts of a group of neighborhood boys (and, through them, the whole neighborhood). Incidentally, all of the notable symbols that recur in the two novels already appear in Faulkner's "A Rose For Emily": an outcast who, in the eyes of the community, has committed a misdeed, who lives the life of a recluse and avoids any socializing with the community, and whose house is an eyesore to the neighborhood but, at the same time, an irresistible stronghold of mysteries that "we" strive to reveal and enter under any pretext.

In *The Virgin Suicides,* the we-narrator's gaze is very clearly male, and it stays that way throughout the whole novel (with minor exceptions). This creates a particular atmosphere as five girls are observed, day and night, at school and at home, by the teenage boys. The boys' lustful eyes stare, for example, at (1) the Lisbon family leaving for church, (2) the girls' movements around the house, or (3) the girls at school:

(1) None of us went to church, so **we had a lot of time to watch them,** the two parents leached of color, like photographic negatives, and then **the five glittering daughters** in their homemade dresses, all lace and ruffle, bursting with **their fructifying flesh.** (Eugenides 1994, 8)

(2) Following the Homecoming dance, Mrs. Lisbon closed the downstairs **shades. All we could see** were the girls' incarcerated **shadows, which ran riot in our imaginations.** (141)

(2) **Through the bronchioles of leafless elm branches,** from the Pitzenbergers' attic, we finally made out Lux's face as she sat wrapped in a Hudson's Bay blanket, smoking a cigarette, impossibly close **in the circle of our binoculars.** (145–46)

(3) They passed beneath the great school clock, the black finger of the minute hand pointing down at their soft heads. We always expected the clock to fall, but it never did, and soon the girls had skipped past the danger, **their skirts growing transparent in the light coming from the hall's far end, revealing the wishbones of their legs.** (100)

What these examples demonstrate, in terms of focalization, is that the we-narrator, when functioning as a focalizer, is capable of doing so in complete unanimity, "as a single mind" governed by a single desire. This observation becomes voyeuristic, however, as "we" peep through windows, closed shades, and branches, and use binoculars for stalking—all of this driven by "our" desire for the girls and by the mystery that surrounds them as their overprotective parents never let them out of the house. (The we-narrator in *Broke Heart Blues* similarly spies on the Hearts' family, especially on John's vagabond grandfather: "Several of us sighted him on a warm spring day wandering, like an upright crow, the marshy no-man's-land beyond Tug Hill Part; we saw, through binoculars belonging to Shelby Connor's kid brother, that Mr. Heart was picky about his findings" [Oates 2000, 86].) The we-narrator's ethics perspectivizes the narrated events and other characters: "We" mystify and objectify the girls when they are alive, and when they kill themselves, in what can be seen as a symbolic escape from under "our" gaze, "we" blame them for making "us" participate in their madness (Eugenides 1994, 248) to only leave "us" so selfishly. In a paradoxical state, "we" couldn't approach "our" fetishized Lisbon girls, but it is they who "hadn't heard us calling" (249). After the Lisbon family tragically disintegrates and the girls' parents leave town, "we" stay there with "our" memories and gaze, admitting "our" own disintegration: "We had no Lisbon girls to spy on. Now and then, of course, as we were slowly carted into the melancholic remainder of our lives . . . , we would stop, mostly alone, to gaze up at the whited sepulchre of the former Lisbon house" (244). This passage captures the essence of this communal narrator-voyeur and the atmosphere of the novel as a whole: As long as the common object of obsession and desire was present, "we" existed as a unity, spying and watching. What remains now (at the moment of narration of this story to an unidentified narratee) and what still holds "us" together are the fading memories of the girls and "our" wish to retain them, even if each of "us" is mostly alone and cannot share these memories with the rest of the former group.

Just as it may be said that Lisbon girls rebelled against their situation, in a way, so does Emily rebel against the ethical norms and values of her community in Faulkner's short story. Emily behaves contrarily to what is expected of a decent woman and thus becomes the center of town's gossip and attentive scrutiny: "Presently we began to see him [Homer, NB] and Miss Emily on Sunday afternoons driving in the yellow-wheeled buggy and the matched team of bays for the livery stable" (Faulkner 1995a, 124). Just as in examples (1) through (3) from *The Virgin Suicides* above, "we" describe how "we" see the couple. The situation of narration remains curious: "We" often shift between first-person plural and third-person references when referring to "ourselves," the townspeople. This exact scene is narrated two more times, with different references and focalization points. These changes reveal the manipulative potential of the we-reference in general: Whenever "we" want to distance "ourselves" from indecent acts, "we" refer in the third person to those of "us" who engage in spying. "We" do not readily admit to taking part in spying and gossiping, and so it is, for example, that "the old people" start talking of Homer and Emily, not "us":

> And as soon as **the old people said, "Poor Emily,"** the whispering began. "Do you suppose it's really so?" they said to one another. "Of course it is. What else could . . ." This **behind their hands**; rustling of craned silk and satin **behind jalousies** closed upon the sun of Sunday afternoon as the thin, swift clop-clop-clop of the matched team passed. (125)

Impersonal constructions like "the whispering began" and the third-person reference mask the plural narrator and move the focal point to a general spot located within the community. In its extreme, like in the last subclause of the quotation, the we-narrator masks itself by not mentioning any observing agent at all, as if the rustling of silk behind jalousies happens on its own as the couple passes through town. Nevertheless, after such passages, which seemingly have nothing to do with "us," the we-reference usually soon expands to reincorporate those who have been singled out. In the next section of Faulkner's story, "we" describe the same scene, but this time by directly mentioning "our" participation in the act of onlooking:

> When **she had first begun to be seen** with Homer Barron, we had said, "She will marry him." . . . Later **we said, "Poor Emily" behind the jalousies** as they passed on Sunday afternoon in the glittering buggy, Miss Emily with her head high and Homer Barron with his hat cocked and a cigar in his teeth, reins and whip in a yellow glove. (126)

Here "we" even use the exact same formulation as "the old people above" ("Poor Emily") and repeat the description of the buggy and the matched team of horses—a technique that unifies the narrating voice throughout the story, regardless of whether or not it is directly designated as "we." The explicitly symbolic image of the jalousies is used here too, recalling the boys in *The Virgin Suicides* as they observed the girls through the tree branches from the window of the house opposite.

An interesting interpretation of the exclusively external perspective on Emily and an obsessive situation of observing and watching by the passive we-narrator is offered by Alice Robertson. Such a perspective, she argues, can be read as paralleling the status of the reader, an outsider to Faulkner's Southern community (Robertson 2006, 158), especially since Faulkner explicitly expressed his concerns of finding the right perspective to get his alien—Northern—readership invested into the unfamiliar world of his stories (154). The reader can only see Emily externally, without access to her consciousness and her motives, just like the narrator. The narrator and the reader are both invested in discovering Emily's story, and so the reader unsuspectingly adopts a complicit perspective and experiences the story-world through the eyes of Jefferson's community. Entering into the perspective of the communal we-narrator alone can be enough to evoke the reader's sympathetic response to this narrator—it is the basic cognitive response of "us" (good) versus "them" (bad) that I briefly discussed in chapter 2. As Stanzel comments, internal perspective is an "effective means of controlling the reader's sympathy, because [it] can influence the reader subliminally in favour of a character in the story. The more a reader learns about the innermost motives for the behaviour of a character, the more inclined he tends to feel understanding, forbearance, tolerance, and so on, in respect to the conduct of this character" (1984, 127–28). This tension between trying to understand Emily's motives (similarly to those of John Reddy Heart or the Lisbon girls in other narratives)—and potentially justify her actions—and being privy to the communal perspective (and potentially being inclined to adopt it) creates much of the ethical ambiguity in the short story, as discussed in the introduction.

Collective versus Individual Perspective: The Problem of Diegetic Levels

Having discussed the plural perspective and voyeuristic tendencies of we-narrators that are communities, I must now consider the final issue of the chapter: a reconciliation of the various perspectival shifts, accompanied by the changes in the we-narrator's involvement in the storyworld, with the homo-/heterodiegetic vocabulary for classifying narrators. The gaze of the collective narrator, I have argued, is *not* the gaze "filtered through individual centre(s) of awareness" (Margolin 2001, 252), but a decentered perspective informed by a communal or collective ethos—decentered insofar as it can be located only broadly, within the we-group. At the same time, a collective perspective is rarely presented as homogeneous: One of the striking features of perspectival dynamics in we-narratives is a correlation of the dominating we-perspective with the perspectives of individual characters, members or outsiders of the we-group. We-narrative thus often navigates complex transitions between collective and individual viewpoints. This creates the psychological dynamism of collective narration, but also makes apparent a problematic aspect of the established distinction of diegetic levels.[7]

While the initial distinction that Genette's "more technical" terms of "homo-" and "heterodiegesis" (1988, 98) make is simply between the narrators' presence or absence as a character in the story they tell, it is the subsequent implications of this distinction that sit uneasily with we-narrators. In the primary sense, we-narrators are indeed characters in the story they tell, or homodiegetic (as defined in Genette 1980, 145). But such involvement in the story implies restrictions when it comes to narrating other characters' mental experiences, for example. Access to the latter has been tightly linked to narrators whose realm of existence is nonidentical with that of the characters, or

---

7. To briefly revisit the classical terminology: Besides the category of "person" (the *relationship* of the narrator to the storyworld in Genette 1980), Genette famously suggested describing the narrator in terms of *level* as extra- or intradiegetic (which contains further, metadiegetic levels). This distinction refers respectively to the first-degree narrative and any narrative(s) it may contain. Stanzel's model for narrators (1984, 90) incorporates only the opposition of "person," which, essentially, is the same as Genette's homo-/heterodiegesis. For Stanzel, and Genette, it is the status of homo- or heterodiegesis that is the main structural difference between narrators, and not their qualities (omniscience or limitations, credibility, etc.). Unlike Genette, however, Stanzel's model allows for a scale of personalization of the narrator: Personalized narrator > dramatized scene without an apparent mediating agent (e.g., pure dialogue) > reflector ("reflection of the fictional events through the consciousness of a character in the novel without narratorial comment") (1984, 48). This gradation is useful for my discussion of intermittent we-narrators.

heterodiegetic (144). In Stanzel's vocabulary, this distinction is decisive for the perspectival choices that are available when the focal point is "located *in* the story, in the protagonist or in the centre of action, or else *outside* the story or its centre of action, in a narrator who does not belong to the world of the characters or who is merely a subordinate figure, perhaps a first-person narrator in the role of observer. . . . In this way an internal and an external perspective can be differentiated" (1984, 49). Rimmon-Kenan even posits a general rule: "The knowledge of an internal focalizer . . . is restricted by definition: a being part of the represented world, he cannot know everything about it" (2008, 81). In other words, the narrator who is also a character in the narrated story cannot justify narration of the mental experience of other characters because if both the character-narrator and the characters are on the same level, they must share the same set of limitations. This, however, is not the case for we-narrators, whose supraindividual nature means that they possess a set of characteristics different from any individual character *of the same diegetic level.*

We-narrators are located in the story, either as protagonists or observers, but their perspective frequently changes between internal and external with respect to themselves (to individual members *of* this narrator) *and* to the events and nongroup characters about whom they narrate. A homodiegetic we-narrator, in other words, is quite different from a homodiegetic I-narrator, to the point that one must ask if it should be called that at all. We-narrators often grant what I would describe as narrative freedom to the narrated characters when strong internal focalization via the character is combined with free indirect discourse. (We-narration thus gives way to narration characteristic of authorial or figural narrative situations.) The distinction between the two types of relation of the narrator to the story is thus difficult to keep separate in we-narratives, as Richardson points out: "These narrations are . . . simultaneously first *and* third person discourses, and transcend either subtly or flagrantly the foundational oppositions set forth in different ways by Stanzel and Genette. Whereas most second person narration oscillates between these two poles, 'we' narration curiously occupies both at once" (2006, 60). A good example of the dynamic status of the we-narrator can be found in *Then We Came to the End*. In Ferris's novel, whenever the narrator presents a communal feeling (in a diegetic summary), it is subsequently split up into individual examples. These general phrases, true of "all of us," open the paragraph on "our" hatred of insecurity: "We hated not knowing something. We hated not knowing who was next to walk Spanish down the hall. How would our bills get paid?" (Ferris 2007, 160) This hatred is immediately particularized into that of individual characters: "Marcia hated not knowing what might come of being caught with Tom Mota's chair" (160), "Larry Novotny hated not know-ing if Amber Ludwig could be convinced that it was in both of their best interests for her to have the abortion" (162), and so on. If extended beyond a few sentences, these passages read as an authorial narration in which the we-narrator does not take part, although we-narration always frames such third-person digressions: "Amber was a Catholic who hated not knowing a lot of the mysterious ways in which God worked. <u>Was it possible, for instance, that God could send Tom Mota back into the office with all of God's wrath to rectify the sins Amber had committed</u> there on desks **we hoped** to god were not **ours**?" (162). This passage demonstrates well the technique of transition from Amber's perspective to "ours": The underlined part of the sentence could read as free indirect speech, giving insight into Amber's state of mind, until it transitions into "our" hopes about her actions. (Notice also the change in the capitalization of "God" which signals the perspectival change from Amber-the-Catholic to "us.") Immediately after this sentence, "we" take over both the focalizing and narrating once more: "We, too, hated not knowing the specifics of Tom's intentions to change history" (163). The seamlessness with which dif-ferent perspectives combine in *Then We Came to the End* can be described as an example of "wandering focalization" (Richardson 2009, 156)—focalization through individual group-members whose perspectives are embedded in a general we-perspective, which thus *seemingly* renders we-narrators homo- and heterodiegetic at the same time. But, since both categories cannot be applied to one and the same phenomenon without losing their meaning, I suggest exploring the tension in this classification in order to better capture the status of the "we."

As I have already noted, many established narratological terms bear the legacy of Saussurean linguistics and are therefore modeled as oppositional pairs, in which the meaning of each element becomes apparent (see, e.g., Stan-zel 1984, 79). The opposition of homo-/heterodiegesis, in particular, has served the concrete purpose of teasing out a distinction between first- and third-person narratives. However, adding a third element to this pair, such as we- or second-person narrative, proves problematic, as Richardson's and my own analyses point out in the case of "we" and as Fludernik has pointed out in the case of you-narratives: "Both Stanzel's and Genette's typologies were designed before second-person fiction became a major concern for narratologists. Stan-zel's typological circle moves from the first-person realm to the third person and back to the first person, which makes it difficult to place second-person narrative anywhere on the circle. Genette's model . . . suffers from the either-or dichotomy of homodiegesis vs. heterodiegesis . . . that does not seem to allow for a third term" (2011, 106). While Fludernik's solution to the classification of you-narratives is to combine both models and add nuance through additional categories (see Reitan's analysis and commentary), I propose testing another model altogether when it comes to the description of we-narratives. Encouraged by Genette's own rethinking of the boundaries between homo- and heterodiegesis in *Narrative Discourse Revisited* (1988, 102–5), I shall address the perspectival shifts in we-narratives via a more flexible rhetorical approach, rather than the grammatical one of "person." Such an approach has allowed Phelan (2005, 117) to combine the notions of voice and focalization—another oppositional pair—in order to more precisely describe the workings of internal focalization. The difficulty of classifying we-narrators in terms of diegesis can, arguably, be resolved via a rhetorical and Platonic understanding of diegesis, in which the we-narrator is a represented (mimetic) instance. In other words, I suggest viewing the we-narrator outside the hetero-/homodiegetic divide because, even when the we-narrator seems to be outside the story-world, the characters it speaks about are still part *of itself,* and if it is inside the storyworld, its transpersonal and transgenerational potential renders insignificant the restrictions typically associated with homodiegetic narration. Even when there is a semblance of homodiegetic limitations, as in *Then We Came to the End,* when only the thoughts of group members are known to the narrator, we-narration also allows for virtually any other arrangement, as in *deadkidsongs.* My suggestion, however, is merely a generalization of the we-narrator's structural qualities. Concrete we-narratives can gravitate more clearly to one of the two poles, with most of the we-narratives analyzed in this book leaning toward homodiegesis.

Toby Litt's *deadkidsongs*

To put all of the above into more concrete terms, let me now turn to Litt's multiperson novel *deadkidsongs* (2001) in detail. Technically, *deadkidsongs* is a first-person narrative because of its framing: The reader is informed by an extradiegetic, heterodiegetic narrator called Matthew that the nearly five hundred pages that follow are a manuscript he found in his father's drawer labeled "TOP SECRET" on the day of his father's funeral, and which Matthew now reads: "Hoisting my feet up onto his oh-so-sacred desk, I flipped the first page and it began—." The structure of the "manuscript" that follows consists of four parts—"SUMMER-AUTUMN-WINTER-SPRING"—with four chapters in each part titled the names of the four protagonists (after the death of one of the boys, only three chapters per part remain). Each of the chapters is further subdivided into variously numbered sections. Each of the four parts uses a different narrative situation: we-narration, authorial narration with reflectorized passages, and first-person narration.[8]

Being a combination of narrative situations, irreducible to a single dominant one, *deadkidsongs* is best described as a multiperson narrative. However, the novel's first part is consistently narrated in the first-person plural, which, I argue, influences the rest of the narrative. The chief function of the first part is to establish the collectivity, Gang, and the rest of the novel is about maintaining this childhood unity amidst the disintegration of the group, the power struggles and internal contradictions that destroy their sense of togetherness. Paul's (unsuccessful) attempts to return to the collective we-voice of the first part in chapter 13, the penultimate chapter of the novel, fail to re-create the initial sense of unity. This failure is apparent not least because of the contrast between the two ways of narrating in "we": the performative of the first four chapters and the predominantly indicative mode of the final chapters.

Besides the contrast between these two uses of the "we," the sense of collectivity and its subsequent disintegration are created with the help of focalization. To describe its dynamics, I rely on the following combinations suggested by Phelan (2005, 117): (1) The narrator narrates and focalizes; (2) the narrator narrates but the character focalizes; (3) focalization and voice both belong to the character (e.g., in stream of consciousness, where no narrator discourse can be recognized); (4) the narrator's and character's focalizations and voices blend (as in, e.g., free indirect discourse); and (5) the narrator focalizes while the character speaks. This vocabulary adds nuance to the opposition between external/internal perspective and allows for a certain decoupling of issues of internal focalization from those of the diegetic levels. The initial feeling of togetherness in Gang is achieved through strong collective (and internal) focalization, which becomes progressively problematized as each of the four boys ends up in dangerous situations. Because Gang members are then on their own, the collective perspective gives way to descriptions of their situations from their respective individual standpoints. The following scene opens in a similar manner to the one in which the boys were hanging from the tree on page 114 (discussed at the beginning of this chapter): The perception and orientation are effected by the group (except this time only three boys are present at the scene), but quickly split into an interplay of collective and individual focalizations as soon as one of the boys gets into trouble. Gang is carrying home a branch of firewood, and they decide to take the route through

---

8. The structural complexity is supported by a variety of paratextual elements that I cannot discuss here at length: telling titles of parts and chapters, three ways of numbering chapter sections, three fonts that mark different types of texts included in the "manuscript," page numbering (two last chapters both start on page 375, signaling two versions of the ending), and so on.

Wychwood to avoid Andrew's father, who might be hiding along one of the paths—a game he often plays with Gang:

> Wychwood was fairly safe territory, **or so we believed,** and thus we moved with less than usual caution, down a well-beaten path. The sun was **high in the sky** and our shadows were fairly definite on the nettly ground **beneath us.** Cow-parsley was **all around us,** fragrant and **almost above head-height.** The grasses **on either side of the path** were already golden and straw-like. . . . The air inside Wychwood **seemed heavier** than outside. (Litt 2001, 44)

All of "us" move along the same path and see the same things (sun, shadows, the nettly ground, cow parsley, grass), the description of which is focalized from within the group, orienting the reader with respect to "our" location. Within this straightforward spatial orientation, the comment on the sensory perception of the air that "seemed heavier" does not require an origin in an individual consciousness. Curiously, the group also offers a certain external view of itself as they walk, which only reinforces the absence of an "I"-speaker:

> As we walked, **two of us** carried the branch on our shoulders. We could have been Zulu tribesmen, back from a hunt, an antelope suspended between us, food for the evening's feast. **The other one, in this case Andrew,** strode a little ahead, scouting for mines, tripwires, ambushes and other dangers. (45)

Even though the fourth member of Gang is under house arrest, "we" remain a group because the physical location of the individual "I"-members is insignificant: "In this case" the arrangement is thus, but in another case it might be different. Yet this initial shared perspective changes radically when Andrew is suddenly ambushed by his father and gets separated from the group. The "two of us" become the focalizer and the observer, looking at Andrew's struggle to free himself: "We saw him trip up, falling sideways into a patch of nettles," "we could see him trying to scramble away, to pull himself free" (46). But even though Gang is reduced to two in this situation, "we" remains the reference to all four boys, not identifiable with any one of them: "We dropped the branch and dashed to help. Matthew grabbed one arm, Peter the other" (46). As the two remaining boys are singled out only by the third-person reference, the individual-transcendent nature of the communal reference is retained.

After the initial splintering of the shared perspective, "our" focalization remains external with respect to Andrew, thus strengthening the temporary split between "us" and him. "We" observe him till the very moment his father throws him into the water of the lake, when the perspective switches to Andrew's. At the same time, "we" remain in control of narration (Phelan's combination (2) as introduced above). The juxtaposition of Andrew's internal perspective and "our" first-person narration produces an unsettling effect: Through Andrew's perception, the reader accesses his feelings and the drama of the underwater struggle, while "our" perspective provides an external view of the scene, creating a sense of anxiety for the boys' friend:

> He opened his eyes under water, in half-hopes of seeing the sun, or light, or lightness. But the water around him was all equally, unequivocally black. His eyes stung on the instant, marsh harshness getting in them. (We were with him, as Gang, though we stood on the bank, alongside the man who had thrown him in. We felt his every thrash, as if from the inside. Yet at the same time, we saw his sandalled feet appearing and disappearing, as he cartwheeled around, never breaking out into the air. This image of his panic combined with our sense of his state.) (48–49)

The first three sentences read like an authorial narration strongly reflectorized through Andrew—that is, a typical heterodiegetic narration. But the we-narrator's comment that follows in the parenthesis contradicts such classification: The narrator is present at the scene and continues to externally observe Andrew's struggle while narrating it. The rest of the description of the struggle to survive in the dirty waters of the lake that follows this passage shifts between Andrew's view inside the lake and "our" external viewpoint. Andrew's perception is accompanied by "our" observation of his movements and creates an effect of continuity between Andrew's individual consciousness and "ours." When he manages to throw up his hand in the air, his sensation of the air on his skin is combined with "our" watching the hand as it appears from the lake. In what follows, it is no longer clear whose perception is governing the telling: "We felt how he next attempted to force the rest of his body to conform. The head, that was the most important thing. The mouth. The nostrils. Get the head where the hand was. Yet at the same time, the hand must not loosen its grasp upon the air" (49). The first sentence features "our" narration and perception, but the second can already be read as "us" wishing Andrew would do it or as Andrew, encouraging himself.

What such dynamics of collective and individual focalizations demonstrate is one of the key features of we-narrative: the irreducible coexistence of collective and individual levels (observed first by Margolin 2000, 592). Ultimately, *deadkidsongs* reproduces on the structural level the tensions within the "we"-group, making them the motor of the plot. On the one hand, "we" are a homodiegetic character-narrator; on the other hand, such homodiegesis abounds in habitual paralepses when we-narration is combined with individual experiences, which are arranged as hidden from the we-narrator or contrasted with it. Phelan qualifies similar techniques as "plausible paralepses" (2017, 59) because occasional expansions in knowledge of character narrators can remain plausible for readers if they are executed in certain ways and, for example, if they enhance the reading experience by presenting crucial information. In the case of we-narratives, such plausible transgressions may be rooted in the group nature of the narrator, which broadens its epistemological scope. However, rather than being occasional, shifts in knowledge and focalization scope are inherent to we-narrators and occur in the direction from homodiegesis to heterodiegesis as well as vice versa. Richardson (2009, 145) describes a similar case of "mutually exclusive narrative stances" in Conrad's *The Nigger of the "Narcissus"* (1899): a character-narrator who is able to narrate thoughts and perceptions of others and step out of the storyworld to give an overview or to concede narration in favor of reflectorization through individual characters.

Arguably, the case of we-narratives brings forth a tension inherent to the Genettian typology itself, as Walsh (2007, 2010) has demonstrated. While remaining typologically useful, the categories of person are combined with those of level (extra-/intradiegesis) and together only *appear* to be distinct pairs of categories that do not determine each other. In fact, as Walsh (2010, 39) observes, they are defined with respect to a shared frame of reference, namely, the notion of *diégèse,* or storyworld. The problem with this typology, for we-narrators in particular, lies in the different functioning of the ontological (narrative) levels in each pair. For the pair extra-/intradiegesis, there can be *no* ontological discontinuity between the narrator and narrated events (see Walsh 2010, 39–41); in other words, according to the transmission logic of the communicative model, the narrator has to be on the same level as the narratee and the story she is telling. The chain addresser–message–addressee cannot work when one of its parties is on a different diegetic level. At the same time, for the pair hetero-/homodiegesis, there *has to be* an ontological discontinuity between levels: A heterodiegetic narrator inhabits a different storyworld from the one about which she is narrating. This results in epistemological limitations as the heterodiegetic status gives the narrator unlimited authority over the narrative act, whereas the homodiegetic does not.

In *deadkidsongs* the distinction of extra-/intradiegesis can be schematized as in figure 1. The I-narrator of the framing narrative, Matthew, should be called an extradiegetic narrator who, according to Genette, is a "fictive editor" (or, in the case of this novel, a fictive reader) of the intradiegetic narrative told by the "we" and a number of other intradiegetic narrators (which I omit in

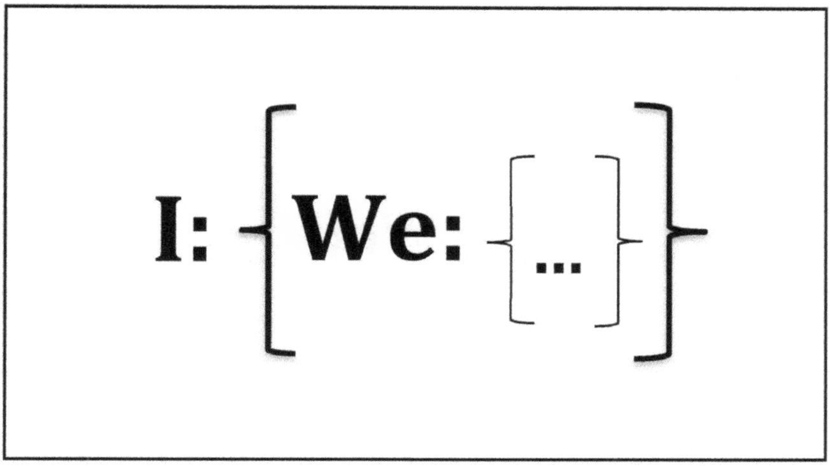

FIGURE 1. Simplified levels of embedding in *deadkidsongs*

the schema for the sake of clarity): "The narrating instance of a first narrative is . . . extradiegetic by definition, as the narrating instance of a second (meta-diegetic) narrative is diegetic by definition, etc." (Genette 1980, 229).[9] Thus, as an extradiegetic narrator, Matthew must be "off-diegesis" (Genette 1988, 85), which is to say, outside the storyworld, yet he is still minimally embedded in *a* storyworld where he has a father who commits suicide and leaves him a manuscript to read, which he does in his father's study. For Genette, extradiegetic narrators must be outside diegesis in accordance with the literal logic of narrative transmission: They have to be "at the same level as their public—that is, as you and me" (1980, 229). However, Matthew is fictive (that is, represented) because, according to the logic of the classification, each narrative instance has a diegetic level that includes it (Walsh 2010, 39). The extradiegetic level thus is and is not a diegetic level.

Genette tries to resolve this paradox by describing the same narrator in terms of two levels. His example from *Mémoires* by Antoine François Prévost goes as follows: The hero of one volume of the *Mémoires,* Des Grieux, has told his story to the Marquis de Renoncourt, who now presents it to the public. The marquis is thus the "author" of the *Mémoires* and an extradiegetic narrator because, "although fictive, he addresses the actual public" (Genette 1980, 229). But "the same Marquis as hero of the same *Mémoires* is diegetic,

---

9. For Genette (1980, 228) intradiegetic equals diegetic and so an intra-intradiegetic narrative (i.e., metadiegetic) can also be described as diegetic.

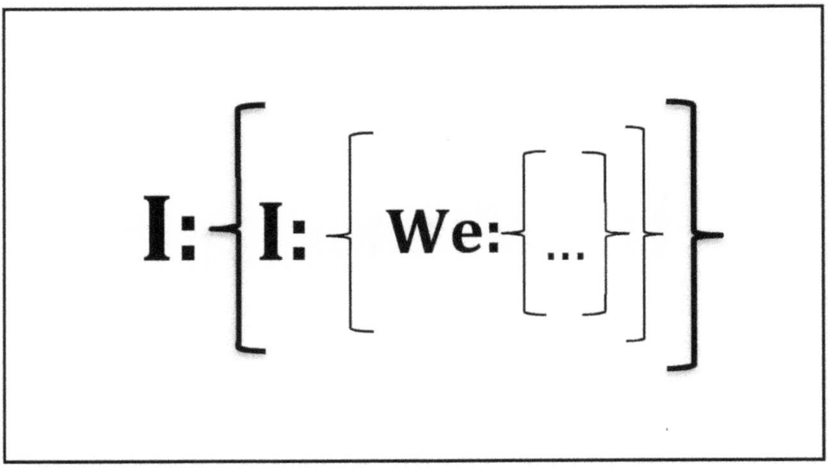

FIGURE 2. Multiplication of the levels of embedding

or intradiegetic" (229). And further: "M. de Renoncourt is not a 'character' in a narrative taken charge of by the Abbé Prévost; he is the *fictive author* of *Mémoires,* whose real author, of course, is Prévost, just as Robinson Crusoe is the fictive author of the novel by Defoe that bears his name; subsequently, each of them (the Marquis and Crusoe) becomes a character in his own narrative" (229). This logic results in a multiplication of levels of embedding that, in the case of *deadkidsongs,* produces the following structure (see figure 2).

Matthew would be treated as the extradiegetic heterodiegetic narrator of *deadkidsongs,* in which he is also an intradiegetic and heterodiegetic instance—a character who sits in his father's study and reads a story by "us," the meta- and homodiegetic narrators. When such logic is applied to any narrative, as Walsh observes, "we face the prospect of an endless series of implicit narrators" (2010, 39). And the question remains: Is the level inhabited by the extradiegetic-heterodiegetic Matthew a *diegetic* level? The problem of the status of extradiegetic narrators is, ultimately, the problem of fictionality itself: This narrator is a theoretical necessity in order to frame the narrative transmission as fictional and, at the same time, to bind it to the real-world level of narrative transmission between the text and the reader. In chapters 1 and 3, I posited the structural superiority of the we-narrator: A we-narrative, as a full-blown narrative situation, maintains the structural dominance of the plural narrative agent; that is, the highest level of narrative embedding is dominated by the we-narrator. The narrator is thus not reducible to a singularity: There is no covert or implicit "I" on the extradiegetic level that "actually" does all the talking, the structuring, and the evaluating. But according to the current model, the (implicit) embedding level has to be that of the (implicit) singular speaker, the "real" utterer of narrative acts (and yet distinct from the non-fictional author). Within the pragmatic rhetorical model of narrative communication, this issue of levels can be resolved by acknowledging the simple recursive ability of one narration to represent another (Walsh 2010, 41), which then serves as a basis to distinguish between diegesis (in Plato's sense, as reworked in Walsh 2007; this corresponds to extra-heterodiegesis in Genette's sense) and mimesis (all other Genettian categories of level). Thus, in *deadkidsongs*, both narrators, Matthew and "we," can be treated as represented, with Matthew being only minimally objectified as a narrator-character. The Genettian extra-heterodiegetic narrator thus turns out to be another name for the author (in the poetic sense, as the narrative function, deep structure, implied author, etc.).

Let me now return to the other pair of distinctions: hetero- and homo-diegesis. In *deadkidsongs*, the we-narrator as focalizer does more than simply represent its own group ethos; it also portrays intimate feelings, and the thoughts of every separate member of the group are easily accessible at any point in the we-narration. This creates a seemingly unlimited (heterodiegetic) report of individual characters' thoughts *as private*—that is, unknown to the narrator, even as the we-narrator continues to exist in the scene when these "private" thoughts are being narrated: "At that moment, Matthew was totally convinced that he was dying" (Litt 2001, 17); "Andrew wouldn't have dared approach his father when he was so explosive-looking. For a moment, but only for a moment, he thought about merely standing aside, and cheering his father on" (23); and so on. In such passages, the perspective of the we-narrator may be said to retreat into the background, while its homodiegetic presence as a character entity is maintained:

> Matthew was having some trouble keeping pace **with the rest of us.** He was feeling very dizzy, and couldn't see quite as well as usual.
> **Whilst we walked,** Paul tried to keep as much distance as he could between himself and his father. There was the terrible possibility that his father might put his arm around him or even kiss him on the cheek. (28)

In this passage, the sentences I have underlined can be read as the contents of Matthew's and Paul's minds, alongside the we-narrator's narration about the scene. In extended passages like these, individual perspectives expand to stretches of figural narration, and classifying the narrator as either homo- or heterodiegetic is not possible—nor is it productive. The narrator exists simultaneously as a somewhat abstract entity (the all-knowing and all-seeing Gang) and as a concrete group of individuals, each of whom has their own concerns and feelings. It is important to note here that, expanding his initial corpus, Genette concedes in *Narrative Discourse Revisited* that he was too hasty to posit "an impassable boundary between the two types, hetero- and homo-diegetic. Franz Stanzel, on the contrary and in a way I often find convincing, insists on allowing for the possibility of a progressive gradation" (1988, 103). Genette then proceeds to consider heterodiegetic narrators "with a touch of homodiegeticity" (103), as in *The Possessed* by Dostoevsky, and "mixed or ambiguous borderline situations" (104) that make the choice between homo- and heterodiegesis impossible altogether, such as the "subsequent historian (the one in *Un Roi sans divertissement*) who tells of events that occurred 'in his district' . . . but well before his birth" (104–5). The we-narrators I have been discussing certainly have an affinity with such subsequent historians, having transpersonal and transgenerational qualities.

One way to describe the situation of narration in the above passage from *deadkidsongs* is as a combination of the we-narrator's voice and focalization ("Paul tried to keep as much distance as possible between himself and his father") with a character's voice and focalization ("There was the terrible possibility that his father might put his arm around him or even kiss him on the cheek"): the combination of various modes of narration and focalization unconstrained by an impassable hierarchy of levels. Whenever passages of internal focalization through individual characters (e.g., through Matthew or Paul) are represented by diegesis—and not by the we-narrator—they are "free" from the narrator's idiom and often give a sense of the voices of the characters as distinct from the narrator's. This creates a double-voicedness of certain passages in the we-narrative part of *deadkidsongs* where one or another of the four boys expresses themselves independently of the narrator's voice and perspective through internally focalized figural narration. Their full voices become clear in the longer stretches of reflectorized narration and in the subsequent parts of the novel narrated in the first-person mode, but the short example above already reveals an interplay of individual and group perspectives.

Consider one last example in which Gang is thinking about the implications of Peter's heroic salvation of Gang's "Archives" from fire. At this moment, Peter is in the hospital and thus is also physically separated from Gang:

> A few late walkers passed us as we stood there, feet planted upon either side of our bicycles. Little could they have guessed **the thoughts that we**

separately had, nor **the single thought that bound us together. Each of us wished that it had been ourself** [sic], rather than Peter, silly Peter, who had heroically been injured. Though each was glad it had been Peter, not anyone else. The setting sun seemed to us the glory of our friend, disappearing awhile out of our collective sight. . . .

Paul silently blamed Andrew for Peter's injuries, whatever they were. Had the afternoon not been such a failure, Peter would never have suggested going home. Had Andrew been a better leader, Peter would have been with us at that moment.

Matthew was consumed with worry for the friend that, among all Gang, he felt most equal to, closest to. They often spent time together when we weren't around, reading and doing experiments. . . .

Andrew wanted to be able to do more than just bring us to this good place. He wanted to turn the incident into a triumph, a triumph for which he could take some credit. . . .

Thus, the morale of Gang lay at a particularly low ebb. Our unity, our Ganghood, for the while, was fractured. It would return, of that, of that more than anything, we were certain. But as the stars came out above our heads, we felt ourselves, for once, as far-distant from one another as they from us. (Litt 2001, 114–15)

This passage brings out the underlying rivalry in Gang and recalls the formally similar expression of in-group tensions in the excerpt from *Then We Came to the End* that opens chapter 2. While "we" stand on top of the hill, to which Andrew has brought "us," looking into the direction of Midford where Peter is hospitalized, each of "us" is consumed with separate thoughts. The perspectival arrangement of this passage thematizes groupness, fatal tensions within it, and its borders: Passers-by (outsiders) cannot not know what "we" are thinking; only "we" know what unites and separates "us." But this time individual opinions are so different and loaded with blame and conflicting desires that "our Ganghood" is threatened—Paul's rivalry and hostility toward Andrew become clear, as does Matthew's secret dislike of their militant group and Andrew's total oblivion to these moods. Still, there is one unifying sentiment left: the way "we" feel about Peter's act and the way "we" all deem him to be of the lowest rank in the group (see the example at the beginning of this chapter from page 10 of the novel), somewhere on the border of the group— better him than "anyone else" to save the sacred "Archives," but the rest of "us" would have brought more glory to Gang with this act. The phrasing that "each of us wished that it had been *ourself*"—not "himself"!—definitively puts Peter outside this group selfhood. And so, even if "we" reaffirm "our" certainty that Gang will prevail in the last paragraph of the quote, this affirmation reads as a forced one, a refusal to fully admit to "ourselves" that the militant ethos of future glory and "our" equality that held "us" together all this time is now disintegrating—perhaps having been false all along.

Frequent focalization shifts in we-narratives between a seemingly homodi-egetic collective narration and individual perspectives of other characters are difficult to reconcile with the homo-/heterodiegetic classification and its implied restrictions of perception and knowledge. However, if focalization is taken as a simple issue of whose perception orients the narration, it can be straightforwardly understood as a construction of a subject position and thus "an implicit premise of the rhetorical focus of the representational act" (Walsh 2010, 52). While readers actively engage in an (ethical) evaluation of what is said (which constitutes an object of representation), focalization is a tacit rhe-torical effect rather than an object of representation itself. In other words, in the examples above, the fictional reality is presented in turns via perspectives of "us," Paul, Matthew, Andrew, and "us" again. These perspectival positions are offered to the reader as access to the many conflicting positions that are necessary to convey the group's disintegration but do not in themselves con-stitute an analytical impasse, contrary to what may be the result of a model based on the hierarchy of narrators and characters according to diegetic levels.

CHAPTER 5

Collective Knowledge

Epistemological Possibilities of We-Narrators, Gossip, and Unreliability

> One thing we knew for certain—despite all our certainties,
> it was very difficult to guess what one individual was thinking
> at any given moment.
>
> —Joshua Ferris, *Then We Came to the End*

HOW THE narrator knows what she knows is a recurrent question in narratological analyses of fiction. Narrators' knowledge claims in first-person narratives (with singular narrators) can send a narratologist on the hunt for explanations as to how the narrator can narrate something she has no way of remembering or knowing because of the limitations of her "human consciousness."[1] This mode of inquiry has been transferred to first-person plural narrators as well. Addressing knowledge construction in we-narratives, this chapter begins with the premise that, in the majority of cases, engagement with a literary narrative does not require the unambiguous ascription of knowledge to fictional agents or a resolution of ascribed knowledge in strict terms of human limitations. Simply put, what narrative communicates often overshadows how this knowledge is distributed among its characters (see also Phelan 2013). Moreover, when it comes to epistemological possibilities of we-narrators, I argue that they have to be viewed through the lens of collective—transpersonal and potentially transgenerational—knowledge because they are group characters.

In what follows, I adopt a stance toward plural narrators' knowledge, based on socio-philosophical understanding of group knowledge. I argue that

---

1. See, for example, Nielsen's (2011) discussion of first-person narration in Apuleius's *The Golden Ass* as "unnatural" because its narrator tells a story his experiencing self could not have memorized.

group" storytelling, as it is constructed in we-narratives, offers insight into a performative act of knowledge creation (comparable to that of the real world, if need be). I suggest approaching we-narration as an especially apt technique for exemplifying the social nature of knowledge, which combines individual and collective aspects of human experience, and for laying bare some of its ideological implications. We-narrators even voice these implications, often in explicit meta-narrative and metafictional commentary. Having briefly discussed the construction of knowledge in general, I then focus on Zakes Mda's novel *Ways of Dying* and the ways in which it combines broad narratorial knowledge with limited, subjective understandings of the state of affairs by the individual characters. Next I look into gossip, epistemological tensions, and unreliability in we-narratives—in particular, in Jeffrey Eugenides's *The Virgin Suicides* and Joyce Carol Oates's *Broke Heart Blues*.

When we-narrators are treated as limited by the conventional scope of human knowledge by virtue of being a variation on a first-person singular narrator (e.g., Marcus 2008c, 1), their collective knowledge is described as transgressive, in the sense that these narrators could not have acquired it under normal human conditions (Richardson 2009, 144–45). For example, the narrator in "A Rose for Emily," being "clearly an individual and a male," is particular in that "he" cannot have gained "access to information which does not come from having watched, eavesdropped and listened to secrets and which simply do not fit in with the implied restrictions of the first-person perspective" (Skei 1999, 155). In line with many other interpretations of this short story, Skei's analysis treats the we-narrator as a singular character that can only narrate what she or he has directly witnessed or heard. Even while recognizing the plural form of narration, Patrick Colm Hogan similarly depicts the issue of collective knowledge as problematic. Hogan distinguishes between three forms of "group narration," similar to Lanser's (1992) tripartite typology of communal voice: (1) an individual speaking for the group in an instantiated voice, (2) a range of group members speaking for parts of the group in a distributed voice, and (3) a collective "we" voice (2013, 235–36; see Lanser's singular, sequential, and simultaneous communal voices, respectively). The distributed voice "allows for diversity of thought and feeling within the group" (Hogan 2013, 235), while the instantiated and collective voices emphasize group connectedness and uniformity. This uniformity renders them problematic, in Hogan's view, since individuals "do not have access to other minds in the relevant way" (249). Hogan then asks to what extent a singular spokesperson for a group can know and truthfully voice the group's thoughts, beliefs, views, and feelings. And to what extent can a collective we-narrator claim uniformity without destroying the group's internal diversity?

These are pertinent questions when it comes to the ideological implications of we-narration and the authority with which "I" speaks for "we." Hogan approaches the collective voice critically, and, indeed, "we" can often be used to manipulate and speak of unity where there is none (see chapter 2). The choice of the pronoun signals both belonging and disavowal: In Mda's novel, for example, one of the characters, Noria, speaks of how her village community treated Toloki. She starts with "they," as she is ashamed to have been part of the bullying herself, but then gathers the courage to admit she was involved as well: "Toloki, I am sorry about the way they treated you back in the village . . . about the way we treated you" (Mda 1995, 157). But while we-narration should be approached with an awareness of its ability to manipulate a group's sense of unity and belonging, Hogan's questioning of the possibility of *any* uniformity of a fictional or real-world group is itself problematic. Collectivities, fictional or otherwise, do not suggest total uniformity simply by presenting homogeneity of opinion or feeling.

Developing the observation that in the real world groups are not as uniform as we-narration implies, Hogan claims that even when a singular narrator speaks about a group as a whole, this raises problems because

> it usually seems implausible that a group would share a particular understanding or emotion—unless the group is very different from groups in the real world. The problem is only worsened when the narration is rigorously focalized. This is because a focalizer, like a limited narrator, cannot have access to the inner life of group members. Thus, even if there is uniformity, he or she could not know. There are, then, two dilemmas for what might be called the *indirect voicing* of groups by narrators, the same two as found in collective and instantiated narration. First, there is the problem of group uniformity. Second, there is the problem of narrator/focalizer knowledge. (2013, 236)

Thus, if a fictional narrative uses a collective voice, it would seem that this voice must from the outset be viewed with suspicion, either as a speaker overstretching her authority or as a manipulation of some other kind. But, while speaking for, about, or *as* a group indeed entails issues of narrative authority and power, Hogan's general suspicion of group uniformity and its expressions is too radical. Uniformity is not limited to fantastical groups—such as, for example, "a set of identically programmed robots" (Hogan 2013, 249)—but rather, *any* group requires a certain convergence between its members in order to come into existence. To repeat A. Cohen's apt description of communities, groups "continuously transform[ ] the reality of difference into the appearance of similarity" (1985, 21)—as long as individuals, despite their differences, share this group's ethos. In other words, without a certain degree of uniformity among their members, there would be no collectivities. In *The Philosophy of Sociality* (2007), Tuomela describes this as the we-mode as compared to the I-mode: Individuals act either in a truly progroup mode or privately, accordingly to their own goals. To act as a member of a group of whatever kind is to abandon the I-mode in favor of the we-mode, which entails a certain depersonalization when an individual accepts the group's commitment, its "affective elements" (the "we"-feeling), and then acts based on these components (3). What we-narratives often do, I argue, is voice the *"we-mode" from the position of the group in the totality of a character.*

Therefore, within narratological frameworks, we-narrators' knowledge should be approached under the collective properties of the group, which transcend the personal ones of individual characters. In this sense, the epistemological possibilities of a plural narrator are more comparable to authorial narrators than to first-person ones because collective knowledge is not limited to any one group member nor to what they could have witnessed, heard, or accessed individually. At this point it may be instructive to turn to the general philosophical conception of knowledge, according to which *all* knowledge is institutional and therefore social and collective. Furthermore, even though knowledge originates in an individual, the individual itself is always already social. In its typical conception, knowledge as a justified true belief (that something is so) originates in an individual (or individuals) but acquires the status of knowledge by being collectively accepted.[2] On this ground, two types of knowledge can be distinguished, (1) "natural" and (2) "social," each of which include:

> (1) group beliefs (viz. beliefs attributed to a group) concerning the external world (e.g. grass is green) and more generally facts that are not at least entirely artificial and thus depend at least partly "upon the way the external world is"; (2) group beliefs and we-mode beliefs about facts which are social and artificial in the sense that they are performatively created and collectively accepted. In the present kind of beliefs it is entirely up to the group members to decide about their truth or, rather, correctness. (Tuomela 2004, 112)

The second type (2) covers what Tuomela calls "constitutive institutional beliefs" (112)—a type of knowledge whose truth is established and whose

---

2. For example, Tuomela (2004, 114); Klauk (2011, 47).

acceptance is justified by the group and only by the group. In a weak sense, this type of knowledge would cover, for example, a group belief that Paul is a traitor (a collective commitment instigated by, e.g., a group leader) or a shared belief of Lvivians that the kerosene lamp originated in their city.[3] The group nature of such kinds of knowledge has several consequences:

- Even if the beliefs or knowledge of individual group members varies, this does not undermine the existence of collective group knowledge (114);
- The authority of group knowledge is higher than that of individual knowledge (115);
- The group's individual members are each capable of voicing a collective position if they share collectively well-established knowledge (114); and
- The "conceptually central ground or conceptual model for institutional beliefs is collective performative speech acts" (115).

Furthermore, knowledge is constructed and distributed unequally in a group: There are operative group members who create knowledge and nonoperative group members who learn it (115–16). According to Tuomela, "a group cannot know unless at least some of its members know the item in question" as "group properties supervene on their members' relevant properties" (112). To reiterate, these properties concern group knowledge in general, but it is instructive to apply them to fictional knowledge claims as well. Such a comparison makes we-narrators seem far less "unnatural" and makes visible their potentially overlooked *group* features.

The use of collective narration might be technically striking in some knowledge claims, but often the we-narrator's knowledge is thematized—naturalized—as learned from individual members through gossip or rumor, as facts of common knowledge—which cancels out the need to specify or justify their source. The communities in "A Rose for Emily," *The Virgin Suicides, Broke Heart Blues,* and *Ways of Dying* possess, create, and express constitutive institutional knowledge through "collective performative speech acts." Their knowledge of protagonists' lives is constructed from information and beliefs that have been established as true within the group and have become common knowledge, even though, technically, not all members are equal in such

---

3. I omit most of Tuomela's argumentation for the sake of brevity, as well as a potentially problematic aspect of his conception of the degree to which the collective creates and influences such knowledge. There is also the issue of competing epistemological theories, which I cannot address here. But what Tuomela's positivistic theory should already make clear is that narratological approaches to the knowledge of the narrator would benefit from considering both its individual and group aspects.

knowledge—some are operative members and some are not, in that the latter learn from the former subgroup what happened without witnessing it themselves. In the case of "A Rose for Emily," for example, Faulkner consistently uses the collective perspective within the story's realist frame: Information about Emily that circulates in the Jefferson community comes from observation, rumor, gossip, and individual accounts of the "we"-group members. Rather than "listening to secrets," as Skei describes it, the community relies on secondhand information from those who visit Emily's house on several occasions, from Emily's servant, and so on. However, when the we-narrator's curiosity is not satisfied, "we" have nothing to tell: A Baptist minister was asked to visit Emily, but "he would never divulge what happened during that interview" (Faulkner 1995a, 126). "We" are thus left to speculate. When the community's role is strongly thematized, then the only epistemological limitation is the community's own reach. In *Ways of Dying*, "we" similarly know everything about everyone in "our" village, but "we" can only guess what goes on in other communities:

> It is rumoured that when Noria was a baby, she already had beautiful laughter. We say it is rumoured because it is one of the few things that we do not know for sure. . . . Since we never had anything to do with the mountain people, we only know about the events there from the stories that people told. (Mda 1995, 31–32)

Zakes Mda's *Ways of Dying*

The narrator in *Ways of Dying* (1995) exemplifies various epistemological features that a group character can have. It is a communal narrator in charge of telling a story about "our" "homeboy" and "homegirl" Toloki and Noria, their life in an unidentified South African village, hardships in the city (potentially Johannesburg), and their unlikely romance: "Both Toloki and Noria left the village at different times, and were bent on losing themselves in the city. They had no desire to find one another, and as a result forgot about the existence of each other. But we never stopped following their disparate and meagre lives" (12–13). The main concern of the novel, however, is the violence during the years of negotiations to end apartheid in South Africa between 1990 and 1994 and the possibilities for the nation's future, which Mda's communal narrator allegorically inscribes into the story of Toloki and Noria. Toloki's village (and the communal narrator that *is* this village) becomes an emblem of the whole nation. Similarly, as Johan van Wyk makes clear in his analysis of the novel, the harbor city in which Toloki lives now merges "various incidents reminiscent of the recent history of different South African cities into one city: The train violence and attacks by migrants on nearby settlements are associated with the Vaal Triangle (Gauteng), the carnival with Cape Town, the tribal chief and his followers with Durban" (1997, 84). Toloki, who earns a living by mourning at funerals, turns into a symbolic figure as well: "He was a Professional Mourner who mourned for the nation, and was paid in return" (Mda 1995, 166). By telling the story of two of "our" own, "we" tell the story of "ourselves," of "our" own struggles, victories, defeats, lives, and deaths.[4] When the novel ends with Toloki and Noria finally getting together and spending New Year's Eve in Noria's newly rebuilt shack—now bigger and brighter than it had been before it was burned down in an act of political revenge—"we" pass by the shack with thoughts of a brighter future. Even though the stench of burnt tires still lingers in the air, it is the smell of celebration and not of a funeral pyre. If some of "us" (Toloki and Noria, in this case) can find peace, so can "we" all.

To tell the story of the nation through that of an individual, Mda relies on constant shifts between collective and individual perspectives: between Toloki and, later on, Noria, the community (Toloki's village), as well as the outsiders (other villages, the city, the rich, the militant groups). The community narrates the story with a firm authority, but also with a certain detachment that can be interpreted as impartiality or naïveté. *Ways of Dying* is narrated in the present tense, which makes the we-narrator an observer. Yet, frequent flashbacks and reminiscing interrupt the progression of the story, and the novel's structure thus approaches the associative chronology typical of other we-narratives discussed here. As a character, the we-narrator performs collective actions, observes, and shares thoughts, opinions, and other mental states. Consider this example of collective action, as Toloki's father locks himself in his smithy, determined to die: "We went to take a look at him, and found him sitting wide-eyed, starring at his figurines. We brought him food and fruit, but these remained untouched" (110). With such descriptions, "we" are firmly inscribed into the same storyworld as Toloki, but, at the same time, "we" have no limitations in knowledge when it comes to narrating Toloki's life, thoughts, and actions. Toloki, however, is often granted a certain narratorial independence as the narration shifts into reflector mode: In the opening scene at the funeral, for example, "we" describe how the funeral proceeds and, at the same time, Toloki describes it and "us" in free indirect speech as he is the main focalizer

---

4. See this very motif in Lee's *On Such a Full Sea* (2014), where the we-community of a colony narrates "our" life through the life of one of "us"; analyzed in N. Bekhta (2015).

in the passage. He moves through the crowd to the podium and "people willingly move away from him" (8) because of his smell. "We" are referred to in the third person as "people" until he makes it to the podium, where "people" turn into "us":

> Toloki is now very close to the makeshift podium where the Nurse defiantly stands, but he still cannot hear a word he is trying to say. Some of us are heckling the Nurse. Some are heckling the hecklers. So, we do not hear one another. Toloki never thought he would live to see the day when a Nurse would be heckled. This is a sacrilege that has never been heard of before. And at the funeral of an innocent little boy, on a Christmas Day too. (8)

This passage mixes two perspectives and two voices, Toloki's and "ours." In addition, the opening sentence and the comment on how Toloki never thought he would see such a scene may be taken as a typical report by an authorial narrator, or an instance of diegesis. Toloki's perspective and an indirect expression of his voice govern the last two sentences. Toloki's role as a reflector character allows Mda to combine a description of the scene from "our" point of view and Toloki's critical view of "our" behavior—a combination that simultaneously characterizes "us," Toloki, and the relationship between the crowd and the outsider.

If described with the help of the diegesis/mimesis model sketched out in chapter 3, this narrative situation can be schematized as in figure 3. The framing box schematizes the act of diegesis (in Walsh's sense, as derived from Plato), which represents both the we-narrator (We) and Toloki (T) and covers third-person descriptions that do not necessarily read as if they originate with the we-narrator. It is especially evident that such descriptions and explanations come from the author-as-narrator when Mda needs to explain a South African custom or the nuances of the country's domestic politics to his readers (e.g., 157, 176)—something that the characters or the we-narrator either do not need to do because it is so well-known, or cannot talk of without sounding implausible. Furthermore, "We," the represented character narrator, tell the story of Toloki (Tw) in "our" own voice (mimesis as designated by the light-gray box). Taken as an idiom, this communal voice describes "us" as characters: scarcely emotional as observers, but also as patient and understanding as if "we" were Toloki's family. This schematic arrangement also describes how Toloki (Tw) figures in "our" account and focalization and, at the same time, acquires a certain narratorial agency of his own as a reflector character (T). Passages of Toloki's (T) perception, the contents of his mind that "we" do not control or narrate, are therefore schematized as part of diegesis, not dependent on the we-narrator.

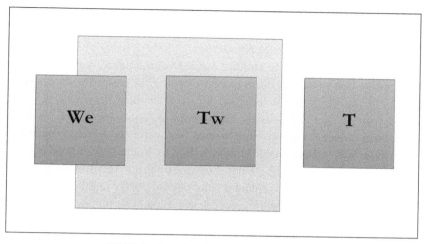

FIGURE 3. Narrative situation in *Ways of Dying*

This approach to descriptions of narrative structures, as discussed in chapter 3, is more productive for we-narratives than the classical communication model because of the changing hierarchies of perspectives and voices that we-narration make possible. *Ways of Dying*, for example, progresses by means of Toloki or Noria sharing stories of the past with one another. The novel combines snippets of direct speech and the report by the we-narrator of most of what Toloki and Noria reminisce about. This "report" often takes the shape of free indirect discourse, thus combining the characters' and the we-narrator's voices and focalization. In the episodes focalized through Toloki, "we" very easily retreat into the background, and reflectorized authorial (i.e., third-person) narration takes over. This move, however, does not undermine the narratorial authority of the communal voice. One of the techniques that reestablishes the we-narrator's authority after passages of third-person narration is direct addresses to the narratee. For example, "we" reappear after a passage of Toloki's musing on the events of the funeral day: "He thinks of the events of today. Of course he is piqued. What self-respecting Professional Mourner wouldn't be? Why did they treat him so at this boy's funeral? He is well-known and well-liked all over the city cemeteries. Only yesterday he surpassed himself at the funeral of a man who died a mysterious death" (16). After a page full of similar thoughts, the we-narrator reappears and takes over the narration in a summarizing and reporting manner: "Yesterday saw the highlight of a career that has spanned quite a few years. **As we have told you,** the man in question died a mysterious death" (17). And thus, even though this piece of information appeared earlier in Toloki's internal monologue, "we" reclaim overarching narrative authority: "We," the community, are in charge of this story; everything he recounts has already been or will be told by "us." Even Toloki's thoughts are not private.

Ultimately, the narrative authority of the communal we-voice lies in the assumption that what "we" deem to be the truth *is* the truth. The deictic complexity of the we-pronoun contributes to the seamless construction of the broad span of "our" knowledge. Throughout *Ways of Dying*, "we" undergo changes in referential scope: The pronoun "we" variously refers to the village as a whole, only to the village children, only to women, or only to a group present at this or that scene. Such fluctuations bring about changes in the narrator's knowledge, since different subgroups are privy to different kinds of information. But the narration proceeds smoothly, with the we-voice's idiom unchanged, even though the "we" who is recounting the given event differs. This generates a unified we-voice that creates a collective narrator who is, nevertheless, capable of knowing (and telling) what happens in various subgroups of the community—without dispersing the sense of unity.

Gossip

> No one in our town has such a thing as privacy. There's always an eye watching, an ear cocked. Each and every one of us generates a whole archive of talk.
>
> —Carsten Jensen, *We, the Drowned*

To return to the question of how narrators know what they know: The narrating community in *Ways of Dying* knows a lot by virtue of being a community, and the novel explicitly thematizes the construction and distribution of collective knowledge:

> It is not different, really, here in the city. Just like back in the village, we live our lives together as one. We know everything about everybody. We even know things that happen when we are not there; things that happen behind people's closed doors deep in the middle of the night. We are the all-seeing eye of the village gossip. When in our orature the storyteller begins the story, "They say it once happened . . . ," we are the "they." No individual owns any story. The community is the owner of the story, and it can tell it the way it deems it fit. We would not be needing to justify the communal voice that tells this story if you had not wondered how we became so omniscient in the affairs of Toloki and Noria. (Mda 1995, 12)

The knowledge of the village transcends that of its individual inhabitants. Commenting on precisely this passage from the novel, Richardson writes: "In an attempt to ground the impossible knowledge of the contents of other minds in a first person form, the speaker playfully locates the source of such knowledge in a more unreliable (yet widely believed) source, village gossip" (2009, 149). However, I would suggest a different reading: Neither the novel on the whole nor this passage in particular features "impossible knowledge." The collective voice in *Ways of Dying* does not imply a singular speaker and thus cannot be deemed unreliable on the grounds that it would be impossible for this speaker to make explicit the contents of other minds. Treating the we-narrator's knowledge claims as part of collective knowledge requires no further justification—and the quote above invites an end to exactly such justifications and to questions as to how "we" can know. Thus, in the spirit of community as the owner of the story, "we," for example, are able to narrate what Toloki himself cannot: "We know all these things, but Toloki does not remember them" (30). His memory can only take him so far, but the collective memory is infinitely vaster than his.

Moreover, the comment above on the nature of storytelling and the circulation of knowledge can be read metafictionally as addressed to those specialized readers who, like narratologists, would rather focus on the enunciative and epistemological plausibilities than on the aesthetic and performative side of the voice of a collectivity. The invocation of gossip is a reminder of just how "possible" or everyday communal knowledge is. Gossip is also commonly employed as a naturalization strategy for a we-voice, as in "A Rose for Emily," *Then We Came to the End, Ways of Dying,* and many other we-narratives. This is especially the case for those narratives where the narrator is a community, as the epigraph to this section succinctly conveys. Gossip's narrative quality is to "interpret fragmentary knowledge about people and events and project it in the form of tellable stories," as Esther Fritsch (2008, 207) observes. And further: "The themes of gossip are mostly transgressions of social norms, making gossip a site where these norms are maintained and negotiated and participation in it becomes a sign of social membership" (207). These characteristics make gossip an appealing technique for we-narration: It is an operation that brings disparate and partial pieces of knowledge into a story. Being a site of socialization, it also creates communities, often at the cost of ostracization. As is the case with many protagonists of the we-narratives discussed in this book, Toloki and Noria defy certain traditions and norms of "our" community. An example of such defiance is Noria's running away to live in a town with a man from another village. Limited to the knowledge of "our" community, the we-narrator recounts what happened during Noria's fifteen-month pregnancy and her marriage to Napu based on what "we" hear and learn from other people.

Passages like this are studded with disclaimers about "our" sources so that the information gains credibility: "**We later learnt** that Noria ran away because she was heavy with child" (Mda 1995, 76); "**Noria later told us** of the things that happened to her in that mountain village" (77). Gossip implies acquiring information that is private or secret and spreading it, but it does not necessarily indicate that this information is false. In this, gossip differs from the less trustworthy rumor, whose source of knowledge is often impossible to identify. In fact, the group narrator of *Ways of Dying* is often very precise about the sources of its knowledge and so, arguably, its narration does not create the impression of unreliability.

Other communal we-narratives almost inevitably mention gossiping to indicate sources of their knowledge. This happens in "A Rose for Emily," *Broke Heart Blues,* and *The Virgin Suicides,* but perhaps the most elaborate example comes from *Then We Came to the End,* where most of narration progresses by gossip about the private lives of "our" colleagues and, by extension, of "ourselves." One of "our" coworkers, Janine, has returned to work after her daughter tragically disappeared and was found dead. "We," fueled by the curiosity and desire for visceral participation in this tragedy, focus on Janine's behavior to try and imagine what it must feel like to grieve:

> We put up bunting and had cake for Janine's return. Next day Joe Pope found her crying in front of the mirror in the men's room. She had gotten confused and gone through the wrong door. It was rare to get news by way of Joe Pope, since he didn't talk to many people, so we probably shouldn't have known that he found Janine in the men's room. But he did talk to Genevieve Latko-Devine, and Genevieve talked to Marcia Dwyer, and Marcia talked to Benny Shassburger, and Shassburger talked to Jim and Amber, who talked to Larry and Dan Wisdom and Karen Woo, and Karen never met anybody she didn't talk to. Sooner or later everyone found out everything. . . .
>
> We talked about Janine wandering into the men's room. No one thought it should be kept a secret, but we were careful not to ridicule the event or turn it into a joke. A few of us did, but not many. It was obviously a tragic thing. We knew about it, but how could we possibly know the first thing about it? Some of us discussed the matter to break up the routine, but most of us used the information to explain why she was quiet at lunch. (Ferris 2007, 26–27)

This passage is a good example of how knowledge about something private— crying in a men's room—becomes a well-known fact: Even if Joe is outside the group, "we" learn about what he saw through a chain of other people, and "we" then interpret this incident to explain Janine's behavior. It is tempting to imagine her unimaginable suffering because, even if "we" *see* how Janine is, "we" cannot know what it *feels* like to lose a child so tragically. This desire to know without really experiencing it "ourselves" is what makes "us" gossip. But, in this case, the information as presented above does not immediately suggest an evaluative judgment, even if "we" admit that those insensitive among "us" may turn it into a joke. Gossip functions as a source of information (see also Paine 1967) that may be presented negatively or positively, but it also may be neutral as far as the message itself goes. It is, of course, a morally questionable source of knowledge, since often one is *not supposed* to know the information it reveals. In this sense, gossipy narrators may be treated as ethically unreliable, but reliable (in the sense of trustworthy) when it comes to the narrated information. In my view, it is useful to distinguish here between the reliability of what is narrated—what "we" know about Janine and how "we" interpret it—and the broader question of the ethics of gossip.

Another feature of interest when it comes to gossip and we-narratives is the social function of gossip: It is relevant only for a specific group (one has to know the people with and about whom one gossips), and it circulates in a selective manner within a specific social network (see Bergmann 1993, 70). Gossiping thus works as a group-binding operation, as one more element of the symbolic construction of in-groups, boundaries, and outsiders, and of reinforcing the group's moral norms and codes of behavior. It occurs within a trusted circle (of, say, friends or neighbors or office workers), but, in principle, any member of that circle can become an object of gossip at any point. Bergmann describes gossip as "the social form of discreet indiscretion" (149) and as a paradoxical form of communication:

> Gossip is publicly despised and at the same time practiced in private with great delight. . . . It is precise and detailed and remains, however, vague and allusive. Authentic presentations are suddenly transformed into exaggerations. Indecency is mixed with decent restraint. Indignation about transgressions is paired with amusement. Disgust with compassion, disapproval with understanding. . . . Gossip is like a moral balancing act, a boundary crossing that is undone with the next step. (149)

This quote brings to mind the Jefferson community in "A Rose for Emily," where at one time it is the old people who are spying and gossiping about Emily because the we-narrator wants to distance itself from this indecent act, but at another time, it is clear that the old people are also "us." At one time, the office "we" in *Then We Came to the End* can say "He knew it because he was one of us, and we knew everything," only to be followed by "We didn't know who was stealing things from other people's workstations" (Ferris 2007, 4). The details and vagueness, certainty and doubt that characterize gossip describe much of we-narration in communal stories.

Epistemological "Transgressions" in We-Narration

All of the above already makes it clear that shifts between we-narrators and characters, as well as broad knowledge claims, are not in themselves structurally or epistemologically transgressive. But it is also the case with any narrative situation that much of the *habitual* compositional complexity tends to be problematized in narratological analyses driven by a narrowly textual focus (rather than rhetorical or readerly). Phelan, for example, observes that so-called improbable plot moves or structural choices occur very often, but go unnoticed by readers—"until some close-reading, probability-obsessed narrative theorist points it out" (2017, 47). In other words, despite the difficulty various shifts discussed so far may pose to narratological models, they often do not have a defamiliarizing effect on the reader. One way to avoid this discrepancy between a theoretical model and a rhetorical effect is to consider, as Phelan does, "*the mutual influence of authorial and readerly agency on the shape of narrative texts*" (34). For example, once the text creates certain expectations in the reader as to its plot progression and dominant thematic focus, the author can move in and out of the textual system of probabilities (e.g., by making a homodiegetic narrator tell more than they should know) without those moves coming across as implausible. The readers "will continue to interpret new information in light of that dominant focus until the textual phenomena provide sufficient recalcitrance to frustrate those efforts" (49). Such recalcitrance is avoided due to various narrative techniques, conventions, and (meta-)rules that govern reading, as well as due to the "dominant system of probability" of a given narrative (for elaboration on these, see Phelan 2017, chapter 2). In theoretical terms, *we-narratives should thus be considered from the perspective of the system of conventions and probabilities—*which they themselves partly establish—*for representing what it is like to live collectively.*

When it comes to collective knowledge, we-narration does not, for the most part, come across as implausible, despite what the attention to its enunciative "unnaturalness" might lead one to conclude. Plausibility governs even such seemingly paradoxical situations in *Ways of Dying*, when, in passages reflectorized through individual characters, "we" suddenly do not know what actually happened with this character, although so far "we," the all-knowing transgenerational narrator, have been framing, controlling, and commenting on similar digressions. The following example comes from a description of Noria's menial jobs, which are not enough to sustain her son and herself. She is forced to become a sex worker, and when "we" notice the change in her financial situation, "we" gossip. Consider how the first paragraph straightforwardly tells about Noria's hotel work, and how the next one already presents "our" speculations about what she might be doing there:

> At the hotel, Noria learnt that art of entertaining white men who came from across the sea. In return, they bought her drinks and paid her a lot of money. Unlike her friend who introduced her to the trade, she did not find it necessary to continue working at the Bible Society. She had no need to preserve a respectable front. . . .
>
> She bought her son new clothes, and school uniform. She enrolled him at a private school. . . . Our tongues began to wag about this whole suspicious affair. . . . Where did she get all the money to spoil the brat, and to buy herself such wonderful clothes that looked like those worn by women in magazines? What kind of work was she doing? We saw her come back from town in the mornings, and leave in the late afternoons. . . . Xesibe added to the mystery when he assured us in the drinking places that none of Noria's new-found wealth came from him. (Mda 1995, 89)

In this case, "our" gossip is malicious, that of a jealous village where one of "us" is suddenly better off than the rest. It is also caused by a lack of knowledge: Even questioning Xesibe, Noria's father, does not help. How can one account seamlessly combine a detailed description of Noria's work and "our" not knowing what she was doing? The smooth transition between these episodes is possible due to a clear distinction between the present time of narrating and the time when the events took place. The passage about Noria can be described either as narrated diegetically (in Walsh's sense), with the we-narrator sidelined, or as the we-narrator's choice (that is, Mda's design) to tell it from the perspective of "our" earlier, unknowledgeable selves. The passage is then followed by the narrating "we" (located in the present), who describes the same events from the perspective of "our" (past) experiencing selves so that they read like a reminiscence and therefore as a plausible account of how—at that moment—"we" did not know what Noria was doing, even though "we" are a vastly knowledgeable community. Either way, this choice does not stand out structurally because of the temporal markers and the smoothness of transitions into and out of the digression, which do not call attention to themselves (the "Rule of Self-Assurance," Phelan 2017, 48). Instead, passages like this add considerably to the reader's mimetic engagement with the narrative since the progression of the story gains from disclosing two pieces of information at the same time: what Noria did and what "we" knew about it at the time (Phelan's "Meta-Rule of Value Added").

Consider the following example from *deadkidsongs*: "We" are sitting in Andrew's bedroom admiring his collection of model planes. In the parenthesis, the information is introduced that Matthew "still slept with the bear upon his pillow, though this was a fact he kept secret from the rest of us" (Litt 2001, 38). This could potentially have a defamiliarizing effect because the we-narrator is telling the reader something "we" cannot know: that Matthew is embarrassed because instead of war-related toys, he has a teddy bear. But even though Matthew's bear is a secret, telling the reader about it does not come across as something out of the ordinary for the we-narrator. The passage is an extremely brief aside, it is arranged in brackets, and it fits thematically into the paragraph in which "we" describe "our" toys. Likewise, another example from *deadkidsongs* (from pages 77–78), which I (a close-reading narratologist) discussed at length in chapter 3, is theoretically curious, but, arguably, not at all defamiliarizing when it comes to its effects.

Obviously, authors choose in what way and to what ends to use a collective narrator-character. In the multiperson novel *Many Pretty Toys* (1999), for example, Hazard Adams problematizes in a laborious manner the very group uniformity questioned by Hogan (2013, 236). Adams lists what feels like all of the opinions and views of his collective narrator (a group of students and faculty members) on the topics they address. "We" mostly agree on the "facts" that "we" report. These items would classify as "natural knowledge" (Tuomela 2004, 112), which depends, at least partly, on the external world and not on "our" beliefs and opinions about it. It is thanks to this agreement of the "majority" that the story seems able to progress at all, because "our" opinions, unlike the facts, are usually too multiple to be shared. When the opinions are presented, the reader goes through pages and pages of lists, as in the following example—a metaleptic comment on the author's views on "us":

> We quarrel at once. Various groups among us claim that the author does not want trouble, does want trouble, does not care one way or the other, wishes to trouble us, does not wish to trouble us, is punishing us, testing us, playing with us or saving us, or is not really involved one way or the other in the matter. Some claim it is not a matter at all. And some claim there never is any matter. (Adams 1999, 15)

Adams continues in this manner for most of the page. Yet sometimes even such meticulous listing cannot quite cover it: "We argue these points vociferously when we attempt to report such events. . . . It is, therefore, not possible for us to report the debate, since no text that we have been able to prepare reflects the tone of events for the majority of us" (35). "It is virtually impossible for us to issue a statement regarding taste, since we represent so many shades of it ourselves" (64). These are examples of how a complete unanimity in a group is impossible, and the narrative thus foregrounds its thematic rather than mimetic component. However, such extreme diversity in the we-narrator's voice is a rare exception in we-narratives.

Other instances of we-narration may opt for another extreme: the complete unanimity of a Greek chorus. This is the case in the chapters written in the we-voice from Peace's *Occupied City* (2010) and Atwood's *The Penelopiad* (2005). In both novels, the victims lament their destiny: They are united in the circumstances of their death, which becomes a strong source of their unanimous voice. Others, like Sontag's short story "Baby," use the transpersonal potential of collective narration to overcome the dual voice and the affective binary structures of the married couple. Generally, however, the group narration of a we-narrative might be located somewhere between monotonously documented dispersion and the strict uniformity of a chorus: "We" in novels such as *Ways of Dying*, *deadkidsongs*, or *The Virgin Suicides* mediates between a collective first-person voice and "our" individual members, creating the alluring possibility of a harmony somewhere between full, totalitarian unanimity and crippling, irreducible individual tensions. Moreover, when read under the collectivity condition as groups and not as individuals, we-narrators demonstrate the creation of transindividual and transgenerational knowledge.

We-Narrators and Unreliability in a Nutshell: Matters of Knowledge, Ethics, and Ideology

I conclude this chapter with unreliability, a major issue in any general discussion of narratorial knowledge. We-narrators often—perhaps more often than other types of narrators—admit their uncertainty, their failing memory, or their inability to recall certain information. But such statements are not automatic markers of unreliability. Much as information originating in gossip is not necessarily incorrect, neither are narrators who admit to doubt necessarily unreliable. Needless to say, the narrative form itself cannot be treated as subjective and unreliable by default, contrary to, for instance, Dieter Meindl's suggestion: "Whatever the configurations of . . . first-person-plural narrative,

there can be no doubt as to [its] potential untrustworthiness" because "we" is "closely related to an 'I,' an enunciating subject, which makes all these texts potentially subjective and unreliable" (2004, 75). Without making such default claims, I focus here on what unreliable narration by a group might mean, but the ambiguity of the very category of unreliability can make this a tricky discussion. In order to keep the focus on we-narrators, I strategically limit my considerations only to one aspect of unreliability.

At the moment there seem to be two competing—and sometimes overlapping—approaches to narratorial unreliability: an axiological approach, proponents of which define unreliability primarily on the basis of moral and ethical aspects of narrative, and the one that defines it through epistemological concerns, such as inadequate narrators' or readers' knowledge about the facts of the fictional world. While it is impossible to completely separate issues of ethics from issues of trustworthiness, my discussion in what follows of we-narrators in *The Virgin Suicides* and *Broke Heart Blues* is guided primarily by the epistemological understanding of unreliable narration: It is a matter of fictional truth, of readerly distrust toward the narrator's account as an interpretive response authorized by the narrative text.[5] (In *deadkidsongs*, for example, the unreliability of its "manuscript" comes from contradictions and increasingly implausible details in the narrators' accounts, with readerly suspicion being corroborated by an alternative ending.) There are several problematic implications of (axiological) unreliability as an ethical discrepancy between the reader and the narrator, although, ultimately, my choice is motivated by the consequences of a group narrating a story. While in first-person narratives, trustworthiness can sometimes be linked to the subjectivity of the narrating character, in we-narratives the narrator is a group, and so their unreliability, arguably, derives less from the "person" of the narrator than from those textual clues that point to a discrepancy between the narrated and the "actual" state of things in the storyworld. In other words, we-narrators often have a complex character image as a group whose individual members can express their own contradictory views, but who, as a group, are at the same time capable of producing strong, universalizing opinions and common knowledge. In the situation of plural narration, truthful accounts may be combined with conflicting ethical positions.

---

5. In its common, dictionary sense, "unreliability" means "that which cannot be trusted." Trusting the narrated is, of course, a complex issue and depends on our attitude toward the one who narrates: their psychological profile, temperament, reputation, or moral disposition. However, I would argue that these issues come in second, after the initial realization, implicitly or explicitly prompted by the narrative, that the narrator is not telling the full story.

Unreliability is much debated[6] because it is heavily based on interpretations involving values, morals, and judgments and thus stands apart from other, more formal and therefore more straightforward categories for describing narrators, such as homo-/heterodiegesis. There is one striking peculiarity about most current publications on this category: Whatever refinements of the concept are proposed, Wayne Booth's definition seems to have prevailed as the standard one since 1961 (see Kindt 2008, 34). This is surprising, given the changes in the theoretical climate, the provisional nature of Booth's definition ("for the lack of better terms"), and its specifically rhetorical orientation.[7] Booth introduced the term to establish the mechanisms by which the reader arrives at an *ethically different* interpretation of the narrator or her story from the one that has been explicitly endorsed by the text.[8] In recent approaches, this ethical dimension has given way to an increasingly dominant epistemological focus,[9] which raises the question of whether it would be practically useful to distinguish between the two phenomena, finding a "better term" for those issues of narrative ethics that can be delinked from issues of truth and trustworthiness currently considered under the heading of unreliability.

---

6. Definitions of unreliability, its areas of application, it effects, and its functions have been debated for quite some time. This really began in the 1960s with Wayne Booth's introduction of the notion, though I shall refrain from reciting its whole history and peculiarities of use here. For an in-depth investigation of the term, see Kindt (2008), especially 28–67. For a shorter, article-length overview, see A. Nünning (2005); Hansen (2007); and Shen (2011). See Köppe and Kindt (2011) and A. Nünning (1999, 56) for a discussion of issues of epistemology and axiology. For a detailed historical survey of the concept's critical development and the existing approaches, see V. Nünning (2013). The most recent collected volume on unreliability, *Unreliable Narration and Trustworthiness* (2015), edited by V. Nünning, approaches the problem from an interdisciplinary perspective and in a variety of genres.

7. To quote the well-known formulation: "For the lack of better terms, I have called a narrator reliable when he speaks for or acts in accordance with the norms of the work (which is to say, the implied author's norms), unreliable when he does not" (Booth 1961, 158–59).

8. In other words, in a Boothian rhetorical approach, unreliability stems from the discrepancy between the evaluative attitudes of narrative agents and those expressed by the totality of the work (which are grounded in the implied author). Another major approach to unreliability, the cognitivist-constructivist one, recently seems to have merged with the former; see A. Nünning (2008). See also Shen (2011) on how the two approaches have never been completely isolated from one another, with the rhetorical approach having exerted greater influence (3.1.3). The defining difference between the two approaches lies in the way they locate unreliability— "as a textual property encoded by the implied author for the implied reader to decode" (the rhetorical stance) or as an interpretive strategy that the reader engages in (the cognitivist/constructivist stance) (3).

9. See Köppe and Kindt: "In the practice of literary studies today, however, a fictional narrator is regarded as unreliable if he distorts the fictional facts. Thus, it is not the 'norms of the work' (however they might be understood) that serve as the standard in determining whether the narrator is regarded as reliable or unreliable, but rather an unobjectionable (accurate, adequate, exhaustive, credible, etc.) description of fictional states of affairs" (2011, 81).

In *The Cambridge Companion to Narrative* (2007), unreliable narration, as introduced by Phelan, is defined in the glossary as a "mode of narration in which the teller of a story cannot be taken at his or her word, compelling the audience to 'read between the lines'—in other words, to scan the text for clues about **how the storyworld really is,** as opposed to **how the narrator says it is**" (Phelan 2007, 282). The reader, having noted unreliability, begins to look for a second version of the story. Tilmann Köppe and Tom Kindt, distinguishing between mimetic—or what I would call epistemological—and axiological unreliability, define "mimetic unreliability" as the effect of a literary work authorizing an interpretation "that the narrator does not provide completely accurate information" (2011, 90).[10] In what follows I examine unreliable we-narrators under the epistemological approach: I take unreliability to mean an inconsistency in the story (world) and interpretive operations for resolving it; a process of arriving at fictional truth by reading against the grain of the narrator's account. This process is triggered by the narrative, which must authorize the reader to interpret the narrator's story as (partly) unreliable.[11]

An axiological understanding of unreliability as the narrator's failure as an "ethical evaluator" (see Phelan 2007, 213) points, on the other hand, to a related but nevertheless distinct set of interpretive issues whose crux lies in the question of how the reader engages with the morals and norms of a literary work and on which basis he concludes that the narrator's evaluation of the

---

10. At its most general, unreliability may be tied to a sense that something is not said or hidden. As Michael Riffaterre notes in his study *Fictional Truth* (1990): "It is common wisdom that the unconscious harbors in symbolic and cryptic form a truth that we repress at the conscious level. The unconscious is therefore assumed to stand in regard to consciousness as does reality in regard to appearances. Consequently, whenever the text seems to hide something, that something is supposed to be true" (85). For the category of unreliability to be used productively, it is also necessary to delimit it, via what can be broadly conceived of as a rhetorical move, by asking what effects are structurally inherent to unreliability. Kindt (2008, 35–36), for example, assumes that the wide popularity of the concept of unreliable narration arises precisely from its vagueness. A divergence between what the text seemingly says and what it actually says is also the basis for irony, humor, and satire. The effect of these phenomena (i.e., their felicity) lies in the reader's immediate recognition of the "double" communication on which they are based. Unreliability, on the other hand, is a deception that often creates effects of incredulity and surprise when discovered. As Theresa Heyd puts it, they lie in "the quintessential moment of 'discovering' the unreliable quality of a narrative" (2011, 7). Typical examples of this effect of discovery—shocking, illuminating and, to some extent, always pleasurable—include Agatha Christie's *The Murder of Roger Ackroyd* (1926) and, to give more recent examples, Yann Martel's *Life of Pi* (2001) or Toby Litt's *deadkidsongs*.

11. To differentiate between the reader's assessment of the character narrator and of the narrated, Stanzel observes that unreliability cannot be reduced solely to the narrator's qualities "as a fictional figure, e.g., character, sincerity, love of truth, and so on" (1984, 89). The mode of telling influences how the unreliability is expressed and experienced, as well as establishes its relevance for interpretation (see Stanzel 1978, 260–61).

state of affairs is wrong. Vera Nünning summarizes this group of conceptions as follows:

> Those narrators who are untrustworthy not mainly because of their incorrect account of the facts within the fictional world but rather because of their faulty interpretations, evaluations and morals. A murderer may gleefully and consistently tell the story of how much he enjoyed torturing and killing his victims; a pedophile may tell the story of his love for a young girl **realistically and truthfully**—but they would both **still have to be considered untrustworthy**. It is possible, of course, that individual readers who enjoy torturing young girls may think of these narrators as perfectly reliable, but by having recourse to the prevalent cultural norms and values one can point out their untrustworthiness. (2015, 10)

Axiological unreliability can be a notion rife with ideological implications. What or who is the source of moral and ethical norms that have to be observed? Why do readers *have to* consider untrustworthy a truthful account of a killer about the joy she derives from killing? The reader may find it disgusting, wrong, and horrible, but might fiction not want to attempt to create a trustworthy image of what it is like to be a killer?[12] Classifying ethically difficult narrators as unreliable is a theoretical move, rooted in the historical context of Booth's definition and aimed at preventing linking the (implied) author to the convincing but ethically flawed views endorsed by morally dubious narrators (also see Hansen 2007, 238). This move by extension implies—via the primary meaning of the word "unreliable"—that their stories are not trustworthy although, paradoxically, their account can be truthful.

In an attempt to solve this contradiction, Greta Olson observes that unreliability often binds the reader to the (implied) author in the sense of "an ingroup that shares values, judgements, and meanings" (2003, 94) and excludes the unreliable narrator.[13] She suggests that instead of being a sign of a lack of truthfulness or mental stability, unreliability in the axiological sense I describe

12. Analyzing the ethics of narration in Nabokov's *Lolita*, Phelan makes a similar point: "Nabokov is doing something extraordinary, however distasteful: occupying the perspective of a pedophile, asking us to take that perspective seriously, and, indeed, through the second story, asking us, at least to some extent, to sympathize with him. In this respect, the ethics of the novel involves performing one of the best functions of art: extending the perceptions and feelings of its dominant audience, doing so in ways that challenge preconceptions even if the challenge makes us uncomfortable and even likely to turn against the artist" (2005, 130).

13. On the ideological implications of this conception of unreliability, see Greta Olson's (2003) analysis of Booth's model and her further development of these implications and historicization of the concept of unreliability in Olson (2018).

here functions to highlight the workings of power, for example by making explicit the reader's own assumptions of moral (or other) superiority:[14] The attribution of unreliability in this sense may "perpetuate[] processes in which the determination of supposedly intrinsic weakness has been used to reify representational privilege" (Olson 2018, 169). Furthermore, for the reader to recognize the inadequacy of the character's judgment or evaluation, she would have to possess a supposedly correct or valid set of moral standards in contrast to that character. These might well be as straightforward as a condemnation of killing, torture, and sexual abuse, but they also may be the prevalent cultural norms of the time. And, for example, "A Rose for Emily" demonstrates that the prevalent norms are not necessarily correct and its character-outsider may actually serve as a vehicle of critique of the communal norms. This critique works regardless of whether the reader recognizes that Faulkner's views differ from those of the we-narrator or not. (However, Faulkner had to include enough nuance into the text to make such recognition possible.) Similarly, it fails if the reader occupies a position similar to Jefferson's community. Ultimately, unreliability as a narrative effect emerges in an interaction of the three elements of the narrative act: author, text, and reader. Within this view of unreliability, I would like to maintain the possibility of treating the norms and values of narrating characters and the trustworthiness of their account separately. This can be analytically productive for distinguishing between those ethical discrepancies that are matters of knowledge and reliability and those that are matters of perspective, understood as the process of apperception where the reader recognizes that she sees X as Y where the narrator or character sees X as Z. Again, however, in practice any such neat separation may be impossible to maintain.

Throughout this book, I have touched upon issues of ethics of the narrating collectivities or communities. Here I consider only a few examples of their potential for (un)reliability in the narrow sense of epistemological trustworthiness. Below I compare texts that are structurally and thematically similar: Eugenides's *The Virgin Suicides* (1994) and Oates's *Broke Heart Blues* (2000). I also draw one final time on Faulkner's short story "A Rose for Emily" (1995a),

---

14. An apt description applicable to such an author-reader alliance that defines rhetorical approaches to unreliability can be found in Barbara Foley's discussion of the ideology of form of *Bildungsroman*: "Readers are drawn willy-nilly into political alliance with authors, who, screening themselves behind omniscient narrators, position readers as coconspirators presumably cognizant of the values towards which the more or less naïve protagonists are fumbling. Both in establishing the 'subject-ivity' of characters and in confirming the 'Subject-ivity' of readers, bildungsromans represent, in the Althusserian paradigm, a quintessentially ideological form of discourse" (1993, 321). In other words, what is defined here as axiological unreliability can be seen as an ideology of form in general literary criticism.

which serves almost as a template for the two novels. The communal we-narrator of Eugenides's novel admits to never having known the story of the Lisbon girls but, nevertheless, cannot be classified as unreliable. The we-narrator of Oates's novel does not explicitly confess that "we" do not remember much of the events, but even so produces an effect of unreliability. The reliability of the Jefferson community ultimately remains unresolvable.

To start with the latter story, the associative chronological arrangement of "A Rose for Emily" makes it impossible to pinpoint the exact temporal location of the narrating "we" and, consequently, to judge the extent to which the community is underreporting about what Emily did. The narrative starts when Emily dies and "we" enter her house, motivated by past affection or curiosity (the beginning of section 1). There "we" discover that Emily was a murderer and, very likely, a necrophiliac (which is described in the last section, 5). These two moments are separated by a series of sections of reminiscent narration about Emily's life in the town of Jefferson. Since the first and the fifth sections are the temporally most recent ones for the narrator, time of narration could be situated as at the moment of discovery of the crime. This would mean that the narrator is underreporting from the very beginning—underreporting being one possible meaning of unreliability (Phelan 2007, 205). However, another equally legitimate temporal scenario might go like this: "We" gather together in Emily's house for her funeral, and "our" memories make "us" recall her life in "our" town. By way of association, the story of Emily unfolds until "we" finally get the chance to look inside the sealed-off room, making "our" discovery at the same time as the reader. In this scenario, the we-narrator would function as a detective, gathering clues in Emily's house to fill in the gaps in "our" knowledge about what happened in her life.

If, in the first scenario, the we-narrator is deemed unreliable, then, as an ethical consequence, the reader's evaluation of the we-narrator may be revised. If the narrator has been aware all along of the true reasons for the narrated events, then the "we"-community appears in a far more positive light. The rare sympathetic comments about Emily can be taken to reveal "our" remaining affection toward her, and the whole account would thus be "our" attempt to explain and rationalize what happened rather than merely prying into the life of a neighbor. In the second scenario, the we-narrator would retain the negative image of a nosy, gossipy community, appalled by someone ignoring its values.

Knowledge of the temporal location of the narrating "we" would help to classify the narration in "A Rose for Emily" as reliable or unreliable, but this classification seems unimportant, since the story—arguably—aims at ethical ambiguity: It offers a scandalous revelation and makes it difficult for the reader to either condemn or justify Emily for the murder. This ambiguity is achieved through a variety of techniques, and having a community narrate the story is one of them: Its mixture of gossip, public opinion, and common knowledge creates a certain type of discourse that seems more appropriately described in terms of ideology (and ethics) rather than reliability (trustworthiness). The we-narrator's ethical position can be interpreted as disapproving of Emily: She lives in contradiction to "our" values and traditions; she comes from an upper-middle-class family with aristocratic ambitions, which explains to "us" her reasons for not wanting to mingle with those socially lower than her and for not marrying one of "our" men. The reader's sympathetic mimetic engagement with the figure of Emily is fueled by the thematization of her as a victim of a tyrannical father, as an orphan, and as a lonely soul. On the one hand, she is obliged by her social position to keep up appearances while being poor, and on the other, she is forced by her community to conform to social rules that are alien to her. With the knowledge of the narrator's initial underreporting, readers may look back and reevaluate their negative position toward the oppressive patriarchal community and recalibrate their sympathy toward the we-narrator, but the figure of Emily would, arguably, remain ambiguous. The two revelations of the locked room are what maintains this ambiguity:[15] First, the reader discovers that she is a murderer. This can be accepted, if seen as an act of desperation or revenge, something that the town drove her to do. But then the reader also realizes that Emily must have slept next to the corpse all these years (the hair on the pillow is gray!), and this is something for which the town is more difficult to blame and that is more difficult to accept.[16]

More direct discursive and textual markers of unreliability abound in we-narratives: We-narrators, especially if they represent communities, exhibit signs of failing memory, admit to lacking pieces of knowledge, correct themselves, speculate, and base their accounts on rumor and gossip. Richardson aptly observes that

> the "we"-form raises interesting issues concerning reliability: insofar as it is a subjective form, it is enmeshed in issues of reliability and discordance, but these are issues that are potentially different from those in first person singular narratives since they may involve more accurate intersubjective beliefs as well as communal misprisions or even mass delusion. (2009, 146)

---

15. I am grateful to Heta Pyrhönen for her detective reading of this story and the distinction between the degrees of acceptability of the two transgressions that Emily committed.

16. See Robert Vogt's argument for distinguishing this case as a specific type of "ambiguous-unreliable narration" (2015, 133), that is, narration in which readers are unable to decide whether the narrator is unreliable or not. See also Behrendt and Hansen (2011).

The issue in question here is the authority of the narrative voice: With a we-voice, such authority is unstable in the sense that "we" can maintain the status of the general truth, common knowledge, "intersubjective beliefs," and, at the same time, spread insinuations. In "A Rose for Emily," the community builds its image of Emily and the events surrounding her on secondhand accounts, which the reader then accesses via the we-narrator's interpretation, and on inferences based on constant observation—inferences and interpretations that reflect the town's changing attitude toward Emily. As discussed above, information circulates in a community in many ways, and one of them is gossip or rumor, which constitutes a peculiar narrative device when it comes to the authority of the narrated, being "characterised by a reduction of complex issues, motivations and behaviour, an uncertain truth status, and rich use of telling detail" (Fritsch 2008, 207). Thus, by definition, "our" gossipy account of Emily's life is uncertain in its truthfulness. My suggestion is to take this observation beyond the category of (un)reliability in either of its two dominant meanings—a category tied, moreover, to one, singular narrating character.

A similar situation is created in Eugenides's novel *The Virgin Suicides* (1994), in which "we" admit "our" uncertainty: As a group of boys at the time of the narrated events, now adults, "we" recall the neighborhood girls, whose story "we" still cannot piece together. The narration in the novel, incidentally, progresses in a manner typical of we-narratives and makes prominent use of one its key features: The we-narrator relies heavily on the attention of the narratee. "We" narrate "our" story by going through a collection of the old documents and photographs of the Lisbon girls, showing the "exhibits" to the narratee as "we" comment on them. The constant presence of an unidentified listener is also a justification for the peculiar mode of narration of the story of the Lisbon girls: It is akin to a presentation of evidence together with "our" inferences and conclusions with a (failed) desire to be as objective as possible. Because the we-narrator is also a character, the narration differs from the so-called *pluralis auctoris* mode of the authorial narrator (*sensu* Stanzel). Consider the following example, in which the first sentence might be read as that of an I-narrator from an authorial narrative (referring to herself as "we"), had the rest of the passage not revealed "our" involvement in the storyworld in a parenthetical comment to the fictional narratee:

> We'd like to tell you with authority what it was like inside the Lisbon house, or what the girls felt being imprisoned in it. Sometimes, drained by this investigation, we long for some shred of evidence, some Rosetta stone that would explain the girls at last. . . . Trying to locate the girls' exact pain is

like the self-examination doctors urge us to make (we've reached that age). (Eugenides 1994, 170)

"We" in *The Virgin Suicides* are fully dramatized both as a narrator, constantly communicating with an unidentified narratee, and as a character, whose main concerns are the mystery of the Lisbon suicides and the pains of growing old. "We" admit that "our" knowledge is mostly theories and reconstructions, "our" memory is now failing, and that no material evidence was ever enough to uncover what was going on:

> Our own knowledge of Cecilia kept growing after her death, too, with the same unnatural persistence. Though she had spoken only rarely and had had no real friends, everybody possessed his own vivid memories of Cecilia. (40)

> Though we felt for the Lisbon girls, and continued to think about them, they were slipping away from us. (185)

> In the end we had pieces of the puzzle, but no matter how we put them together, gaps remained, oddly shaped emptinesses mapped by what surrounded them, like countries we couldn't name. (246)

The effect of such admissions dispersed throughout the narrative, however, does not contribute to a sense of unreliability, but rather to the self-construction of "us" as a collectivity: a group of men united by a common adolescent memory and the need to preserve it. In other words, these uncertainties characterize "us" through "our" voice as idiom without necessarily creating doubts as to the truthfulness of "our" account. The life and death of the Lisbon girls is as much a mystery to the reader as it is to the narrators, and so the effort with which the town boys try to fathom the suicides contributes to the reader's sense of trust in their story. (Ethically, however, their obsessive spying and prying is more questionable.) "We" struggle to gather "exhibits" and pieces of evidence and "we" interview the participants of those events, meticulously reconstructing and documenting the story. When the house of the Lisbon family is cleaned out for sale, for example, "we" acquire some of "our" most precious mementos: "We, of course, took the family photographs and, after organizing a permanent collection in our tree house, divided the rest by choosing straws" (228). Despite the admitted uncertainties, such details add to the frankness and honesty of the we-narrator's effort to tell the story of the Lisbon girls.

But even material evidence proves unstable—just like "our" unity and "our" town. Everything is perishing in time as "we" desperately try to keep a hold of it:

> And us. We aren't even allowed to barbecue any longer (city air-pollution ordinance), but if we were allowed, we might still gather, who knows, a few of us at least, to reminisce about the Lisbon house and the girls whose hair, clotted on brushes we still faithfully keep, has begun to look more and more like artificial animal fur in a natural museum exhibit. All of it is going— Exhibits #1 through #97, arranged in five separate suitcases, each bearing a photograph of the deceased like a Coptic headstone, and kept in our refurbished tree house in one of our last trees. (246)

As "our" observation of the Lisbon girls progresses, "we" reveal that "our" reason for telling their story is not so much to establish once and for all the truth about the girls' suicides, since that is also impossible, as "we" themselves realize: "This is all chasing after the wind" (248). The reason for telling is a need to talk through it, "to coalesce our intuitions and theories into a story we could live with" (241). The story becomes one of "our" bitterness, egotism, midlife crises, unfulfilled dreams and hopes. The never-to-be-had Lisbon girls, in this light, become scapegoats and the cause of all "our" frustrations:

> The essence of the suicides consisted not of sadness or mystery but simple selfishness. . . . They made us participate in their own madness, because we couldn't help but retrace their steps, rethink their thoughts, and see that none of them led to us. . . . And we had to smear our muzzles in their last traces, of mud marks on the floor, trunks kicked out from under them, we had to breathe forever the air of the rooms in which they killed themselves. (248)

As Olson notes in her study of unreliability, terms like "unreliable," "untrustworthy," and "fallible" come from the characterization of narrators as people, against "implicit theories of personality" (2003, 99), which makes such characterization a matter of the story and not a matter of discourse. When treated as a matter of discourse, unreliability may be viewed as a technique that produces surprise, the feeling that there is something "between the lines," the pleasurable discovery of an alternative story (see Heyd 2011). In *The Virgin Suicides,* there is no such hidden story, no surprise in this sense (especially since the novel opens with a scene from the morning on which the last of the Lisbon girls committed suicide). Moreover, as a characterization of "our" communal personality, we-narration in the novel approaches the mode of lyric progression, thus also drawing the reader away from evaluations of "our" account as fallible and inviting her to sympathetically enter into the narrator's perspective and thus imaginatively participate in "our" situation.

My final example in this chapter occasionally produces unreliability to suggest that there is a detective-like discovery to be made. Oates's *Broke Heart Blues* follows what seems like the classic we-narrative routine: An outsider catches the attention of a small middle-class suburban community. Willowsville high school students closely follow the arrival, life, drama, and subsequent departure of the Heart family: Sixteen-year-old John Reddy Heart allegedly kills his mother's lover with his grandfather's gun. John becomes a mysterious celebrity, desired by all the girls (and their mothers) and adored or envied by all the boys. His grip over "us" is so immense that not only do "we" connect all of "our" coming-of-age experiences and sexual awakening to him, but "we" cannot forget John, even decades after leaving the school and the town. As Cologne-Brookes comments, however, quite why "these wealthy, middle-class Americans have so idolized Heart into abstraction" (2005, 209) remains unclear in the novel.

In general, the novel's theme revisits questions brought up in *The Virgin Suicides*: long-lost youth, romanticized past, and that merciless time that takes many of "us" away while leaving the rest to experience the grim onset of age. Similarly, "our" failing memories take "us" further and further away from John, the symbol of "our" youth. Curiously, the theme of decay in *Broke Heart Blues* recalls not only *The Virgin Suicides* but also "A Rose for Emily": "It seemed to us that the Hearts' house, once as distinguished as any house in St. Albans Hill . . . began to deteriorate almost overnight" (Oates 2000, 156). In *The Virgin Suicides*, the decaying house of the Lisbon family disturbs the neighborhood (just as Emily's house is an "eyesore" for the Jefferson community): The emanation of a smell from it that no one can explain, the disturbing rotting of the trees alongside "our" streets, and many other scenes center on the decay these outsiders bring to the neighborhood. In Faulkner's story and *Broke Heart Blues*, these scenes add to an image of an outcast in the eyes of community, while in *The Virgin Suicides* the decay of one family stands for the decay of the whole community.

The occasion for narration in Oates's novel is "our" thirtieth high-school reunion, which places the time of telling long after the killing. The novel uses a familiar set of techniques of plural narration—a communal narrator that encompasses an unstable group throughout the years; associative chronology, which is possible due to the gap between the narrating and narrated times; and a collective external perspective onto the outsider about whom "we" narrate. Oates's communal narrator offers multiple accounts of one and the same event, which often contradict one another, and displays failing memories and uncertain status of knowledge that is acquired through rumor—all of which comments upon the construction of communal knowledge. But, *unlike* Faulkner's and Eugenides's narratives, *Broke Heart Blues* also creates a sense of unreliability via suspicion: It makes the reader wonder whether or not John actually committed the crime.

The novel is structured in three parts: The first part covers all high-school events and the facts about John that "we" managed to learn; the second part reiterates much of the same from John's perspective, with the final part being "our" reminiscence of the events thirty years later. Oates dedicates the middle, very short part of the novel to John Reddy Heart: Here the mode of narrating changes from the first-person plural narrative situation to a figural one and thus, after many digressions, the reader learns what really happened: John's mother, Dahlia, shot the man and John took the blame for her. This move from we-narration to a third-person reflector character is a shortcut to straightforwardly describe the hardships of John's life: how he was taking care of his younger brother and sister, his grandfather, and his alcoholic mother, who sexually abused him as a child. But this change in perspective and mode of narration is also the weakest part of the novel. As one of its reviewers observes: "All this forced background information and disentangling seems unnecessary, a reflection of Oates's tendency not to trust the reader to make the connections. The artistic effect is like someone explaining a joke" (Max 1999, n.pag.). In other words, the explanations of the second part of the novel neutralize one of unreliability's effects: the pleasure of discovery that readers take in recognizing a truth of which the narrator seems to be unaware.

Nevertheless, the part in which John is given a voice is precisely that second version of the story spelled out—the one that corroborates the reader's initial suspicion of narratorial unreliability. The first part of the novel creates an extensive communal image of John-the-idol, a collective infatuation that John never reciprocated. This the reader learns again, when she reaches the second, shorter part. For example, one interaction between Katie, one of "us," and John is described here from his perspective. Katie had multiple sclerosis back in high school, and John once helped her with a wheelchair—an event that in "our" eyes is on par with Jesus touching the leper. Katie bumps into John decades later and asks him to come to the school reunion, which is narrated from John's perspective: "This woman's face was familiar though it had no distinct association for him. One of the rich Willowsville girls. . . . None of them had been real to him and he'd kept his distance from all of them" (Oates 2000, 409). In response to her invitation, "John laughed, the idea was preposterous, but not wanting to seem rude he said, 'Maybe.' He was walking away. He'd forgotten the intense woman's name" (410). Then, back with the communal narrator in the final part of the novel, the reader is returned to the incident: "Kate Olmsted was telling us she'd met John Reddy Heart in the spring and he'd 'vaguely promised almost definitely' he'd try to make it to the next reunion. This was ten years ago, at our twentieth. Some of us had believed Kate, who can be very convincing, and some of us hadn't" (424). Leaving no doubt as to the discrepancy between "our" perspective and John's, Oates reiterates the same incident yet again, this time in Katie's direct speech:

> At our lavish twentieth reunion, too, there'd been the giddy, excited expectation that John Reddy would turn up at the pig roast. As Kate Olmsted told us breathlessly—". . . I was flattered—he remembered me! Pushing me in the wheelchair, I suppose. He seemed surprised that I was walking, so I explained about remission. . . . I invited him to our reunion as a special guest. He said he'd try to make it, he practically promised, and I believe him." (437)

This tiring amassing of perspectives on one and the same event characterizes the we-narrator as a self-involved and deluded group, offering a case study of gossip and interpretation. The sense of unreliability in this novel lurks elsewhere: "We" constantly provide information that suggests that there exists another version of what happened when John Reddy Heart opened the door of his mother's bedroom, which "we" do not or cannot yet tell, underreporting or misinterpreting the events. The reader is told "our" version of the murder and is privy to the court hearing of the matter, which clears nothing up since it also consists of fragmentary reports by those of "us" who managed to sneak into the hearings. Finally, the first part ends with a question: "*Why weren't there any fingerprints on that gun except John Reddy's?*" (298), creating a minor cliffhanger and a first cue for the reader that something is perhaps awry. Thus, on the one hand, the narrator in *Broke Heart Blues* is unreliable in matters of John's crime. It is in this respect that *Broke Heart Blues* "authorizes imagining that the narrator does not provide completely accurate information" (Köppe and Kindt 2011, 90) for whatever reasons—for example, due to a simple lack of knowledge. The sense of mystery surrounding the murder is magnified by the consistent external perspective because "we" do not have access to John's house and are not privy to his thoughts. On the other hand, the over-explanation cancels out the reader's pleasure at the discovery of this epistemological unreliability. With all its multiple angles on the Heart family, all the pieces of gossip, and facts that are often hard to separate from each other, "we" offer a meticulously detailed account of John's role in "our" community. This account characterizes "us" rather than him. Much like many of the recent novels in the we-form, *Broke Heart Blues* seems to offer an extended exercise in we-narration, inflating the narrative structures of Faulkner's popular short story, as well as a useful point of comparison when it comes to the degrees of we-narrator's reliability.

The two novels discussed here, which are structurally and thematically very similar to the paradigmatic we-narrative of Faulkner's "A Rose for Emily," bear an even closer affinity to each other: Both *The Virgin Suicides* and *Broke Heart Blues* deal with themes of time, sorrow, the romanticization of adolescence, and the idolization of an outsider. There is, however, one important structural difference between Eugenides's novel and Oates's, which contributes to a more pronounced sense of unreliability in the latter: *The Virgin Suicides* tends toward a reflectorization of the narration (and thus approaches the mode of lyric progression), whereas Oates's novel stays close to the teller mode (in Stanzel's sense). Thus, *The Virgin Suicides* provides fewer reasons to doubt the narrator on the whole; it remains a story about "us," not an account of the suicides, and thus evokes various ethical judgments of the we-character, but not of its unreliability. *Broke Heart Blues,* by hinting at the narrator's unreliability, maintains the mystery of the murder. It remains to be seen, however, how well epistemological and, especially, axiological meanings of unreliability describe discourses of we-narrators. Being collective or communal, such discourses have a pronounced social agenda, be it on the scale of a nation, as in *Ways of Dying,* or of a petty middle-class suburb, as in Eugenides's or Oates's novels. I have therefore argued that when considering the unreliability of we-narrators, the trustworthiness of the story they tell should be evaluated separately from the norms and values they project, the latter being explicitly matters of ideology and elements of group ethos.

CHAPTER 6

=========

Us versus Them

Community Dynamics in We-Narratives

THROUGHOUT THIS BOOK I have discussed the essential elements and qualities of the first-person plural narrative situation, supporting them with extended examples from various we-narratives, often in comparison with multiperson and other narrative situations. To round off the discussion, this short chapter brings together the most salient of my theoretical observations in a final case study, the short story "Watch the Animals" by Alice Elliott Dark. This text is especially suitable for such a summarizing task because it illustrates well the referential complexity of we-discourses, their peculiar performative use in narratives, and the dramatization of plural narrators as collective characters with a specific scope of perspective and knowledge. While the structural tension between collective and individual voices and perspectives, characteristic of most we-narratives, admittedly does not figure prominently in "Watch the Animals," this short story epitomizes a narrative conflict, typical of contemporary Anglophone we-narratives: a disruption in a small, usually middle-class, suburban community. Hence, the focus on *community* dynamics in this chapter. I start by examining the structural features of "Watch the Animals" and, via a discussion of narrative progression, move on to its ethical conflict.

Published in 1999, Dark's story relies on structural and thematic features that are very similar to those in Faulkner's "A Rose for Emily" (1995a), discussed at the beginning of this book, and, in a sense, corroborates their defining status. Just like in Faulkner's story, in "Watch the Animals" a small-town upper-class community struggles with its nonconformist female neighbor. The story thus brings up anew the complex ethics of social relationships within a closed, conservative community and the fluid dynamics of the division between insiders and outsiders, acceptance and ostracization. Its narrative techniques include an all-knowing, all-seeing we-narrator who acts as a group, who often narrates by means of gossip, and whose external perspective on its neighbor, Diana Frick, creates an intense situation of constant watching of not just her animals, but also their owner.

Diana is an outsider in "our" small town (or suburban village) in a similar way as Emily is in the town of Jefferson: On the one hand, they both belong to "our" communities, their families having been highly respectable members of "our" town, but on the other hand, they flaunt "our" codes of behavior and disregard "our" values, thereby making it difficult to treat them as "one of us." Unlike Emily, however, Diana does not manage to isolate herself completely from her neighbors and has to seek "our" help when she is diagnosed with stage-four cancer—help for her animals, that is, not herself. She has created an animal shelter on her property for abused cats, dogs, and horses, and they will need care after she dies. The community is indignant at first—in her books Diana has been criticizing "us" all her life—but eventually "we" agree to take in her animals, persuaded by her promise of a monetary reward and "our" own growing sense of pity and responsibility. Whereas the main complication of the plot is rather straightforward and directs the reader's attention to the question of whether or not the community will ultimately take care of the animals and thus change their ways, its resolution remains ethically ambiguous. This ambiguity is created through a complex set of social (and ethical) relations that the communal narration brings to the fore. To examine them in more detail, I must first outline how the story's communal character narrator is constructed.

Structure of Communal Narration in "Watch the Animals"

The participant-observer we-narrator in this short story reflects many of the tensions characteristic of small social groups, which I discussed in chapter 1: "We" exist as a community because of a similarity between "our" members or, in other words, "we" possess a shared ethos and a sense of "our" group as a group. At the same time, this ethos is defined in opposition to those who test "our" borders (Diana) or to complete outsiders (animals, the rest of the world). While communities always negotiate between what unifies "us" and a certain amount of differences between the individual members, a difference too great becomes a threat to "our" existence and must be contained—or excluded from the group. The town's attitude toward animals is a good example of how much difference this particular "we" can tolerate. When it comes to household animals and pets, "we" see "ourselves" as compassionate on the whole (although there are some exceptions): "There were few among us who hadn't mourned a loyal dog or put out scraps for a stray cat or developed a smooth working relationship with a horse. Animals had a place in our lives, to be sure, and we took seriously our responsibilities toward them" (91). But Diana goes as far as to claim that animals have souls and deserve rights equal to humans—something "we" cannot accept: "Her calling was low rather than high, down at the level of the animals, and we couldn't help but think it a delusion and a waste" (93). Clear hierarchies define "us": Besides the distinction of species, those of class ("we" take pride in "our" blue blood), age ("our" elders enforce "our" traditions), and gender (only some life choices are acceptable for women) inform "our" perspective. Diana's dedication of her life (and money) to rescuing animals is wasteful and unworthy of someone like "us." Thus, while "we" can tolerate—albeit disapprovingly—"Harold Johnson's shooting of his dog for eating the Thanksgiving turkey" or "someone nail[ing] a cat through its feet to a plank of wood" (94), "we" see Diana's obsession with animal well-being (and, implicitly, radical equality) as an excess that does not belong to "our" ethos. Throughout the story animals become a symbolic test group through which "our" ethos and Diana's attitudes toward "us" are made explicit.

Besides the we-narrator's direct statements about its views, "our" communal ethos is constructed through the use of perspective. The we-narrator as a character is thus described via how "we" see and interpret various events in terms of joint beliefs, opinions, and agreed-upon actions (particularly those that pertain to Diana's request). As I have argued, when the focalizer character is a collectivity, it is more pertinent to talk of its group ethos, rather than its fictional mind. Thus, as a character, "we" are an upper-middle class community with strong attachments to aristocratic family lineages (94). These are also the terms in which "we" describe Diana as one of "our" own kind: She is "a moneyed blue blood" (91), an "artless natural beauty," in whom "we" "see ourselves at our best. She was the sum of our efforts over the last four hundred years in this country, and back into the past to Britain and the continent, Normandy, Saxony, the high, clear springs of our culture" (94). Yet, to "our" great disappointment, Diana lives a secluded life writing children's books and tending to the animals. She refuses to socialize, to decorate "our" communal events with her presence, to live by "our" code, and to lead what "we" consider a respectable life: "We assumed she'd follow the path we all walked: marriage to someone like-minded, a house of her own but similar to her parents', children raised with the traditions that she remembered fondly, all the little habits that connect one generation to the next" (92). Family traditions are what keeps the community alive, even if some of "us" sometimes might not want to adopt them entirely. The group ethos remains stronger than these moments of weakness:

> We'd taken to heart the often repeated caveat from our childhoods that the elders applied to all manner of deviance—*think what would happen if everyone behaved like that!* The consequence was never exactly specified; for most of us, the implication of chaos and breakdown was enough. We knew our own bad thoughts, after all, knew what we had to suppress. We understood why we couldn't indulge our baser natures or the full range of our whims; we might lose what we had if we did. How had it happened that Diana didn't understand what was at stake? (94)

Communities exist by containing differences that would otherwise cause chaos and dissolve them. In the example above, the containment happens via the authority of the elders, and so a serious questioning of the necessity for hierarchies, such as Diana's nonconventional views, questions this authority and threatens the community. While minor deviations are acceptable, excess is threatening—especially since "we" see her excessive views being supported in the "outside" world: "Her arguments were silly, but the book became a hit. Souls, she claimed. That was the crux of what she had to tell the world. As always, she pushed it beyond the beyond" (94). Through comments like these, "we" seem to express a vague realization that "ours" is an outdated form of existence and that Diana's views will outlast "our" own. Thus, the stakes of containing change within this community are indeed high—they are a matter of survival. Mistreated animals and Diana's views on species in general come to sum up various complex social relations in this story, its communal narrator being the site of the ethical conflict.

The narrator of the story is indeed a full-blown group character, not just one member of the community who uses the plural reference to speak on everyone's behalf. The consistent plural self-reference and strong communal focalization, which leads the reader into "our" world view, is supported by a performative use of the we-pronoun when it comes to descriptions of actions, opinions, and so on, from one of the opening scenes, where Diana visits "us" in "our" house, to one of the last, when she comes to "our" church during a joint Christmas mass. While the former visit suggests that only some of "us" can be physically involved in this scene and the church service indicates that all of the small town can potentially be present, both of them are narrated consistently in the plural. Descriptions of encounters between Diana and "us" in small-scale settings do not introduce any tension into the collectiveness of the we-reference or, to put it differently, they do not break the communal "dominant code" (*sensu* Phelan) that governs this narrative because of the way they are executed. Consider the following extended example:

> She first came around to plead her case in autumn, when the lanes swelled with bright leaves. We couldn't help but examine her for signs of the illness, but nothing much showed; she'd always been spare. Her eyes shone blue as ever, that was the main thing. She appeared without calling first, **the way we used to do** when we were liable to be having tea or drinks in the afternoon and could easily accommodate company. **Now we were busy, but we didn't turn her away.** Years of curiosity assured her a vigorous welcome.
>
> "Let's sit outside," she said. "I've got the dogs, and I need a smoke." . . .
>
> When we were all settled and mugs of tea had been handed around, she made her play.
>
> "I'm leaving money to cover their expenses," she told us. The days were over **when it was considered impolite to talk about money,** but she made her offer sound like a bribe. **It was yet another example of how clumsy she was with people.** . . .
>
> We said we'd think it over, then changed the subject. When would she begin treatments? we wondered. (91–92)

First of all, this passage shows very well how the we-narrator's idiom and perspective construct the character of Diana for the reader: She appears without calling first, thereby disregarding the implicit rule that such visits are reserved only for in-group members who, furthermore, know the appropriate time for them. Since she does not, she is both an outsider and a blunt, slightly tactless person compared to whom "we" come across as understanding and accommodating. Some judgments are offered in an impersonal manner ("when it was considered impolite" or "how clumsy she was with people"), which suggests a commonly accepted view and the narrator's effort to get the reader onto "our" side as well. Here Diana comes only to some of "us" to ask about the animals. The flexibility of the we-reference, whose scope can change freely without any morphological modifications, ensures that the "we" in this passage can be both narrower in scope than elsewhere in the story and, simultaneously, remain the same "we" that refers to "all of us." From an expression of communal habits in "the way we used to do" and a particular household's "we" in "now we were busy," the pronoun moves back toward a more general reference in "we didn't turn her away." The "we" in the latter phrase reads both as one particular household and as "we"-the-community who do not turn Diana away—for the reason that "we" have been curious about her life all these years.

Thus, this detailed description of one interaction between some of "us" and Diana functions as a cumulative example of many other similar visits. Individual particularities that are nevertheless narrated in the plural is one of the defining characteristics of we-narrative. Such pluralization contributes to the force of the performative "we" by maintaining the collective reference, even if "we" are talking of individual cases (see *The Buddha in the Attic,* discussed in chapter 3). Eventually, "we" all will share "our" information, observations, and judgments of her with each other, constructing a plausible pool of transpersonal collective knowledge: "When we compared notes on these visits, we couldn't help but bristle" (92). Finally, while the we-reference fluctuates between a concrete subgroup and the whole community, it does not suggest any particular "I" implied in the discourse because of the way the interaction between Diana and "us" is arranged: Diana's direct speech is either followed by impersonal narrative commentary that sums up "our" reaction to what she says, or it is followed by "our" free indirect speech, as in "We said we'd think it over, then changed the subject. When would she begin treatments? we wondered." The we-narrator does not speak directly through a single character—as in a conventional dialogue, an exchange of direct utterances—since it would either singularize "us" or bring about an implausible move within the conventions of this story, a chorus of people chanting to Diana. Such arrangement of direct speech in combination with narration and free indirect discourse assures that the we-narrator remains communal throughout the story, including during conversations.

The above passage also speaks prominently to another quality of we-narrators as characters: "our" fondness of gossip and spying. When it comes to observing Diana, the we-narrator's perspective is not so obsessive as to suggest a voyeuristic undertone (unlike in some of my previous examples) and functions rather as a clarification of the need to gossip: "Nothing we could see in her indicated she was" going to choose a wrong life for herself (92) and so "we" need to continue observing, for instance, to uncover the reasons. Unlike Diana's, "our" decisions need to comply with the prevailing opinion and must be approved by the rest of the community: "On the telephone, in the clubs, shops, and churchyards, we tried to decide what to do" (91). Gossip in "Watch the Animals" functions less as an information-sharing channel (in contrast to, e.g., *Ways of Dying* or "A Rose for Emily") and more as a community-building device: "For the benefit of younger generations and those new to town, at dinner parties and on Sunday walks, we repeated her story" (92). Since the themes of gossip are usually transgressions of social norms that the participants of the gossip support, their discussion of such transgressions becomes a group-binding exercise, a reinforcement of the norms and an assessment of whether "we" still agree on what's right and what's wrong. Gossiping in this short story works as a means of reassuring "ourselves" and coaching those new to "our" community in "our" values. Diana's request for help thus becomes an exciting new topic: Is she changing for the better? Does she finally recognize that "we" are good people? However, "our" delight is mixed with an old indignation at her condescending disregard for "our" habits and conventions—and the mixture informs the main ethical complication of the story.

Ethics of Communal Narration in "Watch the Animals"

To reiterate, in "Watch the Animals" the narrative is set in motion by the question of whether or not the neighbors will help Diana with the animals despite their feud. As Diana presents her request to the we-narrator, "we" start looking for the best response—the best possible configuration of solutions that would remedy not only Diana's situation but also "our" insulted pride, the need to help one of "us" without losing face, and the problem of adopting the animals despite "our" fear and suspicion toward them. This predicament of the we-narrator's explains why the telling is so heavily focused on Diana and the animals: The story may be seen as a review of "our" judgments of her throughout "our" lives, by which "we" attempt to reevaluate "our" stance and decide what to do about her request. As the we-narrator engages in these assessments, the reader also determines her relation toward the story via "interpretive and ethical judgements about [characters], their situations, and their choices" (Phelan 2017, 83) that, furthermore, condition the reader's affective responses and her desires concerning the narrative's progression. In rhetorical terms, narrative ethics is an interaction and synthesis of such readerly and textual dynamics. The governing perspective and the communal nature of the narrator in "Watch the Animals" complicate the textual ethics considerably, to the point that even though "we" eventually agree to take in Diana's animals and even begin helping out in her household, caring for her and the animals on a daily basis, this resolution does not come across as satisfactory for the reader.

To clarify how such ambiguity comes about, I shall divide the progression of the ethical dynamics of the story into three sets: (1) the attitude of the we-narrator toward Diana, (2) the we-narrator's attitude toward the animals, and (3) Diana's attitude toward the we-narrator and the animals. The first group of ethical relations is the most prominent one, but it is continuously influenced by the more abstract opposition of "us" versus the animals, where the animals stand in for outsiders, "them." Diana constantly straddles the line between being like "us" and being a "stubbornly nonconformist" (Dark 1999, 91) outsider. To begin with the third group of relations, the reader only can evaluate them on the basis of the secondhand information that comes from the we-narrator. Diana's character is accessible exclusively via the we-narrator's external perspective, similar to Emily in Faulkner's story. There are no diegetically narrated passages revealing her own opinions and beliefs (unlike in many we-narratives that focus on individual characters), and readerly judgments of her character are not actively corroborated by the text. It is unclear, for example, if there are other, more significant reasons for the hostility between her and the community: "We" mention the accidental death of her brother, after which her father was inconsolable about the loss of his family line and having to leave "all that money, albeit in trust, to a woman" (92). However, such potentially significant details are mentioned *inter alia* as the we-narrator is consumed with Diana's attention to the animals. Not even the fact that she took in a series of foster children in her forties gets much attention in "our" judgment as "we" mull over her reasons for not liking "us." When "we" read in her autobiography how, since her childhood, she has been bothered by the animal cruelty in town, "we" take this to be the decisive explanation of her indifference toward "us": "She'd chosen the company of other species over companionship with her own kind, a preference we naturally took as a rejection" (91). The choice of animals over "us" means that Diana considers *them* better! The we-narrator becomes so consumed with this detail that the reader's focus shifts from the reasons for Diana's choice to the reasons for the narrator's obsession.

"Our" attitudes toward the animals can be read more metaphorically as the attitudes of a conservative community toward outsiders. This interpretation becomes especially strong after the we-narrator acknowledges the following:

> [Diana's animals] were not purebreds, or even respectable mutts. She collected creatures that others had thrown away, the beasts left on the side of the highway or confiscated from horrific existences by her contacts at the ASPCA. . . . She took these animals that otherwise would have ended up euthanized at best, and she trained them and groomed them and nursed them and fed them home-cooked foods until—we had to admit—they bore a resemblance to the more fortunate of their species. They behaved, as far as we could tell. But from a practical standpoint, could they ever be considered truly trustworthy? Who knew what might set them off? (92)

These animals are not simply a lower species, but the lowest of the low, even within their own kind. Diana further offends "us" by having the rescued animals bear the names of their tortures so that "we" cannot forget or ignore their past. And, while "we" have to acknowledge that they resemble and behave like any other animal that "we" may own, "we" cannot accept that these *other* animals are like "ours"—a transparent allusion to any outsider in such a community. They do look like "us," but who can *really* know what is on their mind? The distinction between "us" and "them" is concretely present in how the we-narrator can know any of "our" thoughts, but not the thoughts of outsiders to the group, including Diana. "We" do not consider the ethical equality of all human beings possible, nor can "we" understand and extend compassion to someone as radically different from "us" as a member of another species.

However, neither the possibility of radical equality nor the post-human agenda of demonstrating animal subjectivities and sentience are, ultimately, the concerns of this short story. The most significant—and conflicted—ethical relationship is that of "us" toward Diana. While "we" admire her refined aristocratic beauty and talent, "we" feel insulted and jealous at the same time because Diana does not acknowledge that "we" are like her—the wish to which multiple repetitions of the phrase "our kind" testify. Quite to the contrary, not only does she ignore "our" communal activities, she writes highly popular tales where barnyard animals satirize many recognizable types and ways of "our" life: "We saw ourselves drawn with a harsh, loveless pen and felt stung by her portrayal, especially as we were *proud* of her" (93). The explanation for such a conflicted attitude comes from the we-narrator directly: She is the pinnacle of "our" communal values—rich, beautiful, and popular (with the rest of the world). Even if she rejects "our" company, "we" cannot ignore her in turn because if "we" are like her, "we" also support the causes that she does. The short story offers a direct corroboration of this interpretation: "We" compare Diana in the church to a nun from the 1943 film *The Song of Bernadette*. In this film, a girl has visions of a beautiful lady, whom the community interprets to be Virgin Mary, which makes the girl the center of jealousy and admiration. Notably, it is the community who interprets her visions and then, on the basis of this interpretation, glorifies and despises her. Diana's situation is similar in that her public image is a communally constructed one that, in turn, conditions the communal attitudes toward her.

The trajectories (1) and (3) of the unfolding of the ethical progression come together figuratively and literally when Diana needs to ask for "our" help with the animals. She minimizes the physical distance between herself and "us" by coming to "our" homes, clubs, and churches. "We" are simultaneously delighted and outraged. Delighted because all this time "we" wished for her presence to grace "our" communal gatherings; outraged because she still does not play by "our" rules (of etiquette, in this case). Diana seems uncompromising in her view of "us" as self-centered opportunists and directly offers "us" money to adopt one or more of her animals. But, while "we" want the money, "we" also want to save "our" (deluded) image of "ourselves" as caring and altruistic: "It wasn't that it was unheard of to put conditions on a request, or to shore up a good deed with a financial benefit, but to do so successfully required finesse and subtlety. People want to believe they are high-minded and generous, not greedy and bought. A good monger could have offered us the same deal in terms that would have us not only clamouring to agree to it but also feeling grateful she'd come to us" (92). Interestingly, this passage, besides providing a further insight into the community's mercantile ethos, opens in impersonal and general terms ("it wasn't that it was unheard of," "people want to believe they are high-minded") in an example of the distancing technique of the we-reference: the we-narrator's use of the third-person reference when "we" want to distance "ourselves" from something shameful or inappropriate that "we" nevertheless do. In "A Rose for Emily," the same distancing happens when "we" talk about spying on Emily and Homer. In the end, "we" resist adopting her animals because of the directness of her request: Accepting it would mean confirming "our" hypocrisy.

"Our" change of heart comes about, somewhat abruptly, with Diana's eventual submission—real or assumed—to the ways of "our" community. Again, her actions that make "us" change "our" mind are presented as already interpreted by the we-narrator, so the reader cannot adequately judge if it is "our" desire to see them as such, or if Diana is finally playing the game. She shows up at church on Christmas Eve afternoon and "we" offer to take in her animals, one by one, moved by how pious she looks, how she makes an effort to dress up, how much she reminds "us" of "our" glorious ancestors and mortality. And then "we" start visiting her house, checking on her health, walking her dogs: "She needed us at last, and her need was as good as an apology" (95). Ironically, at the same time "we" describe how Diana is actually physically opposing the intrusion: "'Go away,' she'd shout when we knocked on her windows. It was quite a picture, seeing this frail shrinking creature waving her bird arms at us, as if she could keep us out" (95). But "we" make a copy of her keys and now never leave her alone: "We" lock up her animals and take their place at last. This section of the story is the most explicit in terms of how much the narrator's perspective has been orienting the telling: Diana tries to fight "us" away, but "we" interpret it as her needing "us"; what is described as care might be physical overpowering. However, similarly to "A Rose for Emily," the issue of the narrator's ethical reliability remains unresolvable since "our" perspective and voice are the exclusive ones in the story.

This period of intrusion goes on for a few months until "we" find out one morning that Diana has killed herself during the night, surrounded by her dogs, which presents another interpretive ambiguity for the reader: She did it either to take control over her death, or, in a more radical interpretation, to get away from "us," to regain her independence. In any case, even without the possibility of choosing between the two interpretations, this event contributes to the reader's judgment of the we-narrator's actions. "We" interpret Diana's suicide along the former lines, as her doing things her own way, and clean up the signs of her pill overdose: "The world at large isn't always as understanding as one's own kind" (96). When the news reporter calls about her obituary, "we" tell him that Diana died in her sleep surrounded by friends. It is thus an ultimate reversal: The world has been understanding of her views on animals and she died surrounded by them, but "we" take over the narrative of Diana's life, forcing false interpretations upon her "readers" (i.e., the rest of the world) in the move that fully subsumes the traces of her nonconformist life. And while "we" conclude by claiming to question "our" views on animals—perhaps they do have some sentience and feel grief for Diana—this comes a little too late, "our" final narrative manipulation. Sending the dogs back to their cages with a call "Prison time!," "we" muse: "What could we lose by extending them our empathy; what could we gain by holding back?" (96). Nothing, since at this point Diana's views are not a threat to "us" any longer, having been figuratively and literally imprisoned.

The progression of the ethics of "Watch the Animals," if approached in we-narrative terms, is the progression of a community toward a containment of the disruption, a submission of a rebellious member whom "we" cannot simply expel. This short story, by constructing a fully communal character narrator, moves what would have been an interpersonal conflict into the realm of a larger-scale social interaction; it thus becomes a story about a clash between the power of a social group to which one belongs, nonconformism, and the simultaneous reliance on the community against which one rebels. In anchoring itself in these themes, "Watch the Animals" embodies many of the defining features of we-narration: its peculiar performative use of the first-person plural pronoun, unanimity of communal perspective and judgment despite divergences between individual members, and a consistent group voice and action. Its overarching conflict of the community versus an individual epitomizes the structural and thematic dynamics of we-narratives, where the performative (collective) "we" subsumes the indicative (individual) "we," where plural narration dominates, despite many asides dedicated to individual characters, and where social groups of various scales act, emote, and speak as groups.

CONCLUSION

IN THIS BOOK I have offered a formal definition of we-narrative as an independent narrative form and have given an extensive account of its properties and effects. On the remaining few pages I summarize my main claims and go through the elements of we-narrative once again, point by point, in order to give a manageable overview of its nuances as discussed in the six chapters above. My guiding argument is derived from my close reading of contemporary we-narratives as well as stories that use we-reference extensively:[1] There exists in fiction a distinct first-person *plural* narrative voice. Based on this voice, there is a crucial distinction between we-*narrative* and other instances of we-discourses—a distinction that has been largely unrecognized in previous research. Narrators habitually use we-reference because their social relations inevitably come up in their stories. While such narrators have been typically described as part of homodiegetic/first-person or heterodiegetic/authorial narratives, increasingly texts with more or less frequent mentions of "we," such as Justin Torres's *We the Animals* (2011) or Yevgeny Zamyatin's *We* (1920–1921), are called "we-narratives" instead.[2] This is a puzzling phenome-

---

1. I remain indebted to the initial, extensive bibliographies of such texts compiled by Richardson (2006) and Fludernik (2011), which greatly facilitated my searches for we-narratives.

2. See, for example, Maxey (2015). *We the Animals* is a story about a troubled family from the perspective of one of the three children. Inevitably, "we" comes up all the time because the son is telling about most intimate communities of which he is part, the group of his brothers

non since, at the same time, there are stories that go beyond mere first-person plural references and construct a particular type of speaker, delinked from any type of "I": a fully plural, collective or communal narrator who is a group. Theoretical work is therefore needed to adequately address such differences in the forms and types of we-reference.

Growing theoretical interest in fictional collectivities over the past several years may create the impression that there has been a significant rise in collective characters or plural narrative forms in fiction, too. At the moment, there is no reliable data to substantiate such claims, although one can find a novel or two per year—at least, in English—that either partly uses or is entirely written in the first-person plural narrative situation and that, importantly, is discovered by a motivated literary theorist in the "great unread" (M. Cohen 2002, 23) of the hundreds of thousands of novels published in English every year.[3] And while it may seem a self-defeating move at the end of a book on we-narratives, I must say that without careful archival work, it is too early to make claims about the "rise of the 'we' narrator" in the US or elsewhere (this is *pace* Maxey 2015).[4] My own speculation would be to connect the relative prominence of we-narration in recent US fiction with the theoretical interest and the rise of creative writing programs after WWII, with their institutionalization of the modernist imperative "to make it new" (McGurl 2009, 4) and dynamics of influence, where Faulkner's short stories and acclaimed writers serving as instructors may indeed significantly shape the tendencies of modern prose.[5]

Likewise, without *some* theoretical agreement about the nature of this narrative form, it is impossible to outline its history as distinguished from

---

and his family. For Zamyatin, see Richardson's classification of the text's I-narration as we-narration (2006, 43).

3. See Fredner (2017) for an attempt to roughly account for this number.

4. Maxey (2015, §1), relying on the mixed-bag list of we-narratives and instances of the we-reference circulating in the field of narratology, claims that "an increasing number of American novelists and short story writers have turned to this narrative technique over the past 20 years and particularly since 9/11." The 9/11 reference, however, is based on Costello's (2012) observation that commemoration of this tragedy increases the manipulative *we-references* in public discourse. Taking "the rise and success" of we-narration in contemporary US fiction as a fact, Maxey has little evidence to back up this claim and ends her article on a different note: "Conversely, the rise of the 'we' voice may have little to do with the impact of 9/11. Even when the fiction I have examined post-dates this historic event, it more obviously reflects the powerful legacy of a Faulknerian 'we' and more recently, Eugenides' influential use of this narrator in *The Virgin Suicides*" (2015, §37).

5. Eugenides and Oates, for example, both teach creative writing; virtually all other writers mentioned here are also connected to the creative writing programs in various ways, even if by serving as case studies.

mere appearances of the we-pronoun in fiction.[6] My agenda has been to prove the existence of precisely this structural distinctiveness of collective narrative elements. But, while my analyses may have ended up emphasizing the opposition between plural and singular aspects, this division is, in practice, an impossible one. As Fredric Jameson reminds us, a "structural, experiential, and conceptual gap between the public and the private, between the social and the psychological, or the political and the poetic, between history or society and the 'individual'" is symptomatic of "the reification and privatization of contemporary life" that precludes an understanding of real social change (2001, 4). It is therefore important to stress, once again, that fictional narratives that make groups speak and act as groups also become explicit sites of negotiation of collective (i.e., social) and individual realms of human existence, that plural narrators embody and transform the many individual voices that feed into them. In contemporary Anglophone we-narratives, furthermore, narrating groups almost exclusively take the shape of relatively small suburban communities, symptomatically highlighting the suspicion toward—or the inability to conceive of—other collective forms of life, especially of larger scale, especially in the US. However, giving a synthesis of we-narrative's formal features, I intentionally refrain from providing, at this point, a more detailed theory of the cultural functions of this form or of its affinities with particular national literatures or political agendas. Rather, I wish this book to draw attention to one "strategically limited" insight (Jameson 2001, 5): *the question of formal difference between an I-narrator using we-reference and a "we" speaking as one.* Tackling this question, in my opinion, is the first step toward a (comparative or cultural) history of fictional we-discourses and we-narratives.

I have maintained that fictional uses of the first-person plural pronoun appear in at least two distinct linguistic-philosophical contexts: in we-narratives, where the we-reference transcends the impossibility of the multiplication of the "I," and in other narrative situations, where the we-reference implies the structure of "I + others" similarly to "we" in prototypical nonfictional contexts. (I have described intermediary cases as part of the phenomenon of multiperson narration.) This premise is at the center of my suggestion

---

6. Increased interest in contemporary we-narratives brings about excavations of the literary archive for other examples of this technique, which, however, ignore historical differences in rhetorical function of the we-pronoun and changing literary conventions. Thus, for example, Nathaniel Hawthorne's text "Old News" from 1835 employs the we-pronoun, arguably, in a function of *pluralis modestatis* (examined by Marcus [2008c, 4–5] within his broad approach to what constitutes a we-narrative). Hawthorne's use of "we" has been straightforwardly linked to the we-narration in Eugenides's *The Virgin Suicides* in Maxey (2016, 209) as if the two texts would be examples of the same narrative form.

that it is analytically helpful to distinguish between performative and indicative uses of "we" in fictional narratives. On this basis, a separate narrative situation can be singled out: that of the first-person plural or, in short, a we-narrative.

I have chosen to describe we-narrative as a narrative situation because this theoretical move, while being a critical adoption of Stanzel's typology within a larger pragmatic rhetorical framework, makes it possible to approach we-narratives as an independent form—albeit in relation to first-person or multiperson narrative situations. The Stanzelian taxonomy of narrative situations is capable of offering a synthesis of the various formal elements of a narrative and tracing their mutual influences. Being an ideal abstraction, it provides a useful starting point in distilling structurally significant elements of a hitherto undefined narrative situation from the multitude of its particular manifestations and variations. At the same time, I have not tried to offer a more detailed typology of we-narratives, partly because placing we-narratives alongside other narrative situations already distinguishes them typologically—not to mention that a more nuanced grouping into specific subtypes cannot be maintained—and partly because the Typological Circle itself is not flexible enough for an incorporation of new narrative possibilities.

On these grounds, the following definition of we-narrative was proposed: It is a narrative in which the character narrator is dramatized as a group (of whatever composition) and speaks, acts, and emotes as a collectivity. For an adequate analytical model of we-narration, the consequences of the narrator being a plurality are the following:

1. No (concealed/postulated) I-reference is recognizable nor, indeed, textually justified;
2. The we-reference is used performatively, rather than indicatively;
3. This we-reference is flexible and can expand or contract throughout a narrative, including or excluding various referents from its scope, while morphologically remaining intact;
   - Regardless of such referential shifts, the we-narrator usually achieves strong objectification as a character and rhetorical coherence;
   - This occurs through the consistent and prolonged use of self-reference (as "we") as well as through descriptions of collective actions and mental states and collective address to the narratee, who is often explicitly present;
4. We-narrative, due to its reliance on the force of the performative we-reference, can remain a we-narrative even if it introduces an I-reference

at some point in its progression. If the we-reference, used consistently and repeatedly to refer to a group character narrator throughout the narrative, establishes an overarching sense of a collective character, then this sense is not *automatically* nullified by an I-reference, although the "I"'s significance should be assessed interpretively.

Although not universal or exclusive to we-narratives, two further salient features of the first-person plural narrative situation include:

1. The associative arrangement of the chronology of the narrated events;
2. Progression by means of shifts between the collective and the individual modes of narration and focalization;
   - The most common example of such progression is collective we-narration (Stanzel's teller mode) combined with passages of free indirect speech strongly focalized through individual characters (reflector mode). Often, however, we-narratives also assume lyrical progression (*sensu* Phelan), which can lead to a certain nebulousness of the narrator's identity and (partial) dissolution of the narrator's role as a fully objectified character;
   - The shifts in focalization, furthermore, serve as a means for creating the psychological dynamism of we-narratives. Without such shifts between the narrator-focalizer and character-focalizers (for example, in cases where the we-narrator is an exclusive focalizer), the free indirect speech of individual characters is absent and the narration of mental states thus relies solely on diegetic summaries, obscuring the cognitive diversity of the group and the tensions and disagreements inherent to it.

Such are the main elements of we-narrative. I have argued that it is analytically and interpretively useful to posit the we-narrator as an independent type of narrator (developing Richardson's [2009, 152] crucial insight), not as an implicit "I" who actually speaks on behalf of the group, concealed behind the we-reference. Such a we-narrator, in other words, transcends the individual discourse originator of the first-person singular and functions as a collective speaker (storyteller), in addition to being a collective character (subject). The we-narrator represents a group that often possesses the structure of a community or a collectivity of a higher social order. This makes it possible to talk of communal and collective we-narratives. At the same time, it is important to note that other narrative situations can create a collective narrative, and so this is not an effect exclusive to we-narrative, but rather an interpretive distinction.

What is exclusive to we-narrative, however, is its form, defined by its plural narrator. As a represented group, the narrating "we" should thus be described under the so-called collectivity condition (*sensu* Tuomela 2007, as discussed in chapter 1), which reveals that a we-narrator is a character capable of acting collectively, creating collective (common) knowledge, and expressing shared mental states. These latter are more than mere aggregations of individual beliefs and knowledge and thus are not reducible to any single member of the we-group. The possibility of telling a story in the collective voice, as offered by we-narratives, requires no further justification as to how such a plural but unanimous voice can "actually" come into existence. The need to do so in various narratological analyses of we-narratives is grounded in the implicitly literal logic of narrative communication applied to fictional narratives and bolstered by pan-narrator theories. But to question the enunciative possibility of plural narration and to attempt to analytically resolve the issue within the so-called real-world communicative parameters generates unhelpful speculations or false interpretive problems. In some sense, fictional we-narratives are one such real-world domain where a collective voice *is* possible.

Further consequences of positing a plural narrator become visible in the narrative progression and representation of speech in we-narratives, as well as in the functioning of focalization, knowledge construction, and unreliability. We-narrators do not speak directly as a whole group, and the actualization of their direct discourse—when the speech of many has to be represented—has been deemed impossible. Nevertheless, many we-narratives prove otherwise: Typically, what "we" cannot say directly is presented in a diegetic summary, but this summary can be combined with direct responses from individual characters into a semblance of dialogue. When it comes to focalization, plural narrators can function as focalizers do, especially in terms of spatiotemporal orientation. We-narrators are plural—collective or communal—characters, and so they exhibit collective beliefs, convictions, opinions, and feelings. Rather than calling these group properties a mind in a literal sense (*pace* Palmer 2005), I have regarded them simply as manifestations of a group ethos and thus placed them under the broad rubric of perspective (which covers focalization and knowledge).

Frequent shifts between individual and collective modes of narrating and focalizing, being one of the most salient features of we-narratives, complicate the habitual typology of narrators in terms of homo-/heterodiegesis. In we-narratives, the restrictions associated with and defining of diegetic levels blur as plural narrators are involved in the narrated events as homodiegetic character-narrators (e.g., as witnesses to a crime committed in a community), and, at the same time, possess superior knowledge and selective or full omniscience (a feature of heterodiegetic narration) as transgenerational and transindividual entities, as many of the case studies in this book have demonstrated. The classical homo-/heterodiegetic distinction proves insufficient in describing this fluctuation: We-narrators are indeed part of the storyworld, that is, homodiegetic, but they do not possess crucial properties associated with homodiegetic narrators, and so my suggestion has been to consider them beyond these categories, established on the basis of first- and third-person narratives. I have suggested adopting the approach to the narrator developed by Walsh (2007, 2010), which is based on the Platonic mimesis/diegesis distinction. Accordingly, I have treated we-narrators as represented entities—and not as the ultimate representational instances—whose focalization is also a product of representation. This has allowed me to treat shifts in modes of narration and focalization independently of or in relation to each other, but always as subordinate to the overarching representational logic of the narrative—the authorial rhetorical act of fictive representation. In other words, either we-narrators or the characters about whom they narrate, or both in various combinations, can function as focalizers and narrate or contribute to the narration indirectly as reflectors. One of the possibilities of we-narration as a narrative technique is thus to present a first-person perspective while, at the same time, offering narrative freedom to the narrated characters and thus avoid a single, totalizing position.

As for the issue of collective knowledge, we-narratives can be said to offer insight into performative acts of knowledge creation and distribution rather than to operate with so-called impossible knowledge claims. Relying on the premise that, in the strong philosophical sense, all knowledge is institutional and thus social and collective, I have treated we-narrators as capable of knowing and telling what happens within various subgroups of "our" communities and in the lives of individual members without describing such knowledge claims as transgressive or anti-mimetic. Curiously, communal narrators often exhibit restricted knowledge whenever the narration moves from the actions, beliefs, views, or thoughts of the in-group to those of outsiders (like in the novels *Then We Came to the End* or *Ways of Dying*). Furthermore, when we-narration focuses on the outsider, the narrating community often assumes the role of voyeur. In a strongly focalized we-narrative, the situation of observation transforms the narrators from witnesses into spies and the focalized individuals into objects of unfulfilled desires or scapegoats. The outsider also functions structurally as a strong unifying agent for the group, adding to the creation of a collective gaze and consciousness.

The critical vocabulary for describing we-narratives developed here adds to the comparative study of the forms of contemporary fiction, which include, at least, first-person, authorial, figural, second-person, and, independently, first-person plural narrative situations. This book, being primarily an investigation of one narrative form, lays ground for the broader project of cultural narratology: An establishment of the distinct, independent narrative situation of first-person plural illuminates the inextricable unity of its collective and individual concerns, whose significance I have been able to address only in passing. This, combined with issues pertaining to the uniformity and heterogeneity of collective characters and the possibilities of their narrative representation, can help formulate culturally and politically aware approaches in narratology that avoid constructing easy divisions between collective or social and individual or private aspects of fictional narratives. We-narrative, taken as a distinct form of storytelling, opens up possibilities for such nuanced inquiries.

WORKS CITED

Fiction

We-Narratives, or First-Person Plural Narratives

Dark, Alice Elliott. 1999. "Watch the Animals." *Harper's Magazine*, September 1, 1999: 91–96.

Eugenides, Jeffrey. 1994 [1993]. *The Virgin Suicides*. London: Abacus.

Faulkner, William. 1995a [1976]. "A Rose for Emily." In *Collected Stories of William Faulkner*, 119–30. New York: Vintage International.

Fernandes [pseud.], and Joyce C. Oates. 1975a. "The Brain of Dr. Vicente." In *The Poisoned Kiss and Other Stories from the Portuguese*, 26–28. New York: Vanguard Press.

Ferris, Joshua. 2007. *Then We Came to the End*. New York: Little, Brown and Co.

Lee, Chang-rae. 2014. *On Such a Full Sea*. London: Little, Brown and Co.

Mda, Zakes. 1995. *Ways of Dying*. New York: Farrar, Straus and Giroux.

Nesbit, TaraShea. 2014. *The Wives of Los Alamos*. London: Bloomsbury Circus.

Oates, Joyce Carol. 2000 [1999]. *Broke Heart Blues*. Virago Press.

Otsuka, Julie. 2011. *The Buddha in the Attic*. London: Fig Tree.

Pittard, Hannah. 2011. *The Fates Will Find Their Way*. New York: Ecco.

Sontag, Susan. 1978. "Baby." In *I, etcetera*, 147–86. New York: Farrar, Straus and Giroux.

Walbert, Kate. 2005 [2004]. *Our Kind*. New York, London: Scribner.

Multiperson Narratives

Adams, Hazard. 1999. *Many Pretty Toys*. Albany: State University of New York Press.

Atwood, Margaret. 1980. *The Edible Woman*. London: Virago. (instances of multiperson shifts)

———. 2005. *The Penelopiad: The Myth of Penelope and Odysseus*. Edinburgh: Canongate. (a first-person narrative with sections in the choral we-voice)

Bucak, Ayşe Papatya. 2016. "The History of Girls." *Aster(ix): A Journal of Literature, Art, Criticism*, May 31, 2016. http://asterixjournal.com. (a we-narrative that loses its plural voice in a thematically significant shift to an "I")

Drabble, Margaret. 2003. *The Seven Sisters*. Harvest. Orlando: Harcourt. (instances of multiperson shifts)

Fernandes [pseud.], and Joyce C. Oates. 1975b. "Parricide." In *The Poisoned Kiss and Other Stories from the Portuguese*, 39–49. New York: Vanguard Press. (thematically significant shifts between "we" and "I")

Jensen, Carsten. 2011. *We, the Drowned*. Translated by Charlotte Barslund with Emma Ryder. Boston: Houghton Mifflin Harcourt. (a combination of narrative situations, including we-narrative)

Litt, Toby. 2001. *deadkidsongs*. London: Penguin. (a combination of narrative situations, including we-narrative)

Peace, David. 2010. *Occupied City*. New York: Alfred A. Knopf. (a combination of narrative situations, including we-voice)

Whalen, Tom. 1986. "The Visitation." In *Sudden Fiction*, edited by Robert Shapard and James Thomas, 141–43. Utah: Gibbs M. Smith. (a combination of narrative situations, including we-voice)

First-Person Singular Narratives

Atwood, Margaret. 1994. "We Want It All." In *Good Bones and Simple Murders*, 154–55. New York: Nan A. Talese, Doubleday. (a lyrical, impersonal narrative)

Dybek, Stuart. 1994. "We Didn't." In *Prize Stories 1994: The O. Henry Awards*, 94–107. New York: Doubleday.

Faulkner, William. 1995b [1976]. "That Will Be Fine." In *Collected Stories of William Faulkner*, 265–88. New York: Vintage International.

Theory

Aczel, Richard. 1998. "Hearing Voices in Narrative Texts." *New Literary History* 29, no. 3: 467–500.

Alber, Jan. 2011. "The Diachronic Development of Unnaturalness: A New View on Genre." In *Unnatural Narratives—Unnatural Narratology*, edited by Jan Alber and Rüdiger Heinze, 41–70. Berlin: de Gruyter.

———. 2013. "Unnatural Narratology: The Systematic Study of Anti-Mimeticism." *Literature Compass* 10, no. 5: 449–60.

———. 2015. "The Social Minds in Factual and Fictional We-Narratives of the Twentieth Century." *Narrative* 23, no. 2: 213–25.

Alber, Jan, and Rüdiger Heinze, eds. 2011. *Unnatural Narratives—Unnatural Narratology.* Berlin: de Gruyter.

Alber, Jan, Stefan Iversen, Henrik Skov Nielsen, and Brian Richardson. 2010. "Unnatural Narratives, Unnatural Narratology: Beyond Mimetic Models." *Narrative* 18, no. 2: 113–36.

———. 2012. "What Is Unnatural about Unnatural Narratology? A Response to Monika Fludernik." *Narrative* 20, no. 3: 371–82.

———. 2013. "What Really Is Unnatural Narratology?" *StoryWorlds: A Journal of Narrative Studies,* no. 5: 101–18.

Alber, Jan, Henrik Skov Nielsen, and Brian Richardson, eds. 2013. *A Poetics of Unnatural Narrative.* Columbus: The Ohio State University Press.

Alders, Maximilian. 2015. "Introduction: Social Minds in Factual and Fictional Narration." *Narrative* 23, no. 2: 113–22.

Bakhtin, M. M., and P. N. Medvedev. 1978 [1928]. *The Formal Method in Literary Scholarship: A Critical Introduction to Sociological Poetics.* Translated by A. J. Wehrle. Baltimore: Johns Hopkins University Press.

Bal, Mieke. 1985. *Narratology: Introduction to the Theory of Narrative.* Translated by Christine van Boheemen. Toronto: University of Toronto Press.

Behrendt, Poul, and Per K. Hansen. 2011. "The Fifth Mode of Representation: Ambiguous Voices in Unreliable Third-Person Narration." In *Strange Voices in Narrative Fiction,* edited by Per K. Hansen, Stefan Iversen, Henrik S. Nielsen, and Rolf Reitan, 219–50. Narratologia 30. Berlin: de Gruyter.

Bekhta, Ivan. 2004. *Дискурс наратора в англомовній прозі* [*Dyskurs naratora v anhlomovnii prozi,* Narrator's discourse in Anglophone prose fiction]. Kyiv: Hramota.

———. 2013. *Авторське експериментаторство в англомовній прозі XX століття* [*Avtors'ke eksperymentatorstvo v anhlomovnii prozi XX stolittya,* Authorial experimentation in the 20th-century prose in English]. Lviv: PAIS.

Bekhta, Natalya. 2013. "*Unnatural Narratives—Unnatural Narratology*: A Review." *Germanisch-Romanische Monatsschrift* 63, no. 1: 166–68.

———. 2015. "'Novel 'Forms of Life'—Collective Voices in Narrative Fiction: China Miéville's *Embassytown* and Chang-rae Lee's *On Such a Full Sea.*" In *Emergent Forms of Life in Contemporary English and American Fiction: Conceptual Frameworks, Cultural Contexts, and Aesthetic Explorations,* edited by Michael Basseler, Daniel Hartley, and Ansgar Nünning, 215–30. Trier: WVT.

———. 2017a. "Emerging Narrative Situations: A Definition of We-Narratives Proper." In *Emerging Vectors of Narratology,* edited by Per Krogh Hansen, John Pier, Philippe Roussin, and Wolf Schmid, 101–26. Berlin: de Gruyter.

———. 2017b. "We-Narratives: The Distinctiveness of Collective Narration." *Narrative* 25, no. 2: 164–81.

———. 2019. "Jan Alber's *Unnatural Narrative: Impossible Worlds in Fiction and Drama*: A Review." *Zeitschrift für Anglistik und Amerikanistik* 67, no. 1: 91–96.

Benveniste, Émile. 1971a. "The Nature of Pronouns." In *Problems in General Linguistics,* 218–30. Miami Linguistics Series 8. Coral Gables: University of Miami Press.

———. 1971b. *Problems in General Linguistics.* Miami Linguistics Series 8. Coral Gables: University of Miami Press.

———. 1971c. "Relationships of Person in the Verb." In *Problems in General Linguistics,* 195–204. Miami Linguistics Series 8. Coral Gables: University of Miami Press.

Bergmann, Jörg R. 1993 [1987]. *Discreet Indiscretions: The Social Organization of Gossip*. Translated by John Bednarz Jr. with the assistance of Eva Kafka Barron. New York: Aldine de Gruyter.

Bernstein, J. M. 1984. *The Philosophy of the Novel*. Minneapolis: University of Minnesota Press.

Birke, Dorothee, and Tilmann Köppe, eds. 2015. *Author and Narrator: Transdisciplinary Contributions to a Narratological Debate*. Linguae et litterae 48. Berlin, Munich: De Gruyter.

Booth, Wayne C. 1961. *The Rhetoric of Fiction*. Chicago: University of Chicago Press.

Brooks, Cleanth. 1983. *William Faulkner: First Encounters*. New Haven: Yale University Press.

Brown, Edward K., ed. 2006. *Encyclopedia of Language and Linguistics*. 2nd ed. 14 vols. Amsterdam: Elsevier.

Brown, Roger, and Albert Gilman. 1960. "The Pronouns of Power and Solidarity." In *Style in Language*, edited by Thomas A. Sebeok, 253–76. New York: The Massachusetts Institute of Technology.

Bühler, Karl. 1990 [1934]. *Theory of Language: The Representational Function of Language*. Translated by Donald Fraser Goodwin. Foundations of Semiotics 25. Amsterdam: J. Benjamins.

Caracciolo, Marco. Forthcoming. "Flocking Together: Embodiment and Fictional Engagements with Collective Animal Minds." *PMLA*.

———. 2018. "Fictional Characters, Transparency, and Experiential Sharing." *Topoi: An International Review of Philosophy*: 1–7.

Chatman, Seymour. 1975. "Towards a Theory of Narrative." *New Literary History: A Journal of Theory and Interpretation* 6, no. 2: 295–318.

———. 1978. *Story and Discourse: Narrative Structure in Fiction and Film*. Ithaca, NY: Cornell University Press.

Cohen, Anthony. 1985. *The Symbolic Construction of Community*. London: Routledge.

Cohen, Margaret. 2002 [1999]. *The Sentimental Education of the Novel*. Princeton, NJ: Princeton University Press.

Cologne-Brookes, Gavin. 2005. *Dark Eyes on America: The Novels of Joyce Carol Oates*. Baton Rouge: Louisiana State University Press.

Coste, Didier. 1989. *Narrative as Communication*. Minneapolis: University of Minnesota Press.

Costello, Bonnie. 2012. "The Plural of Us: Uses and Abuses of an Ambiguous Pronoun." *Jacket2*, January 6, 2012. http://jacket2.org.

———. 2017. *The Plural of Us: Poetry and Community in Auden and Others*. Princeton, NJ: Princeton University Press.

Culler, Jonathan. 1975. *Structuralist Poetics: Structuralism, Linguistics and the Study of Literature*. London: Routledge & Kegan Paul.

———. 2007. *The Literary in Theory*. Stanford, CA: Stanford University Press.

DeLillo, Don. 2011 [1985]. *White Noise*. London: Picador.

Dieltjens, Sylvain, and Priscilla Heynderickx. 2007. "Strategic Uses of the Pronoun We in Business Communication." In *Discourse, Ideology and Specialized Communication*, edited by Giuliana Garzone and Srikant Sarangi, 233–49. Linguistic Insights: Studies in Language and Communication 33. Bern: Peter Lang.

Doležel, Lubomír. 1967. "The Typology of the Narrator: Point of View in Fiction." In *To Honor Roman Jakobson*, Vol. 1, 541–52. The Hague: Mouton.

Fillmore, Charles. 1971. "Toward a Theory of Deixis." *Working Papers in Linguistics, University of Hawaii* 3, no. 4: 219–42.

——. 1998. *Lectures on Deixis*. Stanford, CA: Center for the Study of Linguistics and Information.

Fludernik, Monika. 1991. "Shifters and Deixis: Some Reflections on Jakobson, Jespersen, and Reference." *Semiotica* 86, no. 3–4: 193–230.

——. 1994a. "Introduction: Second-Person Narrative and Related Issues." *Style* 28, no. 3: 281–311.

——. 1994b. "Second-Person Narrative as a Test Case for Narratology: The Limits of Realism." *Style* 28, no. 3: 445–79.

——. 1996. *Towards a "Natural" Narratology*. London: Routledge.

——. 2011. "The Category of 'Person' in Fiction: You and We Narrative-Multiplicity and Indeterminacy of Reference." In *Current Trends in Narratology,* edited by Greta Olson and Monika Fludernik, 100–41. Berlin: de Gruyter.

——. 2012. "How Natural Is "Unnatural Narratology"; or, What Is Unnatural about Unnatural Narratology?" *Narrative* 20, no. 3: 357–70.

——. 2017. "The Many in Action and Thought: Towards a Poetics of the Collective in Narrative." *Narrative* 25, no. 2: 139–63.

——. 2018. "Let Us Tell You Our Story: *We*-Narration and Its Pronominal Peculiarities." In *Pronouns in Literature: Positions and Perspectives in Language,* edited by Alison Gibbons and Andrea Macrae, 171–92. London: Palgrave Macmillan.

Foley, Barbara. 1993. *Radical Representations: Politics and Form in US Proletarian Fiction, 1929–1941*. Durham: Duke University Press.

Fredner, Erik. 2017. "How Many Novels Have Been Published in English? (An Attempt)." *Stanford Literary Lab.* https://litlanb.stanford.edu.

Fritsch, Esther. 2008. "Gossip." In *Routledge Encyclopedia of Narrative Theory,* edited by David Herman, Manfred Jahn, and Marie-Laure Ryan, 207–8. London: Routledge.

Fulton, Dawn. 2003. "'Romans des Nous': The First Person Plural and Collective Identity in Martinique." *The French Review* 76, no. 6: 1104–14.

Gallotti, Mattia, and Raphael Lyne. 2019. "The Individual 'We' Narrator." *British Journal of Aesthetics* 59, no. 2: 179–95.

Genette, Gérard. 1980. *Narrative Discourse: An Essay in Method*. Ithaca, NY: Cornell University Press.

——. 1988. *Narrative Discourse Revisited*. Ithaca, NY: Cornell University Press.

Gray, John. 2010. "We the Living." *NewStatesman,* July 19, 2010. https://www.newstatesman.com/books/2010/07/ayn-rand-greenspan-influence.

Hakli, Raul, Kaarlo Miller, and Raimo Tuomela. 2010. "Two Kinds of We-Reasoning." *Economics and Philosophy* 26, no. 3: 291–320.

Halliwell, Stephen. 2013. "Diegesis—Mimesis." In *the living handbook of narratology,* edited by Peter Hühn, Jan C. Meister, John Pier, and Wolf Schmid. Hamburg: Hamburg University. http://www.lhn.uni-hamburg.de.

Hanks, William F. 2008. "Deixis." In *Routledge Encyclopedia of Narrative Theory,* edited by David Herman, Manfred Jahn, and Marie-Laure Ryan, 99–100. London: Routledge.

Hansen, Per K. 2007. "Reconsidering the Unreliable Narrator." *Semiotica* 165, no. 1/4: 227–46.

———. 2011. "Backmasked Messages: On the Fabula Construction in Episodically Reversed Narratives." In *Unnatural Narratives—Unnatural Narratology,* edited by Jan Alber and Rüdiger Heinze, 162–85. Berlin: de Gruyter.

Hartley, Daniel. 2016. *The Politics of Style: Towards a Marxist Poetics.* Leiden: Brill.

Haverkate, Henk. 1984. *Speech Acts, Speakers and Hearers: Reference and Referential Strategies in Spanish.* Amsterdam: John Benjamins.

Helmbrecht, Johannes. 2002. "Grammar and Function of We." In *Us and Others: Social Identities across Languages, Discourses and Cultures,* edited by Anna Duszak, 31–49. Pragmatics & Beyond Series 98. Amsterdam: John Benjamins.

Herman, David, James Phelan, Peter J. Rabinowitz, Brian Richardson, and Robyn R. Warhol, eds. 2012. *Narrative Theory: Core Concepts and Critical Debates.* Theory and Interpretation of Narrative. Columbus: The Ohio State University Press.

Heyd, Theresa. 2011. "Unreliability. The Pragmatic Perspective Revisited." *Journal of Literary Theory* 5, no. 1: 3–17.

Hicks, Granville. 1974. "Complex and Collective Novels." In *Granville Hicks in the New Masses,* edited by Jack A. Robbins, 26–32. Port Washington, NY: Kennikat Press.

Hogan, Patrick C. 2013. *Narrative Discourse: Authors and Narrators in Literature, Film, and Art.* Theory and Interpretation of Narrative. Columbus: The Ohio State University Press.

Jahn, Manfred. 2012. "Comment on Klauk and Köppe." In Tilmann Köppe and Tobias Klauk "Puzzles and Problems for the Theory of Focalization," in *the living handbook of narratology,* edited by Peter Hühn, Jan C. Meister, John Pier, and Wolf Schmid. Hamburg: Hamburg University. http://www.lhn.uni-hamburg.de/.

Jakobson, Roman. 1987. *Language in Literature.* Edited by Krystyna Pomorska and Stephen Rudy. Cambridge, MA: The Belknap Press of Harvard University Press.

Jameson, Fredric. 2001 [1981]. *The Political Unconscious: Narrative as a Socially Symbolic Act.* London: Routledge Classics.

———. 2017. Foreword to *Simple Forms,* by André Jolles, translated by Peter Schwartz, vii–xviii. London: Verso.

Jespersen, Otto. 1958 [1924]. *The Philosophy of Grammar.* London: George Allen & Unwin.

Kempton, Kenneth P. 1947. *The Short Story.* Cambridge, MA: Harvard University Press.

Kindt, Tom. 2008. *Unzuverlässiges Erzählen und literarische Moderne: Eine Untersuchung der Romane Ernst Weiss.* Studien zur deutschen Literatur 184. Tübingen: Max Niemeyer.

Klauk, Tobias. 2011. "Can Unreliable Narration Be Analyzed in Terms of Testimony?" *Journal of Literary Theory* 5, no. 1: 37–56.

Klauk, Tobias, and Tilmann Köppe. 2013. "Reassessing Unnatural Narratology: Problems and Prospects." *StoryWorlds: A Journal of Narrative Studies,* no. 5: 77–100.

Köppe, Tilmann, and Tom Kindt. 2011. "Unreliable Narration With a Narrator and Without." *Journal of Literary Theory* 5, no. 1: 81–93.

Köppe, Tilmann, and Jan Stühring. 2011. "Against Pan-Narrator Theories." *Journal of Literary Semantics* 40, no. 1: 59–80.

Korthals Altes, Liesbeth. 2014. *Ethos and Narrative Interpretation: The Negotiation of Values in Fiction.* Lincoln: University of Nebraska Press.

Lanser, Susan S. 1992. *Fictions of Authority: Women Writers and Narrative Voice.* Ithaca, NY: Cornell University Press.

Marcus, Amit. 2008a. "A Contextual View of Narrative Fiction in the First Person Plural." *Narrative* 16, no. 1: 46–64.

———. 2008b. "Dialogue and Authoritativeness in 'We' Fictional Narratives: A Bakhtinian Approach." *Partial Answers: Journal of Literature and the History of Ideas* 6, no. 1: 135–61.

———. 2008c. "We Are You: The Plural and the Dual in 'We' Fictional Narratives." *Journal of Literary Semantics* 37, no. 1: 1–21.

Margolin, Uri. 1996. "Telling Our Story: On 'We' Literary Narratives." *Language and Literature* 5, no. 2: 115–33.

———. 2000. "Telling in the Plural: From Grammar to Ideology." *Poetics Today* 21, no. 3: 591–618.

———. 2001. "Collective Perspective, Individual Perspective, and the Speaker in Between: On 'We' Literary Narratives." In *New Perspectives on Narrative Perspective*, edited by Willie van Peer and Seymour Chatman, 241–54. Albany, NY: SUNY Press.

———. 2011. "Narrator." In *the living handbook of narratology*, edited by Peter Hühn, Jan C. Meister, John Pier, and Wolf Schmid. Hamburg: Hamburg University. http://www.lhn.uni -hamburg.de.

Mathiesen, Kay. 2007. "Introduction to Special Issue of Social Epistemology on 'Collective Knowledge and Collective Knowers.'" *Social Epistemology* 21, no. 3: 209–16.

Max, T. D. 1999. "Class Reunion: A Review of *Broke Heart Blues*." *The New York Times*, August 8, 1999. https://archive.nytimes.com/www.nytimes.com/books.

Maxey, Ruth. 2015. "The Rise of the 'We' Narrator in Modern American Fiction." *ejas* 10, no. 2. https://dx.doi.org/10.4000/ejas.11068.

———. 2016. "National Stories and Narrative Voice in the Fiction of Joshua Ferris." *Crit* 57, no. 2: 208–16.

McGurl, Mark. 2009. *The Program Era: Postwar Fiction and the Rise of Creative Writing*. Cambridge, MA: Harvard University Press.

Meindl, Dieter. 2004. "(Un-)Reliable Narration from a Pronominal Perspective." In *The Dynamics of Narrative Form: Studies in Anglo-American narratology*, edited by John Pier, 59–82. Narratologia 4. Berlin: de Gruyter.

Miller, J. H. 2005. "Henry James and 'Focalization,' or Why James Loves Gyp." In *A Companion to Narrative Theory*, edited by James Phelan and Peter Rabinowitz, 124–35. Blackwell Companions to Literature and Culture 33. Malden, MA: Blackwell.

Miller, Laura. 2004. "The Last Word; We the Characters." *New York Times*, April 18, 2004. https://www.nytimes.com/2004/04/18/books.

Neumann, Birgit, and Ansgar Nünning. 2008. *An Introduction to the Study of Narrative Fiction*. Stuttgart: Klett Lernen und Wissen.

Niederhoff, Burkhard. 2011a. "Focalization." In *the living handbook of narratology*, edited by Peter Hühn, Jan C. Meister, John Pier, and Wolf Schmid. Hamburg: Hamburg University. http://www.lhn.uni-hamburg.de.

———. 2011b. "Perspective—Point of View." In *the living handbook of narratology*, edited by Peter Hühn, Jan C. Meister, John Pier, and Wolf Schmid. Hamburg: Hamburg University. http://www.lhn.uni-hamburg.de.

Nielsen, Henrik Skov. 2011. "Unnatural Narratology, Impersonal Voices, Real Authors, and Non-Communicative Narration." In *Unnatural Narratives—Unnatural Narratology*, edited by Jan Alber and Rüdiger Heinze, 71–88. Berlin: de Gruyter.

———. 2013. "Naturalizing and Unnaturalizing Reading Strategies: Focalization Revisited." In *A Poetics of Unnatural Narrative*, edited by Jan Alber, Henrik Skov Nielsen, and Brian Richardson, 67–93. Theory and Interpretation of Narrative. Columbus: The Ohio State University Press.

Nünning, Ansgar. 1999. "Unreliable, Compared to What? Towards a Cognitive Theory of *Unreliable Narration*: Prolegomena and Hypotheses." In *Transcending Boundaries: Narratology in Context*, edited by Walter Grünzweig and Andreas Solbach, 53–73. Tübingen: Narr.

———. 2001. "On Perspective Structure of Narrative Texts: Steps toward a Constructivist Narratology." In *New Perspectives on Narrative Perspective*, edited by Willie van Peer and Seymour Chatman, 207–24. Albany, NY: SUNY Press.

———. 2005. "Reconceptualizing Unreliable Narration: Synthesizing Cognitive and Rhetorical Approaches." In *A Companion to Narrative Theory*, edited by James Phelan and Peter Rabinowitz, 89–107. Malden, MA: Blackwell.

———. 2008. "Reconceptualizing the Theory, History and Generic Scope of Unreliable Narration: Towards a Synthesis of Cognitive and Rhetorical Approaches." In *Narrative Unreliability in the Twentieth-Century First-Person Novel*, edited by Elke D'hoker and Gunther Martens, 29–76. Narratologia: 14. Berlin: de Gruyter.

Nünning, Vera. 2013. "*Unreliable Narration* als Schlüsselkonzept und Testfall für neue Entwicklungen der Postklassischen Narratologie: Ansätze, Erklärungen und Desiderata." *Germanisch-Romanische Monatsschrift* 63, no. 1: 135–60.

———, ed. 2015. *Unreliable Narration and Trustworthiness: Intermedial and Interdisciplinary Perspectives*. Narratologia 44. Berlin: de Gruyter.

Nünning, Vera, and Ansgar Nünning. 2000. "Von ‚der' Erzählperspektive zur Perspektivenstruktur narrativer Texte: Überlegungen zur Definition, Konzeptualisierung und Untersuchbarkeit von Multiperspektivität." In *Multiperspektivisches Erzählen: Zur Theorie und Geschichte der Perspektivenstruktur im englischen Roman des 18. bis 20. Jahrhunderts,* edited by Vera Nünning and Ansgar Nünning, 3–38. Tier: Wissenschftlicher Verlag Trier.

Oliver, John. 2014. "Last Week Tonight." Season 1, Episode 19. October 9, 2014. HBO.

Olson, Greta. 2003. "Reconsidering Unreliability: Fallible and Untrustworthy Narrators." *Narrative* 11, no. 1: 93–109.

———. 2018. "Questioning the Ideology of Reliability in Mohsin Hamid's *The Reluctant Fundamentalist*: Towards a Critical, Culturalist Narratology." In *Narratology and Ideology: Negotiating Context, Form, and Theory in Postcolonial Narratives*, edited by Divya Dwivedi, Henrik S. Nielsen, and Richard Walsh, 156–72. Columbus: The Ohio State University Press.

Paine, Robert. 1967. "What Is Gossip About? An Alternative Hypothesis." *Man*, no. 2: 278–85.

Palmer, Alan. 2005. "Intermental Thought in the Novel: The Middlemarch Mind." *Style* 39, no. 4: 427–39.

———. 2011. "Social Minds in Fiction and Criticism." *Style* 45, no. 2: 196–240.

Patron, Sylvie. 2009. *Le Narrateur: Introduction à la théorie narrative*. Paris: Armand Colin.

———. 2010. "The Death of the Narrator and the Interpretation of the Novel: The Example of 'Pedro Páramo' by Juan Rulfo." *Journal of Literary Theory* 4, no. 2: 253–72.

———. 2011. "Enunciative Narratology: A French Speciality." In *Current Trends in Narratology*, edited by Greta Olson and Monika Fludernik, 312–35. Berlin: de Gruyter.

———. 2017. "Narrator." Talk at the conference "Fictionality in Literature: Core Concepts Revisited," Aarhus, Denmark, May 3.

Patron, Sylvie, and Susan Nicholls. 2013. "Unspeakable Sentences: Narration and Representation in Benedetti's 'Five Years of Life.'" *Narrative* 21, no. 2: 243–62.

Phelan, James. 1994. "Self-Help for Narratee and Narrative Audience: How 'I'—and 'You'?—Read 'How.'" *Style* 28, no. 3: 350–65.

———. 1996. *Narrative as Rhetoric: Technique, Audiences, Ethics, Ideology.* Columbus: The Ohio State University Press.

———. 2001. "Why Narrators Can Be Focalizers—and Why It Matters." In *New Perspectives on Narrative Perspective,* edited by Willie van Peer and Seymour Chatman, 51–64. Albany, NY: SUNY Press.

———. 2005. *Living to Tell about It: A Rhetoric and Ethics of Character Narration.* Ithaca, NY: Cornell University Press.

———. 2007. "Rhetoric/Ethics." In *The Cambridge Companion to Narrative,* edited by David Herman, 203–16. Cambridge: Cambridge University Press.

———. 2011. "Rhetoric, Ethics, and Narrative Communication: Or, from Story and Discourse to Authors, Resources, and Audiences." *Soundings: An Interdisciplinary Journal* 94, no. 1/2: 55–75.

———. 2013. "Implausibilities, Crossovers, and Impossibilities: A Rhetorical Approach to Breaks in the Code of Mimetic Character Narration." In *A Poetics of Unnatural Narrative,* edited by Jan Alber, Henrik Skov Nielsen, and Brian Richardson, 167–84. Theory and Interpretation of Narrative. Columbus: The Ohio State University Press.

———. 2017. *Somebody Telling Somebody Else: A Rhetorical Poetics of Narrative.* Columbus: The Ohio State University Press.

Poague, Leland A., and Kathy A. Parsons. 2000. *Susan Sontag: An Annotated Bibliography, 1948–1992.* Modern Critics and Critical Studies 22. New York: Garland.

Prince, Gerald. 1982. *Narratology: The Form and Functioning of Narrative.* Berlin: Mouton.

———. 1988 [1987]. *A Dictionary of Narratology.* Aldershot: Scolar.

Rabinowitz, Peter J. 1977. "Truth in Fiction: A Reexamination of Audiences." *Critical Inquiry* 4, no. 1: 121–41.

Reitan, Rolf. 2011. "Theorizing Second-Person Narratives: A Backwater Project?" In *Strange Voices in Narrative Fiction,* edited by Per K. Hansen, Stefan Iversen, Henrik S. Nielsen, and Rolf Reitan, 147–74. Narratologia 30. Berlin: de Gruyter.

Richardson, Brian. 1994. "*I Etcetera*: On the Poetics and Ideology of Multipersoned Narratives." *Style* 28, no. 3: 312–28.

———. 2006. *Unnatural Voices: Extreme Narration in Modern and Contemporary Fiction.* Theory and Interpretation of Narrative Series. Columbus: The Ohio State University Press.

———. 2009. "Plural Focalization, Singular Voices: Wandering Perspectives in 'We'-Narration." In *Point of View, Perspective, and Focalization: Modeling Mediation in Narrative,* edited by Peter Hühn, Wolf Schmid, and Jörg Schönert, 143–59. Narratologia 17. Berlin: de Gruyter.

———. 2011. "What Is Unnatural Narrative Theory?" In *Unnatural Narratives—Unnatural Narratology,* edited by Jan Alber and Rüdiger Heinze, 23–40. Berlin: de Gruyter.

———. 2015. "Representing Social Minds: 'We' and 'They' Narratives, Natural and Unnatural." *Narrative* 23, no. 2: 200–12.

———. 2016. "Unnatural Narrative Theory." *Style* 50, no. 4: 385–405.

Riffaterre, Michael. 1990. *Fictional Truth.* Parallax: Re-Visions of Culture and Society. Baltimore: Johns Hopkins University Press.

Rimmon-Kenan, Shlomith. 2008. *Narrative Fiction: Contemporary Poetics*. 2nd ed., reprinted. London: Routledge.

Rivarola, José L. 1984. "¿Quién es nosotros?" *Estudios de Lingüística*, no. 2: 201–6.

Robertson, Alice. 2006. "The Ultimate Voyeur: The Communal Narrator of 'A Rose for Emily.'" *ESTSF* 6, no. 2: 154–65.

Sapolsky, Robert M. 2017. *Behave: The Biology of Humans at Our Best and Worst*. New York: Penguin Books.

Shaw, Harry E. 2005. "Why Won't Our Terms Stay Put? The Narrative Communication Diagram Scrutinized and Historicized." In *A Companion to Narrative Theory*, edited by James Phelan and Peter Rabinowitz, 299–311. Malden, MA: Blackwell.

Shen, Dan. 2011. "Unreliability." In *the living handbook of narratology*, edited by Peter Hühn, Jan C. Meister, John Pier, and Wolf Schmid. Hamburg: Hamburg University. http://www.lhn. uni-hamburg.de.

Skei, Hans. 1999. *Reading Faulkner's Best Short Stories*. Columbia: University of South Carolina Press.

Skinner, John L. 1985. "'A Rose for Emily': Against Interpretation." *JNT* 15, no. 1: 42–51.

Sontag, Susan. 1966. "Against Interpretation." In *Against Interpretation and Other Essays*, 2–14. New York: Farrar, Straus and Giroux.

Stanzel, Franz K. 1978. "Second Thoughts on 'Narrative Situations in the Novel': Towards a 'Grammar of Fiction.'" *NOVEL: A Forum on Fiction* 11, no. 3: 247–64.

———. 1981. "Teller-Characters and Reflector-Characters in Narrative Theory." *Poetics Today*, no. 2: 5–15.

———. 1984. *A Theory of Narrative*. Cambridge: Cambridge University Press.

———. 1991 [1979]. *Theorie des Erzählens*. 5th ed. Göttingen: Vandenhoeck & Ruprecht.

Steffens, Niklas, and Alexander Haslam. 2013. "Power through 'Us': Leaders' Use of We-Referencing Language Predicts Election Victory." *PloS ONE* 8, no. 10: e77952. https://dx.doi. org/10.1371%2Fjournal.pone.0077952.

Stockwell, Peter. 2002. *Cognitive Poetics: An Introduction*. Hoboken: Routledge.

Sullivan, Ruth. 1971. "The Narrator in 'A Rose for Emily.'" *JNT*, no. 1: 159–78.

Tanaka, Kei. 2004. "Japanese Picture Marriage and the Image of Immigrant Women in Early Twentieth-Century California." *The Japanese Journal of American Studies*, no. 15: 115–38.

Towner, Theresa M., and James B. Carothers. 2006. *Reading Faulkner: Glossary and Commentary*. Jackson: University Press of Mississippi.

Tuomela, Raimo. 2004. "Group Knowledge Analyzed." *Episteme* 1, no. 2: 109–27.

———. 2007. *The Philosophy of Sociality: The Shared Point of View*. Oxford: Oxford University Press.

———. 2013. "Who Is Afraid of Group Agents and Group Minds?" In *The Background of Social Reality*, edited by Michael Schmitz, Beatrice Kobow and Hans B. Schmid, 13–35. Dordrecht: Springer Netherlands.

van Peer, Willie, and Seymour Chatman, eds. 2001. *New Perspectives on Narrative Perspective*. Albany, NY: SUNY Press.

van Wyk, Johan. 1997. "Catastrophe and Beauty: 'Ways of Dying,' Zakes Mda's Novel of the Transition." *Literator* 18, no. 3: 79–90.

Vogt, Robert. 2015. "Combining Possible-Worlds Theory and Cognitive Theory: Towards an Explanatory Model for Ironic-Unreliable Narration, Ironic-Unreliable Focalization, Ambiguous-Unreliable and Alterated-Unreliable Narration in Literary Fiction." In *Unreliable Narration and Trustworthiness: Intermedial and Interdisciplinary Perspectives,* edited by Vera Nünning, 131–53. Berlin: de Gruyter.

Walsh, Richard. 1997. "Who Is the Narrator?" *Poetics Today* 18, no. 4: 495–513.

———. 2007. *The Rhetoric of Fictionality: Narrative Theory and the Idea of Fiction.* Theory and Interpretation of Narrative. Columbus: The Ohio State University Press.

———. 2010. "Person, Level, Voice: A Rhetorical Reconsideration." In *Postclassical Narratology: Approaches and Analyses,* edited by Jan Alber and Monika Fludernik, 35–57. Columbus: The Ohio State University Press.

———. 2017. "Beyond Fictional Worlds: Narrative and Spatial Cognition." In *Emerging Vectors of Narratology,* edited by Per Krogh Hansen, John Pier, Philippe Roussin, and Wolf Schmid, 461–78. Berlin: de Gruyter.

Williams, Raymond. 1985 [1983]. *Keywords: A Vocabulary of Culture and Society.* Oxford: Oxford University Press.

Woller, Joel. 1999. "First-Person Plural: The Voice of the Masses in Farm Security Administration Documentary." *Journal of Narrative Theory* 29, no. 3: 340–66.

INDEX

action, collective, 9–10, 25, 77, 84, 96, 101, 139, 180

Aczel, Richard, 72n10, 73n12

Adams, Hazard, 33, 46, 148–49

"Against Interpretation" (Sontag), 95

Alber, Jan, 41, 42n14–42n15, 42n18, 111n5

"Allouma" (Maupassant), 70n5

Anthem (Rand), 32n9

antimimesis, 42n15, 69

Apuleius, 70n5, 133n1

Atelier de Marie-Claire, L' (Audoux), 2n1

Atonement (McEwan), 35n10

Atwood, Margaret, 37, 51–52, 51n4, 97–98, 149

Audoux, Marguerite, 2n1

author: fictive, 128; "I" of, 70; implied, 72, 85, 129, 151n8; narrator and, 70–71, 71n8, 73–75, 74n14, 140; in *pluralis auctoris*, 54; unreliability and, 154, 154n14

authorial narrator, 136, 140, 157

authorial voice, 23, 23n2

"Baby" (Sontag), 68, 84–86, 91–98

Bal, Mieke, 71n8

Barthes, Roland, 41, 44

Bekhta, Ivan, 68n2, 82n20

Benveniste, Émile, 57, 57n9, 58

Bergmann, Jörg R., 145

Bernstein, J. M., 53

Booth, Wayne, 151, 153n13

Borges, Jorge Luis, 35n10

"Brain of Dr. Vicente, The" (Oates), 22, 24–25

Broke Heart Blues (Oates), 2, 40, 45, 76, 134, 137; associative chronology in, 95; collective knowledge in, 144, 150, 160–63; as communal, 33; focalization in, 114–16; voyeurism and, 114–18

Bucak, Ayşe Papatya, 52n5

Buddha in the Attic, The (Otsuka), 2, 52, 64, 68; as communal, 33; direct speech in, 98; lyric progression in, 84–86; plural narrator in, 86–91

Carothers, James B., 5n4

cataphoric we-reference, 27–28, 56n8

character dialogue, 91n25, 92–93, 99, 102, 182

Chase, Joan, 23n3

Chatman, Seymour, 68n3, 70n6, 107

chorus, 51–52

Christie, Agatha, 152n10

Cohen, Anthony, 30, 33, 135–36

collective action, 9–10, 25, 77, 84, 96, 101, 139, 180

collective identity, 16, 53, 90

collective knowledge. *See* knowledge; collective

collective voice, 1–3, 6n6, 23, 29, 53, 83–84, 134–35, 143, 182

collectivity condition, 15–16, 112, 149, 182

communal narration, 166–75

communal voice, 2n1, 7, 21–23, 23nn2–3, 26, 29, 134, 140–42

communication: gossip as, 145; narrative, 43, 50, 69–71, 70n6, 74, 74n13, 75, 81, 129, 182; unreliability and, 152; "we" and, 59

community: in *Broke Heart Blues*, 160; in *Buddha in the Attic, The*, 87–88; collective knowledge and, 142–44; defined, 30; institutional, 33; as narrator, 2–3; in "A Rose for Emily," 7, 115, 117–18, 138, 145, 155–57; in *Virgin Suicides, The*, 110; voice and, 76; in "Watch the Animals," 166–75; in *Ways of Dying*, 139, 142–43; "we" and, 53

Conrad, Joseph, 2n1, 69, 74n12, 126

Coste, Didier, 69, 70n5, 71n8, 72, 178n4

Costello, Bonnie, 29n7, 32n9, 48n1, 51

Country of the Pointed Firs, The (Jewett), 2n1

Cranford (Gaskell), 2n1, 23n3

Culler, Jonathan, 42n18

Dark, Alice Elliott, 165–75

deadkidsongs (Litt), 36, 68–69, 84n22, 103, 106, 110; collective knowledge and, 148; community in, 33–34; ethos and, 113; focalization in, 122–32, 127 fig. 1, 127 fig. 2; narrative situation and, 6n8, 40; plural narration and, 76–83; unreliability and, 150, 152n10

deixis, 56–60, 56n8

DeLillo, Don, 91, 96

dialogue, 91n25, 92–93, 99, 102, 182

diegesis, 14, 81, 81n19, 82n21, 140, 183. *See also* heterodiegesis; homodiegesis

diegetic levels, 119–22, 119n7

diegetic voice, 81, 81n19

direct speech: in *Broke Heart Blues*, 162; in "That Will Be Fine," 28; in "Watch the Animals," 170; in *Ways of Dying*, 139, 141; in we-narratives, 83–86; of we-narrator, 98–102. *See also* character dialogue

Dorris, Michael, 22, 37

Drabble, Margaret, 37

During the Reign of the Queen of Persia (Chase), 23n3

Dybek, Stuart, 61–62

Edible Woman, The (Atwood), 37

Embassytown (Miéville), 2

epistemology. *See* knowledge

Erdrich, Louise, 23n3

ethics, 4n3; of communal narration, 171–75; focalization and, 107; and reader-narrator engagement, 71, 82, 85; unreliability and, 150–56

ethos, 113–14, 113n6

Eugenides, Jeffrey. See *Virgin Suicides, The* (Eugenides)

Fates Will Find Their Way, The (Pittard), 2

Faulkner, William. *See* "A Rose for Emily, A" (Faulkner); "That Will Be Fine" (Faulkner)

Ferris, Joshua. See *Then We Came to the End* (Ferris)

fictionality, 70–75, 71n7, 80–81, 82n21, 83, 128

figural mode, 40

figural narrative situation, 41, 78, 120, 130, 161, 184

first-person narrative: in *deadkidsongs*, 122; focalization and, 106; "I" in, 57–58; knowledge claims in, 133; with plural narration, 26; "we" in, 24, 28–29, 50; we-narrative *vs.*, 19, 39–40. *See also* I-narrator

first-person plural narrative. *See* we-narrative

first-person plural pronoun. *See* "we"; we-reference

Fludernik, Monika, 13n15, 19, 19n17, 22–23, 42nn14, 17, 42–43, 45, 52, 72n10, 121–22, 177n1

focalization, 9–10, 69, 103–6; in *Broke Heart Blues*, 114–18; collective, 26–27, 90, 105,

109, 111; in *deadkidsongs* (Litt), 122–32, 127 fig. 1, 127 fig. 2; defined, 103, 107, 107nn3–4, 132; ethos and, 113–14, 113n6; external, 27, 44, 120; internal, 40, 76, 120; narration and, 78; social mind and, 111–12, 111n5; voice and, 82n21; voyeurism and, 114–15; we-narrators as focalizers, 77, 106–14. *See also* perspective

Foley, Barbara, 33, 154n14

Fritsch, Esther, 143

Fulton, Dawn, 59, 63

Gaskell, Elizabeth, 2n1, 23n3

gendering, of narrator, 5–6

Genette, Gérard, 13, 41, 43–44, 60–61, 68, 70, 72, 76, 106–7, 107n2, 119, 119n7, 127–28, 127n9

Golden Ass, The (Apuleius), 70n5, 133n1

gossip, 142–46, 170–71

Greimas, Algirdas Julien, 41

group narration, 134, 149

groupness, 16–17, 29, 90, 131

Guérillères, Les (Wittig), 2n1

Hansen, Per Krogh, 43

Haslam, Alexander, 49

Hawthorne, Nathaniel, 179n6

Heinze, Rüdiger, 41, 42n15

Helmbrecht, Johannes, 53

Hernadi, Paul, 13n13

heterodiegesis, 14, 78, 80, 119–21, 128, 182–83

Heyd, Theresa, 152n10

Hicks, Granville, 33–34, 90

"History of Girls, The" (Bucak), 52n5

Hogan, Patrick Colm, 134–35

homodiegesis, 14, 44, 50, 76, 79, 106, 119–21, 125–26, 132, 182–83

I-mode, 15, 24n5, 136

I-narrator: focalization and, 109; knowledge claims with, 133; we-narrator as covert, 57–58; we-references by, 16, 19n17, 22–24, 24n5, 39, 50, 61; as yardstick for we-narrative, 21–22. *See also* first-person narrative

Iversen, Stefan, 42n14

Jameson, Fredric, 61n16, 179

Jensen, Carsten, 30n8, 142

Jespersen, Otto, 59–60

Jewett, Sarah Orne, 2n1

Kindt, Tom, 151n9, 152, 152n10

Klauk, Tobias, 42n14, 71

knowledge: philosophical conception of, 136–37

knowledge, collective, 183; community and, 142–43; gossip and, 142–46; groupness and, 135–36; as problematic, 134–36; thematization of, 137–38; as transgressive, 134, 146–49; unreliability and, 149–63; in *Ways of Dying*, 138–44, 141 fig. 3

Köppe, Tilmann, 42n14, 68n2, 71n7, 81n19, 151n9, 152

Korthals Altes, Liesbeth, 113n6

Labov, William, 42, 42n17

Lanser, Susan, 2n1, 3n2, 18, 21–23, 23n3, 134

Lee, Chang-rae. See *On Such a Full Sea* (Lee)

Life of Pi (Martel), 152n10

Lintvelt, Jaap, 73n11

Litt, Toby. See *deadkidsongs* (Litt)

Lolita (Nabokov), 153n12

Lorentz, Pare, 31

Love Medicine (Erdrich), 23n3

lyric poetry, 51–52

lyric progression, 62, 64, 67, 83–86, 181

lyricality, 84n22

Many Pretty Toys (Adams), 33, 46, 148–49

Marcus, Amit, 18, 22–23, 39

Margolin, Uri, 3n2, 8, 16n16, 18, 21–22, 24n5, 25n6, 34, 36, 50, 58, 61n17, 98, 99n26, 108–9

Martel, Yann, 152n10

Maupassant, Guy de, 70n5

Max, T. D., 45

Maxey, Ruth, 177n2, 178, 178n4, 179n6

McEwan, Ian, 35n10

Mda, Zakes, 2, 6n6, 33, 134–44, 146–48

mediacy, 12–13, 29, 37n11, 72, 72n9, 75n16, 78, 81

Meindl, Dieter, 149–50

Merrill, James, 29n7

Miéville, China, 1–2

Miller, J. H., 108

Miller, Laura, 32

mimesis, 42n15, 44–45, 45n20, 74, 80–82, 140, 183; mimetic voice (Walsh), 74, 80–82

mimetic component of narrative (Phelan), 6n6, 45–46, 82. *See also* synthetic; thematic

multiperson: *deadkidsongs* as, 123; examples of, 34; narration, 36–37, 37n11, 179; narrative, 35n10, 36–41, 180; types of, 37; we-narrative *vs.*, 16–17, 22; we-references in, 24

multiperspectivity, 37n11

Murder of Roger Ackroyd, The (Christie), 152n10

Nabokov, Vladimir, 153n12

narration: communal, 166–75; group, 134, 149; mediacy and, 13; multiperson, 36–37, 37n11, 179; narrative *vs.*, 39, 39n13; perspectival choices and, 103

narrative: narration *vs.*, 39, 39n13; natural, 42–43, 42n17; second-person, 13n15, 19, 35n10, 52n6, 120; third-person, 29, 39, 57n9, 70, 105, 121, 141, 183; "unnatural," 41–46. *See also* multiperson

narrative communication, 43, 50, 69–71, 70n6, 74, 74n13, 75, 81, 129, 182

narrative discourse, 39, 58, 60–61, 68n3

narrative freedom, 106, 120, 183

narrative progression, 8, 63, 82, 84–85

narrative representation, 71–74, 74n14, 80–81, 184

narrative situation, 12n11, 13–14, 13n15, 36, 41, 56, 72, 85, 123, 146, 180. *See also* figural narrative situation; first-person narrative; we-narrative; *specific narrative situations*

narrator: author and, 70–71, 71n8, 73–75, 74n14, 140; authorial, 136, 140, 157; existence of, 68–69; fictionality and, 70–72, 71n7; gendering of, 5–6; mediacy and, 13, 72; mimetic bias and, 44. *See also* I-narrator; plural narrator; we-narrator

Nesbit, TaraShea, 2, 33

Neumann, Brigit, 107n4

Niederhoff, Burkhard, 107

Nielsen, Henrik Skov, 41, 42n14, 42n18, 133n1

Niffenegger, Audrey, 35n10

Nigger of the "Narcissus": A Tale of the Sea (Conrad), 2n1, 69, 74n12, 126

nonfiction, 17, 37, 50, 52–54, 70–71, 71n7, 109, 129, 179

number (grammatical), 59n13

Nünning, Ansgar, ix, 37, 103, 151n6, 151n8, 107n4

Nünning, Vera, 37, 151n6, 153

Oates, Joyce Carol, 178n5. *See also* "Brain of Dr. Vicente, The" (Oates); *Broke Heart Blues* (Oates); "Parricide" (Oates)

Occupied City (Peace), 52, 149

"Old News" (Hawthorne), 179n6

Olson, Greta, 153, 153n13, 154, 159

On Such a Full Sea (Lee), 2

Otsuka, Julie. See *Buddha in the Attic, The* (Otsuka)

Our Kind (Walbert), 2

Palmer, Alan, 72, 103, 111

"Parricide" (Oates), 22, 25–28, 34, 36–37, 40, 63, 65

Parsons, Kathy A., 94

Patron, Sylvie, 68n2, 73–74, 74n14

Peace, David, 52, 149

Pedro Páramo (Rulfo), 73

Penelopiad, The (Atwood), 51–52, 51n4, 149

performative mode, 11, 65

performative "we," 14–15, 19, 25, 36, 49–50, 50n2, 52–53, 60–65, 83, 90, 96, 100, 168, 170, 180–81

personal voice, 23n2

perspectival shifts, 37n11, 119–22. *See also* focalization

perspective: in "A Rose for Emily," 4, 10, 118, 138; in *Broke Heart Blues*, 115, 161–62; in *Buddha in the Attic, The*, 87–88; collective *vs.* individual, 119–22; communication and, 58; in *deadkidsongs*, 82, 123–25;

defined, 103, 107, 107n3; ethos and, 113; in *Lolita*, 153n12; mixing of, 80; multiperson narration and, 37; narration and, 13; narrative progression and, 85; in "Parricide," 26–27; speech and, 98; unreliability and, 106, 160; in *Virgin Suicides, The*, 110; in "Watch the Animals," 161–62, 167, 170–72, 174, 177n2; in *Ways of Dying*, 139–41. *See also* focalization

Phelan, James, 4n3, 5, 6n6, 35, 45, 68n2, 70n6, 84, 95, 108, 123, 126, 146, 152, 153n12

Pittard, Hanna, 2

Plato, 13n13, 42n15, 81, 129

plural autodesignation, 54–55

plural narrator: in *Buddha in the Attic, The*, 86–91; consequences of, 180–81; in *deadkidsongs*, 80–83; direct speech and, 83–86; focalization and, 69; lyric progression and, 83–86; narrative voice and, 76–83; rhetorical possibility of, 68–76; we-discourses and, 50–56. *See also* we-narrator

"plural of approximation," 59–60

pluralis auctoris, 16, 54–55, 157

pluralis majestatis, 54, 65

pluralis modestatis, 54, 179n6

Poague, Leland, 94

poetry, lyric, 51–52

Prince, Gerald, 39n13, 57, 58, 69n4

progression: lyric, 62, 64, 67, 83–86, 181; narrative, 8, 63, 82, 84–85

pronominal alteration, 40–41

Pyrhönen, Heta, 156n15

Rabinowitz, Peter, 68n2, 86n24

Rand, Ayn. See *Anthem* (Rand)

representation, narrative, 71–74, 74n14, 80–81, 184

Richardson, Brian, 2n1, 3n2, 5, 13n15, 17–19, 22–23, 35n10, 36–37, 42n15, 52n6, 69–70, 111, 111n5, 126, 156, 177n1

Riffaterre, Michael, 152n10

Rimmon-Kenan, Shlomith, 68–69, 70n6, 120

Robertson, Alice, 6, 10, 118

"Rose for Emily, A" (Faulkner), 2–11, 45, 74, 115, 117–18; associative chronology in, 94–95; collective action in, 9–10; collective knowledge in, 134, 144, 154–57; community in, 30; construction of narrator in, 6–7; knowledge in, 137–38; lyricality in, 84n22; as paradigmatic we-narrative, 4–11; readings of, 4–5; "we" in, 4, 6–8, 14

Rulfo, Juan, 73

second-person narrative, 13n15, 19, 35n10, 52n6, 120

"Self-Portrait in a Tyvek™ Windbreaker" (Merrill), 29n7

Seven Sisters, The (Drabble), 37

"Shape of the Sword, The" (Borges), 35n10

Shaw, Harry E., 68n2, 70n6

Shen, Dan, 151n8

Skei, Hans, 6n7, 9, 134, 138

social mind, 111–12, 111n5

solidarity, 48, 51, 54, 63

Sontag, Susan, 68, 84, 86, 91–98

speech, direct: in *Broke Heart Blues*, 162; in "That Will Be Fine," 28; in "Watch the Animals," 170; in *Ways of Dying*, 139, 141; in we-narratives, 83–86; of we-narrator, 98–102. *See also* character dialogue

speech act theory, 18, 60

Stanzel, Franz Karl, 12–13, 12n11, 13, 13n13, 36, 40–41, 71–72, 72n9, 75n16, 76, 81, 85, 119n7, 120, 152n11, 157

Steffens, Niklas, 49

Stühring, Jan, 68n2, 71n7, 81n19

subjectivity, 108, 154n14; collective, 1, 3, 11, 21, 24, 40; focalization and, 108; indicative "we" and, 52–53; perspective and, 103; unreliability and, 150; we-references and, 52–53

synthetic component of narrative, 6n6, 45–46, 51, 78. *See also* mimetic; thematic

Tanaka, Kei, 87

"That Will Be Fine" (Faulkner), 22, 28–29, 36, 61, 63, 65

Then We Came to the End (Ferris), 2, 36, 41, 47–48, 63n18, 113, 131, 133; collective knowledge in, 143–46; community in, 33; direct speech in, 99–100; focalization in, 105–6, 109; as homodiegetic, 122;

I-references in, 34–35, 35n10; individual characters speaking in, 40; performative "we" in, 62; perspective in, 80, 120–21

thematic component of narrative, 6n6, 149. *See also* mimetic; synthetic

third-person narrative, 29, 39, 57n9, 70, 105, 121, 141, 183

Time Traveler's Wife, The (Niffenegger), 35n10

Todorov, Tzvetan, 41, 43, 61n16

Torres, Justin, 177–78, 177n2

Towner, Theresa M., 5n4

Trilling, Lionel, 4

Tuomela, Raimo, 15–16, 24n5, 136–37, 137n3

Twelve Million Black Voices: A Folk History of the Negro in the United States (Wright), 31

"unnatural" narrative, 41–46; "natural" narrative *vs.* 42–43; we-narrators as "unnatural," 41–42

unreliability, 20, 20n18, 80, 84, 106, 114, 143–45, 149–63, 150n5, 151nn6–9, 152nn10–11, 153nn12–13, 154n14

van Peer, Willie, 107

Virgin Suicides, The (Eugenides), 2, 22, 67, 109–10, 134, 178n4, 179n6; associative chronology in, 94–95; collective knowledge in, 137, 144, 157–60, 163; as communal, 33; ethos and, 113; focalization in, 115–18; unreliability in, 150; voyeurism in, 115–16

"Visitation, The" (Whalen), 37–38, 40–41

Vogt, Robert, 156n16

voice: authorial, 23, 23n2; collective, 1–3, 6n6, 23, 29, 53, 76–84, 134–35, 143, 182; communal, 2n1, 7, 21–23, 23nn2–3, 26, 29, 134, 140–42; diegetic, 81, 81n19; personal, 23n2; shared, 2; unreliability and, 156–57

voyeur, we-narrator as, 114–18, 170–71

Walsh, Richard, 14, 68n2, 71nn6–7, 73–74, 74n14, 79, 82n21, 107, 126, 129, 183

"Watch the Animals" (Dark), 165–75

Ways of Dying (Mda), 2, 6n6, 33, 134–44, 141 fig. 3, 146–48

We (Zamyatin), 177–78

"we": as an amplified "I," 59–60; and Collectivity Condition, 15–16; in definition of we-narrative, 11–12; deictic features of, 56–60, 56n8; desired, 54; distrust of, 31–32; existence of, 14; in first-person narrative, 24; hortatory, 55; I-narrator references to, 16, 19n17, 22–24, 24n5, 39, 50, 61; indicative, 19, 28–29, 52–53, 60–65, 60n15, 92, 96, 100; in lyric poetry, 51–52; lyrical, 16n16; narrative, 16n16; in nonfiction, 52–54; non-narrative, 50–51; in oral context, 53; performative, 14–15, 19, 25, 36, 49–50, 50n2, 52–53, 60–65, 83, 90, 96, 100, 168, 170, 180–81; pseudo-inclusive, 54; referential scope of, 48–49, 53–54; subgroups in, 17. *See also* we-reference

"We Didn't" (Dybek), 61

We the Animals (Torres), 177–78, 177n2

We, the Drowned (Jensen), 30n8, 142

"We Want It All" (Atwood), 97–98

we-discourses: in first-person narrative, 28; narrative situation and, 36; types of, 50–56; we-narrative *vs.*, 19, 24–25, 39–40, 83–84, 177

we-mode: in narrative, 52, 62, 111–12, 136; in social philosophy, 15–16, 24n5

we-narrative: collective, 29–34; collective voice in, 76–83; communal, 29–30; communal voice and, 22–23; contemporary resurgence of, 2n1; defining, 1, 11–18, 19n17, 23, 35n10, 39, 60–65; direct speech in, 83–86; features of, 180–81; first-person narrative *vs.*, 19, 39–40; individual voice in, 76–83; multiperson narrative *vs.*, 16–17; as narrative situation, 13–14; person and, 13–14, 13n14; "A Rose for Emily" as paradigm for, 4–11; senses of, 22–23; simultaneity in, 23, 23n3; as unnatural, 3, 17–18, 22, 41–46, 69–70. *See also* plural narrator

we-narrator: in definition of we-narrative, 11; direct speech of, 98–102; as focalizer, 106–14; gendering of, 5; as intrafictional enunciator, 75–76; mental functioning of, 111–13; perceptions of, 108–9; singularization of, 5; as "unnatural," 41; as voyeur, 114–18, 170–71; in we-mode concept, 16. *See also* plural narrator

we-reference: cataphoric, 27–28; contexts of, 24; and definitions of we-narrative, 19;

distancing technique of, 174; generalization of, 88; manipulative potential of, 117; narrator empowerment and, 24n5; in nonfiction, 50; nonprototypical types of, 53–56, 60; subjectivity and, 52–53. *See also* "we"

Whalen, Tom, 37–38, 40–41

White Noise (DeLillo), 91, 96

Williams, Raymond, 29–31

Wittig, Monique, 2n1

Wives of Los Alamos, The (Walbert), 2, 33

Woller, Joel, 31–32

Wright, Richard, 31

Yellow Raft in Blue Water, A (Dorris), 22, 37

Zamyatin, Yevgeny, 177–78

THEORY AND INTERPRETATION OF NARRATIVE

JAMES PHELAN, PETER J. RABINOWITZ, AND KATRA BYRAM, SERIES EDITORS

Because the series editors believe that the most significant work in narrative studies today contributes both to our knowledge of specific narratives and to our understanding of narrative in general, studies in the series typically offer interpretations of individual narratives and address significant theoretical issues underlying those interpretations. The series does not privilege one critical perspective but is open to work from any strong theoretical position.

We-Narratives: Collective Storytelling in Contemporary Fiction by Natalya Bekhta

Debating Rhetorical Narratology: On the Synthetic, Mimetic, and Thematic Aspects of Narrative by Matthew Clark and James Phelan

Environment and Narrative: New Directions in Econarratology edited by Erin James and Eric Morel

Unnatural Narratology: Extensions, Revisions, and Challenges edited by Jan Alber and Brian Richardson

A Poetics of Plot for the Twenty-First Century: Theorizing Unruly Narratives by Brian Richardson

Playing at Narratology: Digital Media as Narrative Theory by Daniel Punday

Making Conversation in Modernist Fiction by Elizabeth Alsop

Narratology and Ideology: Negotiating Context, Form, and Theory in Postcolonial Narratives edited by Divya Dwivedi, Henrik Skov Nielsen, and Richard Walsh

Novelization: From Film to Novel by Jan Baetens

Reading Conrad by J. Hillis Miller, edited by John G. Peters and Jakob Lothe

Narrative, Race, and Ethnicity in the United States edited by James J. Donahue, Jennifer Ann Ho, and Shaun Morgan

Somebody Telling Somebody Else: A Rhetorical Poetics of Narrative by James Phelan

Media of Serial Narrative edited by Frank Kelleter

Suture and Narrative: Deep Intersubjectivity in Fiction and Film by George Butte

The Writer in the Well: On Misreading and Rewriting Literature by Gary Weissman

Narrating Space / Spatializing Narrative: Where Narrative Theory and Geography Meet by Marie-Laure Ryan, Kenneth Foote, and Maoz Azaryahu

Narrative Sequence in Contemporary Narratology edited by Raphaël Baroni and Françoise Revaz

The Submerged Plot and the Mother's Pleasure from Jane Austen to Arundhati Roy by Kelly A. Marsh

Narrative Theory Unbound: Queer and Feminist Interventions edited by Robyn Warhol and Susan S. Lanser

Unnatural Narrative: Theory, History, and Practice by Brian Richardson

Ethics and the Dynamic Observer Narrator: Reckoning with Past and Present in German Literature by Katra A. Byram

Narrative Paths: African Travel in Modern Fiction and Nonfiction by Kai Mikkonen

The Reader as Peeping Tom: Nonreciprocal Gazing in Narrative Fiction and Film by Jeremy Hawthorn

Thomas Hardy's Brains: Psychology, Neurology, and Hardy's Imagination by Suzanne Keen

The Return of the Omniscient Narrator: Authorship and Authority in Twenty-First Century Fiction by Paul Dawson

Feminist Narrative Ethics: Tacit Persuasion in Modernist Form by Katherine Saunders Nash

Real Mysteries: Narrative and the Unknowable by H. Porter Abbott

A Poetics of Unnatural Narrative edited by Jan Alber, Henrik Skov Nielsen, and Brian Richardson

Narrative Discourse: Authors and Narrators in Literature, Film, and Art by Patrick Colm Hogan

An Aesthetics of Narrative Performance: Transnational Theater, Literature, and Film in Contemporary Germany by Claudia Breger

Literary Identification from Charlotte Brontë to Tsitsi Dangarembga by Laura Green

Narrative Theory: Core Concepts and Critical Debates by David Herman, James Phelan and Peter J. Rabinowitz, Brian Richardson, and Robyn Warhol

After Testimony: The Ethics and Aesthetics of Holocaust Narrative for the Future edited by Jakob Lothe, Susan Rubin Suleiman, and James Phelan

The Vitality of Allegory: Figural Narrative in Modern and Contemporary Fiction by Gary Johnson

Narrative Middles: Navigating the Nineteenth-Century British Novel edited by Caroline Levine and Mario Ortiz-Robles

Fact, Fiction, and Form: Selected Essays by Ralph W. Rader edited by James Phelan and David H. Richter

The Real, the True, and the Told: Postmodern Historical Narrative and the Ethics of Representation by Eric L. Berlatsky

Franz Kafka: Narration, Rhetoric, and Reading edited by Jakob Lothe, Beatrice Sandberg, and Ronald Speirs

Social Minds in the Novel by Alan Palmer

Narrative Structures and the Language of the Self by Matthew Clark

Imagining Minds: The Neuro-Aesthetics of Austen, Eliot, and Hardy by Kay Young

Postclassical Narratology: Approaches and Analyses edited by Jan Alber and Monika Fludernik

Techniques for Living: Fiction and Theory in the Work of Christine Brooke-Rose by Karen R. Lawrence

Towards the Ethics of Form in Fiction: Narratives of Cultural Remission by Leona Toker

Tabloid, Inc.: Crimes, Newspapers, Narratives by V. Penelope Pelizzon and Nancy M. West

Narrative Means, Lyric Ends: Temporality in the Nineteenth-Century British Long Poem by Monique R. Morgan

Understanding Nationalism: On Narrative, Cognitive Science, and Identity by Patrick Colm Hogan

Joseph Conrad: Voice, Sequence, History, Genre edited by Jakob Lothe, Jeremy Hawthorn, James Phelan

The Rhetoric of Fictionality: Narrative Theory and the Idea of Fiction by Richard Walsh

Experiencing Fiction: Judgments, Progressions, and the Rhetorical Theory of Narrative by James Phelan

Unnatural Voices: Extreme Narration in Modern and Contemporary Fiction by Brian Richardson

Narrative Causalities by Emma Kafalenos

Why We Read Fiction: Theory of Mind and the Novel by Lisa Zunshine

I Know That You Know That I Know: Narrating Subjects from Moll Flanders *to* Marnie by George Butte

Bloodscripts: Writing the Violent Subject by Elana Gomel

Surprised by Shame: Dostoevsky's Liars and Narrative Exposure by Deborah A. Martinsen

Having a Good Cry: Effeminate Feelings and Pop-Culture Forms by Robyn R. Warhol

Politics, Persuasion, and Pragmatism: A Rhetoric of Feminist Utopian Fiction by Ellen Peel

Telling Tales: Gender and Narrative Form in Victorian Literature and Culture by Elizabeth Langland

Narrative Dynamics: Essays on Time, Plot, Closure, and Frames edited by Brian Richardson

Breaking the Frame: Metalepsis and the Construction of the Subject by Debra Malina

Invisible Author: Last Essays by Christine Brooke-Rose

Ordinary Pleasures: Couples, Conversation, and Comedy by Kay Young

Narratologies: New Perspectives on Narrative Analysis edited by David Herman

Before Reading: Narrative Conventions and the Politics of Interpretation by Peter J. Rabinowitz

Matters of Fact: Reading Nonfiction over the Edge by Daniel W. Lehman

The Progress of Romance: Literary Historiography and the Gothic Novel by David H. Richter

A Glance Beyond Doubt: Narration, Representation, Subjectivity by Shlomith Rimmon-Kenan

Narrative as Rhetoric: Technique, Audiences, Ethics, Ideology by James Phelan

Misreading Jane Eyre: *A Postformalist Paradigm* by Jerome Beaty

Psychological Politics of the American Dream: The Commodification of Subjectivity in Twentieth-Century American Literature by Lois Tyson

Understanding Narrative edited by James Phelan and Peter J. Rabinowitz

Framing Anna Karenina: Tolstoy, the Woman Question, and the Victorian Novel by Amy Mandelker

Gendered Interventions: Narrative Discourse in the Victorian Novel by Robyn R. Warhol

Reading People, Reading Plots: Character, Progression, and the Interpretation of Narrative by James Phelan